Music for Young Children

BARBARA ANDRESS

Harcourt Brace College Publishers

Fort Worth   Philadelphia   San Diego   New York   Orlando   Austin   San Antonio
Toronto   Montreal   London   Sydney   Tokyo

Publisher	Earl McPeek
Acquisitions Editor	Jo-Anne Weaver
Developmental Editor	Linda Blundell
Project Editors	Amy Schmidt, Mike Norris
Production Manager	Annette Wiggins
Art Directors	Melinda Welch, Lora Knox

ISBN: 0-15-503071-X

Library of Congress Catalog Card Number: 94-79966

Address for Editorial Correspondence: Harcourt Brace College Publishers, 301 Commerce Street, Suite 3700, Fort Worth, TX 76102.

Address for Orders: Harcourt Brace & Company, 6277 Sea Harbor Drive, Orlando, FL 32887-6777. 1-800-782-4479.

Website Address: http://www.hbcollege.com

Harcourt Brace & Company will provide complimentary supplements or supplement packages to those adopters qualified under our adoption policy. Please contact your sales representative to learn how you qualify. If as an adopter or potential user you receive supplements you do not need, please return them to your sales representative or send them to: Attn: Returns Department, Troy Warehouse, 465 South Lincoln Drive, Troy, MO 63379.

Printed in the United States of America

7   8   9   0   1   2   3   4   5   6   066   9   8   7   6   5   4   3   2   1

Preface

Adults who teach music to young children have varying degrees of experience and ability both in general education and in music education, so writing a book that serves as a resource for all educators places the author in a quandary. Should the author address the needs of music specialists who are well versed in music but may not be as familiar with the developmental needs of preschool children, or should the author present materials for early childhood generalists who may have limited musical understanding and skills but are more knowledgeable about young children? Yet another consideration for the author is whether the educators are music or early childhood undergraduates, graduates, or care providers in preschool centers and specially funded projects who daily serve the needs of children but often have less formal training in teacher education. Ultimately, the author must write a book that meets the needs of the children to be served. Ideally, the author must offer a model that reflects exemplary early childhood music experiences, and educators at all levels must take and implement whatever they can from the model.

The purpose of this book is to introduce, explain, and clarify new techniques, terminology, and concepts through definition and example. I also intend to provide many ideas that I have presented over the years in workshops and publications, as well as to provide new insights about how to share the joy of music with very young children. In other words, this book represents a practitioner's approach to implementing music in various care and instructional settings. Although the suggestions contained in this book are based on developmental and instructional theories, I have made no attempt to report comprehensively on the literature in these fields; it is more important to provide readers with models and materials they can use immediately to impact children's experiences in the classroom.

The task of *writing* about music sets forth limitations from the start because music is sound. One does not talk or write successfully about sound; one needs to hear it. The success of this book, then, also depends on the care providers and teachers who can make the program described herein come alive for their students.

ACKNOWLEDGMENTS

It is with gratitude that I acknowledge the generous support of the following organizations and publishers: the Music Educators National Conference; Holt, Rinehart and Winston, Inc.; and the Arizona Early Childhood Music Collaborative Project. Without their kind permission to reprint previously published materials, this textbook would not have been possible. My thanks also to co-authors on earlier publications and to colleagues for their inspiration, sharing, and caring during the preparation of this book.

Table of Contents

1

The Young Child

Inside of me there is a song
I've known it oh so very long.
I hear it sing inside my head
Wish it would come out instead.
If I could hum . . . would it come?
Hm mmmmmmmmmmmm
Or la-ti-dah-di-dah____, la la la la la____
La ti dah dah dah____.
I could sing doo de doo doo doo____
doo de doo____doo de doo____.
If my song would sing for me
I'd give it to a friend for free.

Inside a young child are many songs, some of which are waiting to be heard by others and some of which are for the child's own special playful use. In addition to singing are many other forms of musical performance to be experienced and joyfully shared. Music is an important means of communication that young children use intuitively, and caring adults are challenged to provide exploratory and participatory music play experiences that nurture children's natural propensity for music. Adults' interest in and approval of music are readily transmitted to curious children who eagerly imitate the adults. Such positive early experiences can give children a lifelong disposition toward music and musical learning—a gift truly worth giving.

Who are these children, and who is responsible for guiding their musical experiences? The National Association for the Education of Young Children (NAEYC) defines early childhood as infancy to eight years old. This wide age range indicates that many individuals are involved in the music education of young children. Certainly, music education begins in the home, where, ideally, *all* family members are involved in nurturing an awareness of how music enters their daily lives. Today's families, however, are diverse, and the primary caregivers may be a single father, a single mother, grandparents, or members of an extended family. Regardless of family structure, children are greatly influenced by their primary caregivers and highly motivated to please and emulate the value system of these important people. Caregivers become the first and most important music teachers for children.

Many children, from infancy on, spend most of their waking hours in a care center because both parents work. Skilled and semiskilled personnel charged with the care of these children may be found in settings such as family home care, private, and commercial daycare. Public and private preschools with certified general and music educators are also options for educating preschool and school-age children. The adults in these diverse settings, whether certified or noncertified, skilled or semiskilled, are responsible for guiding the quality of musical experiences for their young charges.

Planning and implementing a developmentally and musically appropriate program for young children is a multifaceted task that requires not only adult musicianship and appropriate resources, but information about how children learn at particular time periods. Knowledge about young children's motor skills, how they cognitively experience their world, their stages of social and emotional development, and their rapid rate of language acquisition is necessary to implement musical interactions. In teaching music education to young children, educators must first understand the developing child before they can plan the musical content to be taught.

The Developing Child[1]

It has been said many times that young children are not miniature adults, yet many of our instructional approaches are merely watered-down versions of what has been proven successful with older children and adults. Materials are somewhat adapted or chosen for younger learners, and we indulgently tolerate more errors, but far too often we do not effectively plan for the optimal success level for these children. We have not fully taken into account considerations that inhibit or propel young children's learning at various stages of development.

Many diverse theories in the field describe, explain, and attempt to predict the developing behaviors of young children. New theories emerge that often are based on previous discoveries. Investigators from many disciplines submit notions that are then subjected to scrutiny, challenge, and refinement. There is no single truth in understanding how children develop, merely studied opinions. Researchers such as Jean Piaget have had a profound influence on curriculum planners, yet even his work is now being questioned. Does this make his findings unusable? Not at all. Piaget's work is still respected by many and it provides valuable insights, but now it must be viewed with certain modifications.

The developmental profile of a child is acquired through an interdisciplinary approach involving psychologists, sociologists, anthropologists, and biologists. Experts in the applied fields, such as educators, then enter the equation and attempt to base their practices on those theories that seem most viable. The work of five academic and instructional theorists is briefly reviewed in the next sections. Also interjected within each review are notions about the resultant musical implications held either by the theorists and/or the author of this textbook. The opinions of the theorists, in part or in total, have been most important in organizing this framework for the music education of young children.

A Review of Developmental Theories

JEAN PIAGET: COGNITIVE DEVELOPMENT[2]

Piaget, a noted cognitive psychologist, developed a cognitive framework that has been used extensively by educators in planning curriculum for young children. Piaget's theory provides insights about young children's ability to think rationally, a process of biological maturation that unfolds in a stage-like sequence. According to Piaget, children actively construct mental schemes as they progress through four broad stages of development: sensorimotor—birth to 2 years; preoperational—2 to 7 years; concrete operations—7 to 11 years; and formal operations—11 to 15 years.

Piaget held basic assumptions about the way children learn. He said that they

◆ do not think like adults.

◆ learn by becoming involved with concrete objects.

◆ learn intrinsically (from within), not extrinsically (from without).

◆ evolve intellectually through the generative nature of prior experience and the quality of current experience.

◆ learn through the adaptation of new schemas (formation of concepts; categorizing perceived data).

◆ use two interdependent activities, assimilation and accommodation, in this adaptive process. Assimilation is taking in perceptual data; accommodation is a modification in the way of thinking to accommodate newly perceived data.

◆ strive to establish equilibrium when assimilating and accommodating new data.

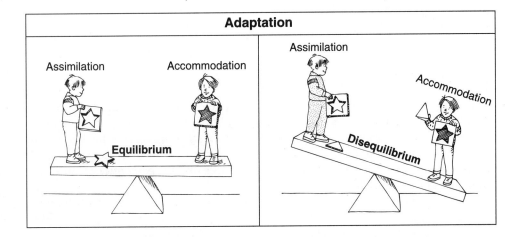

Although Piaget divided intellectual development into four stages, concrete and formal operations will not be discussed here, because children's cognitive growth at these ages is not the focus of this book. The sensorimotor and preoperational stages discussed here are hierarchical and involve a maturation process; thus, characteristics of prior stages are not entirely displaced by characteristics of new stages. Children develop intellectually in the same manner but not necessarily at the same ages.

Sensorimotor Period

The sensorimotor period is the prelanguage period. During this time, infants utilize their senses and motor reflexes to begin building an image of the world. Children are egocentric, see the world only from their own point of view, and are unaware that other points of view exist. During this stage, children learn by acting on the environment. Piaget believed sensorimotor operations are the basis for language development.

Sensorimotor Period

Begins to orient self to objects, space, and time

Causality—Learns about cause and effect

Object Permanency—Knows objects can exist without being seen

Intentional Behavior—Initiates goal-directed activities

Preoperational Period

This stage is characterized by language development and rapid conceptual growth. Children move from functioning largely with concrete objects to symbolic representation (words). Piaget stated that intelligence appears long before language and that intelligence is based on the manipulation of objects; that is, in place of words and concepts, intelligence is indicated by perceptions and movements organized into action schemes.

Two- to four-year-olds work very hard to acquire language, and language accelerates the rate at which experiences take place. According to Piaget, children move through two language stages—egocentric and socialized.

Piaget also said that characteristics of the preoperational stage that prevent children from being capable of completely logical, mature, or adult-like thought are egocentrism, centering, transformation, and irreversibility. *Egocentrism* means children are unable to see any point of view other than their own. They do not deliberately strive to be egocentric, but they are unaware that there are alternative ways of thinking. *Centering* is the way children fix their attention on one perceptual feature at a time. *Transformation* means that children focus attention on each

Preoperational Period

Egocentric Speech— Tends to think actions out loud; has conversations with self in presence of others

Socialized Speech— Exchanges ideas deliberately

element in a sequence rather than on how each element transforms one state to another. *Irreversibility* is the inability to reverse thought; that is, children cannot reason back to the point of origin of a thought or event. Problems with conservation also occur from this inability to reverse thought. Conservation is the awareness that the amount or quantity of an object remains constant even though that object may change in shape or position.

Children's cognitive development moves steadily along during the preoperational stage. The process of assimilating and accommodating proceeds as children refine schemas or categorize new data by discriminating, categorizing, ordering, and improvising.

Near the end of the preoperational stage, children begin to demonstrate some rather sophisticated mental processes such as recalling, reordering, and conceptualizing. Abstract thought begins during this stage, and children move from dealing almost exclusively with concrete objects to using symbols (language) and concepts in a most effective manner. Consequently, this period in children's total development is most significant.

Implications for Music Education: Understanding Responses

Piaget provided clues to how children process and acquire information, which leads to how the learning environment should be structured. Certainly, hands-on interaction is necessary. Tasks that prompt children to discriminate, categorize, and order musical sounds as a part of assimilating sounds, ideas, and forming schemas can be given. We may conclude that improvisational play is possible during the early cognitive stages, but that the more sophisticated mental processes involved in recalling, reordering, and conceptualizing are higher-order skills. So, according to Piaget's thinking, expecting very young children to respond to musical notation or perform repeated patterns on instruments may not be developmentally appropriate.

The following examples are drawn from musical interactions with children of various ages and illustrate their ability or inability to function cognitively when interacting with specific materials and ideas.

Music Interaction 1

The intent of the adult is to focus the child's attention on a piece of music played on a cassette tape recorder. For the adult, this tape recorder is present merely as a sound source. The child, however, chooses to center on the on/off buttons. Music is perceived only as something to control, not as something to hear. Attempts by the adult to redirect attention to the music are ignored by the child. (Centering)

Centering was identified earlier as a characteristic of the preoperational stage. It describes the way children fix their attention on one perceptual feature at a time. Thus, regardless of what the adult may see as the focus of the activity, the child determines what is attended to, or centered upon.

Music Interaction 2

The teacher sets up an activity to explore musical concepts dealing with dynamic changes (soft to gradually louder) using the idea of a train coming from afar to very close as the basis of the play. While soft to loud may seem to be a very basic idea, there are many intertwined concepts confronting the child: big-little, near-far, gradually becoming louder.

The teacher prepares a train puzzle using light- to heavy-textured sandpaper. The play evolves around how the train engine is transformed from one state to another. Amy is not yet ready for this musical play because she focuses attention on each element in the sequence rather than on how they are transformed from one state to another.

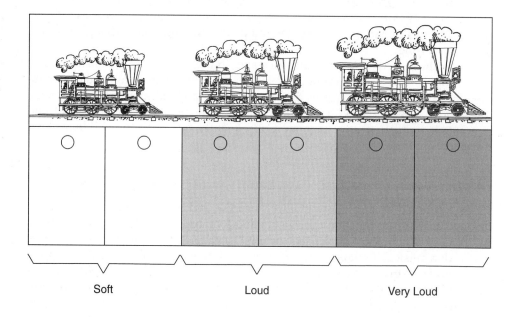

Soft · Loud · Very Loud

The teacher offers a sound game to four-year-old Amy saying, "Here are some train sounds." Amy explores the sounds beneath each of the train engines by swishing the sandpaper starter over the various textures of sandpaper. Amy comments, "This is a little soft train. This is a big, loud train. This is a very big loud train." Though playing with loud and soft sounds is enjoyable, it does not occur to Amy that the pictures could represent one train. She does not appear to think, "This is the little train. It is far away and very soft. This is the same train coming closer, and getting louder. This is the same train, very close and very loud." (A music crescendo) Amy is very successful, however, in expressing appropriate sounds for something very small or large, which represents an astute musical response for her stage of development. (Transformation)

Music Interaction 3

Four-year-old children are playing an accompaniment using pentatonic pitches (C-D-E-G-A) on Orff-type xylophones. Lovely pitter-patter raindrop sounds are played randomly while they sing "Rain, Rain Go Away." The teacher endeavors to unify the xylophone part by asking children to play a simple accompaniment pattern consisting of the repeated pitches C, D, E, and G. Unable to recall the pitch set, the children soon abandon the play. (Irreversibility)

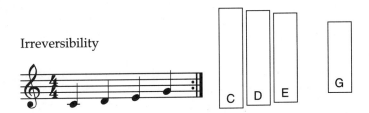

Irreversibility

Children who are asked to play a repeated pitch sequence must be able to reason back to where the pattern began. In the early stages of development, they are not likely to do this because they cannot reverse thought. Losing interest in the activity is a predictable outcome.

Understanding Piaget's theories can help us prepare developmentally appropriate musical activities that will allow children to be successful. The four-year-olds in Interaction 3 may not be able to perform repeated patterns, but they can certainly explore instrumental sounds, play improvised tunes, use sounds to express ideas in nature, and perform drone-like accompaniments (same continuous sound).

Challenges to Piaget's Theory

Some theorists still accept Piaget's theory with the modification that changes in children's thinking take place much more gradually than Piaget proposed. Others believe that Piaget underestimated infants' and preschoolers' ability to understand. Critics feel his findings on competency were the result of a flawed design that presented unfamiliar objects or too much developmentally inappropriate information. Those who are disenchanted with Piaget's theory have abandoned it altogether in favor of a continuous approach to development rather than Piaget's segmented four stages.

Whether one questions or accepts Piaget's theory, all agree that his ideas stand as one of the dominant twentieth-century positions on cognitive learning:

Piaget's stated theory of cognitive development revolutionized the field with its view of children as active beings who take responsibility for their own learning. (Berk 1994, 22)

SEMANOVICH VYGOTSKY: SOCIOCULTURAL THEORY

Vygotsky believed that joint discussion and problem solving between children and more knowledgeable members of the social group help children acquire ways of thinking and behaving that enable them to function within their culture.[3] His *zone of proximal development* refers to tasks that children cannot yet handle alone but can accomplish with the help of adults. Once young learners internalize the essential features of a dialogue, they are able to independently guide their own actions and skills. Vygotsky believed that these dialogues involve continuous, step-by-step changes in children's thought and behavior and vary greatly from culture to culture.

Children's play was deemed most important by Vygotsky. He felt there are two critical features of play:

Representational play creates an imaginary situation that permits the child to grapple with unrealizable desires, and . . . that it contains rules for behavior that children must follow to successfully act out the play scene. [4]

Vygotsky believed that pretend play is greatly enhanced when adults and children interact. The importance he placed on the benefits of direct adult-child interaction is in contrast to the Piagetian theory of discovery learning (self-directed interaction with concrete objects). Both theories, however, strongly support the use of play as a vehicle or approach to learning. Developmentally appropriate teacher intervention becomes more acceptable within Vygotsky's concept of how children learn.

Implications for Music Education: Interactive Adult-Child Play

Appropriate adult intervention as children play in various music learning environments is readily justified for those who wish to use a more eclectic approach in their instructional practices. Combining Vygotsky's theories with Piaget's concerns about children's involvement with concrete objects, or Montessori's self-education (see page 12), provides an opportunity for adults to embrace an interactive play approach within the music learning setting. An example of such interactive play follows.

Four-year-old Tameika randomly strums the open strings of an autoharp with a commercially prepared pick. After a time, the teacher enters the play by saying, "I hear your beautiful music, Tameika. Your music makes my fingers want to dance!" The teacher's fingers dance in response to Tameika's lovely harp sounds. Dropping an assortment of topically prepared autoharp picks into the play area, the teacher says, "I have some more dancers for you." Stickers of animals and ballerinas have been placed on specially prepared picks that the teacher previously cut from plastic margarine lids. Tameika begins to carefully select picks and creates music for the various depicted characters. Teacher enters the play by asking, "How would this silly frog dance?" Tameika hits at the strings, making staccato sounds. The teacher makes a hopping finger dance. "How would this pretty girl dance?" Tameika gently strums across the strings as the teacher's dancing fingers glide through air.

In this example, adult intervention playfully moves the activity from random sound making to expressive accompaniments for dances. The activity extends Tameika's options for creating sounds on the autoharp, and helps her become aware that music can be used for expressive purposes. The teacher intervenes to extend the range of tasks that the child cannot yet handle alone but can accomplish with the help of an adult.

HOWARD GARDNER: MUSICAL INTELLIGENCE

Since the 1900s, society has measured intelligence with a paper-and-pencil IQ test. Gardner posited the theory that people have not just one intelligence but rather multiple intelligences. The intelligences are identified as linguistic, musical, logical-mathematical, spatial, bodily kinesthetic, and personal. This notion of multiple intelligences provides a positive model to explain the different intellectual strengths displayed by people.

Human intellectual competence must entail a set of skills of problem solving—enabling the individual to resolve genuine problems or difficulties that he or she encounters and, when appropriate, to create an effective product. . . .[5]

It is significant that Gardner viewed musical intelligence as a distinct "way of knowing." He stated that "of all the gifts with which individuals may be endowed, none emerges earlier than musical talent."[6] Discussing music intelligence from the time of infancy, Gardner addressed notions about children's spontaneous songs and the production of "characteristic bits" from familiar tunes. The following would be a typical example of such observations.

[The adult sings a song while spinning a dreydl. (A dreydl is a four-sided top with a Hebrew character on each side.)]

> Little dreydl made of clay
> With this dreydl we will play
> Dreydl, dreydl, dreydl, dreydl,
> With this dreydl we will play.

(Three-year-old Rosalie joins in only on the most prominent "characteristic bits," such as the repeating of the word dreydl *in the third line of the song.)*

On the subject of musical competence, Gardner noted that

. . . more so than in language, one encounters striking individual differences in young children as they learn to sing . . . but by school age, most children in our culture have a schema of what a song should be like . . . . Except among children with unusual musical talent or exceptional opportunities, there is little further musical development after the school years begin.[7]

Gardner defined in great detail the components of musical intelligence. They are (1) the development of musical competence (e.g., presenting a sequence of song acquisition from babbling to cultural song responses), (2) evolutionary and neurological facets of music (e.g., discussing one evolutionary parallel in the animal kingdom to human music as observed in similar elements in bird song), and (3) its relation to other intellectual competencies (e.g., relating music in a variety of ways to the range of human symbol systems and intellectual competencies, yet interestingly not using it for explicit communication or for other evident survival purposes). Gardner proposed that normal people are in a position to develop any number of intellectual competencies if they are adequately stimulated.

Implications for Music Education: Multiple Intelligences

Although this discussion has focused on Gardner's thoughts about musical intelligence, it should be understood that all of the other multiple intelligences are a part of the total learning process within a quality music program. Most notable is bodily kinesthetic intelligence, which is enhanced through creative and structured movement responses to music.

The innovative notion that music is one of the multiple intelligences is important for educators to ponder because it gives even more credence to the idea that music should be a part of young children's lives. Gardner's descriptions of how children acquire musical competency contribute to a usable framework for educators who are responsible for developing musical profiles of their young students. When assessing the application of intelligences, Gardner opted for the problem-solving approach, which amounts to "creating intriguing puzzles and allowing children to take off with them."[8] An example follows.

Several small groups of second-grade children are working cooperatively in their music class to solve a musical puzzle. They are asked to create a ten-second composition for three triangles and one drum. Their music is to include a time of silence, with instruments gradually becoming louder, and then gradually becoming softer. Involved discussions occur as the piece is planned, rehearsed, and then performed for others in the class. The teacher tape records each composition as it is presented. After each performance, the class assesses the compositions, often referring back to the recording. Using their own descriptive terms, the children discuss if all the puzzle pieces had been used, when the changes in volume had occurred, and the overall effect of the music.

Validating music in early childhood and school music programs is an ongoing task for advocates of the art. Gardner reinforced the concept that the early childhood years are a critical time for learning, thereby providing one more reason to support quality musical experiences for this age group.

A Review of Instructional Theories

JEROME BRUNER: THEORY OF INSTRUCTION[9]

Jerome Bruner contributed much to a rationale for curriculum development. His theory merged what is known about intellectual growth and theories of instruction. Because each of these domains alone is complex, he concluded that development issues extend beyond education or child rearing to a more global concern of how culture is transmitted and how, during transmission, it produces more effective and zestful people.

The following statements briefly outline Bruner's view of intellectual growth and his theory of instruction.

1. Growth is characterized by increasing independence of response from the immediate nature of the stimulus.
2. Growth depends on internalizing events into storage systems that correspond to the environment.
3. Intellectual growth involves an increasing capacity to say to oneself and others, by means of words or symbols, what one has done or what one will do.
4. Intellectual development depends on a systematic and contingent interaction between a tutor and a learner.

5. Teaching is vastly facilitated by the medium of language because language is the medium through which the learner can bring order into the environment.

6. Intellectual development is marked by increasing capacity to deal with several alternatives simultaneously.

Bruner identified three sequential stages in which people translate experiences into a model of the world.

1. *Enactive Stage—Sensing and Doing.* This is a concrete, hands-on stage of learning.

2. *Iconic Stage—Imaging.* This stage depends on visual or other sensory organization and on summarizing images. This is a stage of internalization; that is, children can retain images when they are no longer present. The icon is an instructional device that helps children internalize. We may infer that, for children to internalize an image in music, the icon must be as *visually descriptive* of the sound as possible.

3. *Symbolic Stage—Representation.* At this stage, communication of thought takes place through language and mutually agreed upon visual systems; certain images and words stand for particular ideas or objects.

Bruner's theory of instruction principally concerns how to arrange environments to optimize these stages of learning. He has suggested that curriculum planners follow these guidelines: (1) Specify the experiences that effectively create interest in learning; (2) specify ways in which knowledge can be most readily grasped by the learner; (3) use effective sequences; (4) specify nature and pacing of rewards and punishments; and (5) shift from extrinsic reward (teacher praise) to intrinsic reward (pupil achievement).

Bruner concluded that almost all children possess intrinsic motives for learning and do not need rewards other than the achievement that performing the activity brings. Such motives intrinsically include curiosity, the drive to achieve competence, admiration of competent models (e.g., someone whose respect the learner wants or standards the learner wishes to adopt), and reciprocity, the deep human need to respond to others and to work with them toward a common objective. (Bruner 1971)

Implications for Music Education: Three Learning Stages

Bruner's three stages of learning can be an effective child-centered learning cycle that takes into account children's development and ability to understand a musical idea. Certainly, very young children need many experiences in just sensing and doing, responding to the wholeness of the musical event. Through many hands-on experiences at the enactive stage, such as manipulating music-related objects, playing instruments, or moving to music, children are introduced to new musical ideas.

The child must move, do, sense, play,

and act upon his or her environment.

Information gained enactively during the iconic stage provides children with developmentally appropriate visual tools (icons), such as pictures of rhythmic and melodic ideas rendered in a *topical* form (e.g., rabbits represent long or short rhythmic ideas in a bunny song) or in a *generic* form (e.g., long and short lines represent rhythmic ideas for any simple song). This playful step in the process strengthens children's understanding of concepts that would otherwise be overly abstract.

The iconic stage is important because it forms the basis of understanding concepts that will later be given mutually agreed upon symbols (i.e., traditional musical notation).

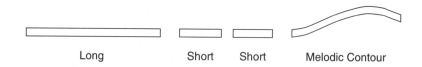

The symbolic stage is significant because it expedites communication and learning. Mutually agreed upon symbols, such as quarter and half notes, are more efficient and accurate for written music than are icons. We would readily agree that one could not capture the necessary musical information required to perform Beethoven's *Fifth Symphony* by using icons of bunny rabbits or long and short horizontal lines. Traditional symbols provide more precise information, enabling longer and more complex musical ideas to be shared.

It is important to note that Bruner's instructional sequence is not only applicable to how young children learn music. Older children and adults, when confronted with new information in any field, tend to go through the same process, usually in less time, depending on the nature of what is to be understood.

MARIA MONTESSORI: SELF-EDUCATION[10]

Maria Montessori, a physician and noted biologist, became interested in the learning process through working with mentally disabled children, and her theories and methods are based on her observation of them. She felt that children's progress is a result of their interaction with objects and ideas within the classroom.

One of the strengths of her program is its power to motivate learning through self-teaching and self-corrective materials. Montessori set forth several principles on the education process:

1. Children are not miniature adults, but are in a stage of continuous and intense change.
2. Children cannot be educated by other people; they self-educate, freely choosing from materials designed to instruct.
3. The teacher's role should be primarily that of observer, intervening as necessary and setting the environment to encourage the spirit of inquiry.

4. Methods are based on practical life experiences. Children are actors in a living scene.

5. Methods are designed not so much to give new impressions as to give order to impressions already received.

6. Children's goals must be respected. The doing of the act may in itself be the aim. Children are not necessarily product oriented.

Montessori used music as an integral part of her curriculum at all phases of learning. With colleague Anna Marie Maccheroni, she created specially designed sound sources and didactic materials for the children's use. Didactic materials, such as sound cylinders, described on page 14, are designed to instruct. Montessori and Maccheroni devised a program that included music theory and ear training by having children participate in varied activities such as playing instruments, auditioning (listening to music), moving expressively, and singing.[11]

In a Montessori program, materials are placed in the environment, and children are led by their own curiosity to use them. Such skills as auditory discrimination, tonal memory, and the ability to order and classify sounds are all part of the exploratory process. Typical Montessori didactic music materials used by children are mushroom and bar bells, sound cylinders, dummy keyboards, visual rhythmic materials, staff boards, note-head discs, and wooden notes.

Mushroom Bells

Mushroom bells are individual bells shaped like small mushrooms. The bells form the equivalent of two sets of the chromatic scale. One set of mushroom bells can be ordered according to scale by using visual and auditory clues. As these bells become higher in pitch, they decrease in size. The bell bases are painted black and white, correlating to piano keys. This set is identified as the *control bells* in sound-matching games.

The second set of bells contains only auditory clues; thus, it may be ordered only by listening and determining which sounds are relatively higher or lower. These bells are visually alike and are mounted on brown bases. They are called the *working bells*. The following examples illustrate how mushroom bell games can help children solve problems: A child plays with one bell, transfixed by a single sound. The child may handle the bell in varied ways: by tapping the bell

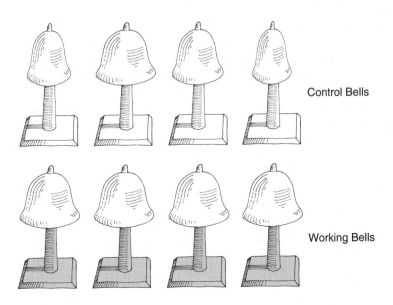

Control Bells

Working Bells

repeatedly; by holding it nearby or far away; by listening to vibrations; by listening to the sound soften to silence; by playing the bell on its edge or in its middle; or by exploring the appearance of the bell.

To play a matching game, several children are each given a white bell, and an equal number of children are given a brown bell. Initially, only two or three random pitches are used, but gradually the complexity of the game is increased until the children are working with the eight pitches of the major scale.

A child with a brown bell finds the child who has the matching sound from the white bell. The two children with the same bell pitch stand together and play their bells; the teacher hears that the pairing is correct.

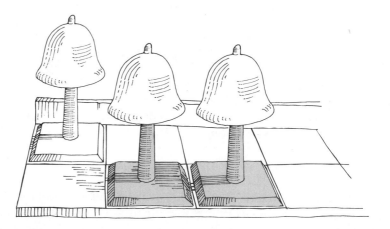

After many experiences of matching bells at random, the child is ready to organize sounds independently in sequence on a game board. The board has white and black spaces that are the same size as the bases of the bells. The board provides a model for the tonal relationships of the major scale—the half steps between three and four and between seven and eight are spatially closer together. The black and white bells are used as controls and are placed at the rear edge of the board; the brown bells are the working bells.

Sound Cylinders

Two sets of cylinders containing such diverse materials as salt, rice, or corn are placed in the environment. The cylinders are wood, thereby allowing no visual clue as to what they contain. The child must rely solely on hearing to match and order the sounds. The child plays with the cylinders to determine "same" and "different" to order sounds from softer to louder.

The concept of rhythm is approached with the use of wooden rods of varying lengths. Traditional music symbols are printed on white rods; brown rods are used as spacers.

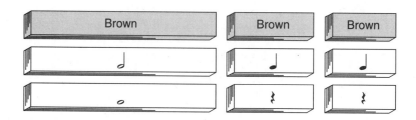

Montessori used the word *hooking* to mean linking one experience to another. It is crucial to children's growth that each experience be purposeful and that it lead to another of greater challenge. Children, though freely choosing, work within the scope and sequence of the selected instructional materials.

Implications for Music Education: Didactic Self-teaching Materials

Montessori developed instructional materials to support her learning theory. There is much in her basic theory that reflects today's thinking about developmentally appropriate practices, including emphasis on hands-on learning. Often, however, Montessori didactic music materials are not readily available to today's teachers. The idea of didactic music materials is very significant for today's planners, however, as such materials provide clues for developing exploratory, problem solving centers. Today's teachers are challenged to adapt the *idea* of didactic materials and create their own manipulative items for independent or small-group play.

Translating Theory into Practice

This chapter's review of but a few of the existing theories and instructional practices has been deliberately limited and is intended only to motivate readers to research further the vast array of available literature. These brief overviews are designed to help you begin to understand *why we do what we do* in early childhood music programs. Having an understanding of existing developmental and instructional theories can help early childhood music curriculum planners better determine their own approach to guiding young children. A planner's decisions may reflect a "buy-in" approach to a single developmental theory or they may reflect a combination of several theories to form a more eclectic approach to guiding children's music education. Following either course of action, planners must also trust their own intuition and common sense gleaned from their personal experiences with children.

A PROPOSED BASIC PHILOSOPHY

Adults who guide children's interactions with music must have a strong sense of purpose and a solid understanding of what is appropriate for children. The following statements are based on developmentally and musically appropriate child-centered concerns.[12]

We believe that early interaction with the joys of music can positively affect a child's life. An important goal in early childhood education is helping children develop a disposition for music—a curiosity about and a desire to be involved with it—that will be carried with them throughout life. Toward this goal, the following nine-point credo is proposed as a philosophical stance:

1. Each child will bring his or her own unique interests and abilities to the music learning environment. *Each child will take away that bit of knowledge that*

he or she is uniquely capable of understanding. We do not fully know how young children process and cope with information; at best, we can second-guess the process and extent of this assimilation. The child must be left, as much as possible, in control of his or her own learning. Appropriate amounts of adult intervention may be used to reinforce or redirect the child's efforts. The master teacher is sensitive to the differences between intervention and interference.

2. Children must experience only exemplary musical sounds, activities, and materials. *The child's learning time is valuable and must not be wasted on experiences with music of trite or questionable quality. Musical selections should include music of many styles and cultures; activities should involve singing, moving, listening to music, and playing instruments; materials must be hands-on items such as music manipulative characters (e.g., wooden figures representing musicians and their instruments) and both orchestral and traditional classroom instruments.*

3. Children must not be encumbered with the stress of meeting performance goals. *Opportunities are available for each child to develop in-tune singing, rhythmic responses to music, instrumental awareness (play and hearing), and to interact (listen and move) with music of his or her culture. Every child's attainment of a predetermined performance level, however, is neither essential nor appropriate.*

4. Children learn through play. *Children learn within a playful environment. Play provides a safe place to try on the roles of others, to fantasize about powerful things, to explore new ideas, and to fit parts and pieces of things and the world together. The child's play involves imitation and improvisation; a play-oriented environment is the most effective route for this method of learning.*

5. The child evolves through several developmental stages of interactive play. *According to Parten, these stages form a scale beginning with play that is solitary and progresses to cooperative experiences within the large group.*[13] *An early childhood music program must accommodate the child's ability to function within each of these social parameters.*

6. It is crucial that the child learn through developmentally appropriate activities and materials. *Hands-on, manipulative materials are essential learning tools. The environment and things in the environment (people and objects) are critical elements as the child engages in much self-teaching.*

7. A given learning environment will serve the developmental needs of many individual children. *Each child interacts with the material in his or her own fashion, based on the child's unique gifts and the developmental stage at which he or she is functioning. A child may display sophistication and confidence in creating songs in response to dolls. Another child, in the same setting, may move the dolls around without uttering a sound—but this "silent participator" leaves the area content in having shared in the musical play. The silent participator often is later heard playing in another area, softly singing to a different set of dolls, thus demonstrating a delayed response.*

8. Musical modeling by family members, other adult friends, and peers is an essential element because of the child's propensity to imitate. *That which the child chooses to imitate must reflect exemplary musical behavior.*

9. The parent/family is the child's most effective teacher, as bonding of love and trust is firmly established. *The musically effective parent is the most powerful route to the child's successful involvement in the art. In an early childhood music program, the teacher must often work in concert with the parent to establish a music-making bond with the young child.*[14]

SUMMARY

A credible music program for young children must be based on solid research. Often, we are tempted to "cut to the core" and proceed only on acquired knowledge and common sense, implementing what we feel is a good program for children. We cannot deny that it is more professional and reassuring to know that there is a valid rationale for why we do what we do. New theories emerge and enhance or supplant those that have been formulated, thus our view of why children grow and respond in a given manner is in a state of flux. Therein lies the excitement of being a teacher. The selected developmental and instructional theories discussed in this chapter are intended to provide a rationale for the methodologies, activities, and responses noted throughout this book. Readers will recognize activities supporting various theories, such as Piaget's notions about cognitive development, Bruner's three stages of learning, and Montessori's use of hands-on didactic materials. For example, what have we discussed in this chapter that helps us understand the learning of this second-grade child's simple essay on "What Is Music?"?

MUSIC
by Becky

In a few words, we learn that Becky's attitudes about music have been influenced by her family members. More important, we recognize that our goal of helping children acquire a disposition for music has truly been met with this child, because for Becky to relegate music to the same status as Christmas is a significant achievement.

THINGS TO DO

1. Test one of the following Piagetian theories by observing an infant in the sensorimotor stage:

    a. *Object permanency*—Show an infant a ball or rattle, then hide it under some covers or behind you. Record the child's chronological age. Observe and notate the child's behaviors. Report back to class on the child's response.

    b. *Cause and effect*—Play blocks or another game that has an obvious cause and effect with a child. Record the child's chronological age. Observe and notate the child's behaviors. Report back to class on the child's response.

2. Observe children at the preoperational stage of development. Notate examples of (1) egocentric and (2) socialized speech that take place. Be prepared to share the child's comments or dialogue with classmates.

3. Prepare a music activity/play area, such as a matching-instrument game, using manipulative items (small percussion instruments or game pieces) that are typical of Montessori's didactic materials. Place your music play activity where your classmates can observe it.

NOTES

[1]This chapter is a revision of an earlier work by Barbara Andress, *Music Experiences in Early Childhood* (New York: Holt, Rinehart and Winston, 1980), 131–144. Used by permission.

[2]Jean Piaget and Barbel Inhelder, *The Psychology of the Child* (New York: Basic Books, 1969).

[3]Laura Berk, *Child Development* (Boston: Allyn and Bacon, 1994), 22.

[4]Laura Berk, "Vygotsky's Theory: The Importance of Make-Believe Play," *Young Children* (November 1994): 31.

[5]Howard Gardner, *Frames of Mind: The Theory of Multiple Intelligences* (New York: Basic Books, 1983), 60.

[6]Ibid., 99.

[7]Ibid., 109.

[8]Ibid., 387.

[9]Jerome Bruner, *Toward a Theory of Instruction* (Cambridge, MA: Harvard University Press, 1971).

[10]Maria Montessori, *Dr. Montessori's Own Handbook* (New York: Schocken Books, 1976), 111–117.

[11]Anna Maccheroni, *Developing the Music Senses* (Cincinnati: Greenwood Press, World Library, 1950).

[12]Barbara Andress, "A Parent-Toddler Music Program," in *Promising Practices: Prekindergarten Music Education,* ed. Barbara Andress (Reston, VA: Music Educators National Conference, 1989), 26–27. Used by permission.

[13]Mildred Parten, "Social Participation among Preschool Children," *Journal of Abnormal and Social Psychology* 23 (1930): 243–269.

[14]Op cit.

2

The Young Child and Music

The infant is cradled in mother's arms as she rocks and sings "Twinkle, Twinkle, Little Star." The baby coos, gurgles, babbles, and otherwise displays enjoyment of the rhythmic and melodic play.

The two- or three-year-old plays with a tray containing specially prepared jingle bell stars. He stacks, shakes, arranges patterns, and swishes stars high and low while singing his own version of the song: "Dis star ringy dingy . . . gonna fly in the sky . . . twinky dis way . . . yeh! yeh! yeh!" As time goes on, the child's ability to sing the song more accurately increases, but first he sings only the anticipated global properties such as "Twinkle, twinkle," and the adult completes the remainder of the song.

A four-, five-, or six-year-old is capable of performing the song accurately and can arrange the stars to make an up-and-down picture of the first phrase of the melody (low-low-high-high-higher-higher-lower). The child points to the sequence of stars as she sings the song.

A seven- or eight-year-old vacillates between following iconic representations (pictures of sound, such as the stars) and traditional music notation when performing this or another song.

Children acquire musical understandings and communication skills as they progress developmentally from enactive hands-on experiences, to meaningful pictorial representations, and finally to the use of abstract mutually agreed upon symbolic representations of sound ideas. This three-phase cycle is repeated with various degrees of emphasis at each phase as each new learning experience is encountered. The appropriateness of the learning process and content is predicated on the child's developmental level.

The behaviors discussed in this chapter describe children's typical musical responses at various chronological ages. This method of describing behaviors according to age groups is for convenience only; it is assumed that readers are aware that all children in a given age group are not at the same developmental stage because of individual differences. Descriptive information for infants through eight-year-olds is included; however, the major focus is on two-, three-, and four-year-old children as this age group does not have the same curricular history as that which has been provided for the public school-age child. Well-defined, time-tested curriculum and resources have been available for teachers of five- to eight-year-old children for many years. Thus, references for materials for this group are cited, but all inclusive information is not included.

The Infant's Behaviors

Infants (6 to 18 months old) begin very early to explore their vocal sounds—bubbling, cooing, and gurgling. Typically, there is much parent-infant preverbal communication with baby talk. Papousek describes the nature of baby talk in terms of its many musical elements:[1]

1. Baby talk is simple in structure and contains many invitations to dialogue and/or warnings.

2. Melodic contours are more expressive than normal speech, and they contain enhanced rhythms and word stress.

3. The pitch of baby talk is higher than normal speech, nearer that of the infant's range.

4. Parts of baby talk are sung rather than spoken.

5. Rising contours are used to attract attention; falling contours are used to calm the baby.

6. The baby is provided opportunities to compare his or her own vocal productions with others through imitative vocal play between adult and child.

7. Repetitive musical patterns are consistently uttered by parents.

THE INFANT'S MUSICAL PLAY

Musical interaction is obvious in very young infants. They respond in the following ways:

◆   *They enjoy being sung to*—They like to hear lullabies, songs with surprises, such as "Pop! Goes the Weasel," songs of their culture, songs that mommy and daddy sing for their own enjoyment and share with the baby.

◆   *They participate in musical baby talk play*—(1) The mother hears the baby coo and echoes the sound, initiating more coos from the baby; (2) the mother drops a toy in the bath water, making high to low "kersplash" vocal sounds. The game is repeated several times, and the baby listens or adds his own squeals; (3) the parent and infant participate in a dialogue, alternating, but not necessarily imitating, a variety of nonverbal sounds; (4) the mother speaks low and soft as the baby is quieted.

◆   *They enjoy the adult's singing while being rocked, stroked, and/or gently patted*—The baby will respond to a lullaby while being rocked and rhythmically patted.

◆   *They respond happily to rhythmic play during body touch, singing, and chanting games*—The body touch game, "This Little Pig Went to Market," can be chanted or sung as an up-the-scale song. The infant shows great delight each time the words *Wee! Wee! Wee!* are squealed.

◆   *They enjoy tactile modeling play in response to music*[2]—The adult guides the one-year-old child's hands or body in movement responses such as rhythmic swaying, clapping, rubbing baby's hands, or dancing while carrying the baby.

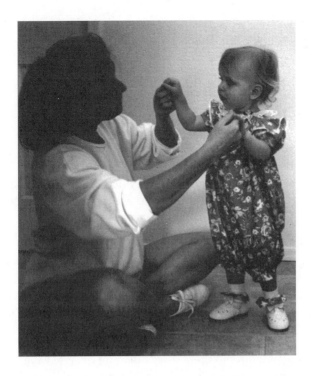

- *They enjoy bouncing motion*—The literature is rife with chants that probably originated from gentle knee-bouncing games traditionally played with infants.

> Ride a cock horse to Branberry Cross
> To see a fine lady on a white horse.
> With rings on her fingers and bells on her toes
> She will have music where ever she goes.

- *They hear recorded music of many styles and from many cultures*—The infant's home environment is full of recorded music from television, radio, and the stereo.
- *They exhibit curiosity about where the song or sound is coming from by touching the singer's or whistler's lips*—The father holds the baby and whistles the tune "Heigh Ho, Heigh Ho" from the Disney movie *Snow White*. The baby listens but is more interested in the father's pursed lips. She places her pointer finger over the lips to stop and start the sounds the dad is making.
- *They experiment with gestures such as clapping and pointing*—The infant will clap in a delayed fashion (often missing hands) as the adult sings and claps a song such as "Clap Clap Clap Your Hands."
- *They can bounce or awkwardly jump while holding the hands of the adult*—The adult extends both index fingers to help balance the infant during the song play. The infant awkwardly performs a knee-bending jump, where her feet do not leave the floor. New words are sung to the traditional song, "Here We Go Round the Mulberry Bush":

> This is the way we jump and jump
> Jump and jump, jump and jump.
> This is the way we jump and jump
> So early in the morning.

◆ *They enjoy sounds of rattles, bells, and toys such as music boxes*—The infant attends raptly to the color, shape, movement, and sound of music-making toys. He will most often reach out to touch and grasp the object.

The Toddler's Behaviors[3]

Toddlers' acquisition of language highlights this developmental stage. They start to speak sentences, which are characterized by a predominance of nouns. They also repeat words frequently, use fewer nonsense sounds, and say two- and three-word sentences more often. Examples are "Me go!" "Daddy hold!" and "Brian go nighty-night!" One-word labeling of objects occurs frequently.

This stage is also characterized by egocentric speech, with the toddler talking to himself more than he actually uses speech in a dialogue. They show rapidly increasing vocabulary and can follow simple directions. Speech is often accompanied by body movements, such as refusing by shaking her head while saying "no." Toddlers play with language, which is often used rhythmically and repetitively.

In addition, toddlers point and gesture when language is inadequate. They appreciate rituals, enjoying the same story over and over. Delayed responses characterized by an outward passivity and watchfulness during the activity and a response sometime later are also typical of this age. A concrete bond with objects that the child can actually hold instead of just imagine is another characteristic of the stage.

THE TODDLER'S MUSICAL PLAY

Toddlers musically respond in the following ways:

◆ *They are distinctly aware of musical and nonmusical sounds*—The toddler freely initiates a dance upon hearing music.
◆ *They create their own made-up songs*—The child makes up songs during play, such as a put-the-baby-to-sleep lullaby.
◆ *They sing simple one- or two-word songs depending on the stage of language acquisition*—A typical one-word song might be a random melody using one word repeatedly, such as kitty, kitty . . . , baby, baby . . . .
◆ *They enjoy voice inflection games*—Singing or chanting a nursery rhyme with added voice inflection on key words delights the toddler.

Jack and Jill went up the hill to fetch a pail of water.

Jack fell d   and broke his crown,
      o
        w
          n

And Jill came tumbling after. Doo-wop!
                              Doo-wop!
                                        Doo-wop!

- ◆ *They ritualistically demand repetition of a song, story, or instrumental sound*— When the adult strikes a drum and cymbal in a silly way, the toddler laughs and demands, "Again!" This demand is repeated many times.

- ◆ *They sing global perimeters of traditional songs*—When singing the song "Skip to My Lou," the toddler may sing only the words *skip* or *Skip Lou,* occasionally adding the final word *darling.*

- ◆ *They combine bits of traditional songs with their own improvised songs*—Typical song lyrics might be, "Goin' store, buy bananas, MacDonald had a, I'm hungry!"

- ◆ *They display curiosity about body touch and finger-play song games*—Labeling body parts is of great interest to the toddler. An example is the chant "Up so, down so, who can find a little toe? Fiddle-fy, in the sky, who can find a little eye?"

- ◆ *They are curious about sounds and shapes of all classroom and orchestral instruments*—The toddler freely explores sound sources by strumming, plucking, striking, and bowing instruments.

- ◆ *They love to make random sounds on the keyboard while an adult is performing*— The mother plays a traditional tune on the piano and the child joins in by adding random sounds.

- ◆ *They move gleefully as recorded music plays*—The child performs standing-still dances, random steps, and awkward turns. She demonstrates little or no concern for rhythmic content of the music while dancing, but does respond to its overall expressive nature.

- ◆ *They enjoy tactile modeling play with an adult*—The parent sings "Row Row Row Your Boat." The parent and child sit facing one another, and the child holds his parent's hands while the parent gently pulls and pushes the child in rhythm with the music.

- ◆ *They need real-looking objects to manipulate during musical play*—A song play about mommy and daddy is more effective when female and male dolls are used rather than two wooden dowels called "mommy" and "daddy."

- ◆ *They often display a delayed response during music time*—The child seemingly is not interested or participating when a song is sung at the childcare center, yet he will sing the song repeatedly to his mother when they are driving home.

Realistic
Representations

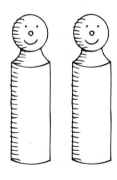

Abstract
Representations

The Three-Year-Old's Behaviors

Three-year-olds have more command of the language than toddlers, and they use language fluently and with confidence. They use words to control, and they can be controlled by words. Three-year-olds listen when reasoned with and attend to adult conversations with interest. Their ideas often formulate faster than they can form the words to express them.

Three-year-olds typically use a word or phrase to stand for a combination of several concepts, such as "dog" for all animals. They are sociocentric in speech; that is, they address the hearer, consider his point of view, try to influence him, or actually exchange ideas with him (deliberate communication). Three-year-olds are excited by challenges, such as walking backwards without peeking. They no longer walk with arms outstretched, and they can gallop, jump, run, and walk with relative ease.

Children at this age are better able to run fast or slow with more smoothness and can negotiate sudden stops. They have better defined, less diffuse, and less repetitive hand movement. Finally, three-year-olds are able to listen to and understand simple instructions better.

THE THREE-YEAR-OLD'S MUSICAL PLAY

At this age, children are becoming more competent in performing music. Cooperative play in large-group music sessions, as well as individual play, are effective ways for these children to interact. They musically respond in the following ways:

◆   *They are more able to reproduce a recognizable song*—The child can now sing recognizable words or melodic fragments that indicate a simple song, such as "Jingle Bells."

◆   *They are more likely to sing a tuneful song when they are allowed to begin on their own comfortable pitch*—The child begins singing the song. The adult joins in, using the pitch range that has been established. Depending on the complexity of the song, the adult will probably still be modeling a more accurate rendition of the song than the child is capable of performing.

◆   *They are gaining the ability to sing a more recognizable song, though many musical inaccuracies still occur*—The child may perform all the words of the song accurately, but continue to make some melodic and rhythmic errors. Overall, the song is very recognizable.

◆   *They perform with an increasing ability to match pitches when singing with others*—The child enjoys being in a group and is becoming more skillful in producing the song that others are singing. Still, the child continues to lag behind others if tempos and melodies are too fast or complicated.

◆   *They recognize the correct rhythmic and melodic contour of a song, but cannot always reproduce what was heard*—The child may sing a lengthy song he has heard on television with recognizable words but limited musical accuracy. When the adult precisely repeats the child's version, the child impatiently says, "That is not the way it goes." The child then insistently sings the song incorrectly again, expecting the adult to perform it correctly.

◆   *They enjoy manipulating hands-on play objects while creating songs*—The child will move a mother or father figure around while singing about mommy going to work or daddy making cookies.

◆   *They continue to improvise songs but now incorporate musical ideas recalled from traditional melodies*—The child sings, "Rock a bye baby . . . gonna go sleep . . . bye!"

◆   *They begin to reflect a sense of musical phrasing when improvising songs*—The child's ability now to shape sentences rather than use just one or two words influences the length of the improvised song statements. The child now sings, "I'm going to the store. Gonna buy broccoli and strawberries."

◆ *They enjoy creating songs that accompany play*—The child improvises random pitched songs while making clay snakes: "This is my great big snake. He goes ssss. . . ."

◆ *They create songs that reflect musical controls*—The child sings softly to put baby to sleep and sings loudly to wake baby up.

◆ *They explore expressive use of their voice*—The child can speak expressively by using voice inflection:

> The wind blows low,
> The wind blows high,
> It tickled my nose as it went by!
> Tickle, tickle, tickle!

◆ *They enjoy repeatedly singing familiar songs*—A large repertoire of songs is not necessary because the child most loves to repeat songs he or she has sung before.

◆ *They enjoy music time with others*—This is a time for having a special friend. Doing things together, such as group singing or sharing instrumental play during choice time, becomes more enticing.

◆ *They move spontaneously to many styles of music*—The child moves with swinging arms and wiggles to pop tune music.

◆ *They successfully imitate the simple movements of others*—The child copies gestures such as up-and-down arm movements and foot stamping that are modeled by the group leader.

◆ *They enjoy having their own movement ideas copied by others*—The teacher comments on a specific gesture the child makes. The child's pleasure is evident as others take note. The child, so reinforced, often continues this same gesture even though the music has changed.

◆ *They use movement to describe the more obvious ideas heard in music*—The child stamps her feet upon hearing loud, boisterous music and tiptoes to soft, staccato sounds.

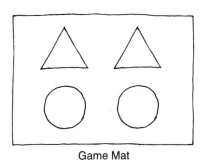
Game Mat

◆ *They demonstrate an emerging music vocabulary*—The child names musical instruments he has had contact with and uses word combinations such as *loud-soft* and *fast-slow* after hearing the adult use such terms in the context of a musical experience.

◆ *They play matching/classifying games*—Several instruments (e.g., two drums and two triangles) and a tag board game mat are placed in the play area. Pairs of matching geometric shapes (circles for drums, triangles for musical triangles) are marked on the mat. The child explores sounds, finds pairs, and places them together in the matched spaces on the mat.

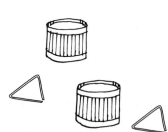

◆ *They can more easily tap or pat their hands on their thighs rather than repeatedly clap their hands together*—Hand tapping on thighs requires less energy than clapping hands together, thus the child begins to maintain a steady beat more readily by using the tapping gesture as an accompaniment to singing.

◆ *They can handle mallets and drum beaters in a more coordinated manner*—The child's striking aim and up-and-down action are better, thus she can begin to maintain a more regular beat when playing small percussion instruments.

◆ *They are increasing their ability to maintain a steady beat accompaniment*—The child often can begin tapping, patting, or clapping a steady beat, but then as his muscles tire, the beat wavers, lags, or stops.

One - two

tie my shoe

◆ *They respond to sound and silence games*—The older three-year-old uses drums or an xylophone (pitches C–G) when playing a game of "Time to play and time *not* to play." The child chants, "One-two, tie my shoe, three-four shut the door . . . ." Hands or mallets are held high in the sky on number words, and the instrument is rhythmically played on all other words.

◆ *They enjoy listening to music*—The child follows attentively as the teacher guides the musical play of "The Dance of the Sugar Plum Fairy" from the *Nutcracker Suite* by Tchaikovsky. The teacher uses dancing puppets to guide the listening experience. Although the child is not held accountable for recognizing the form of the music, the puppets are moved in response to the initial musical idea (A section), a new idea (B section), and the return of the first idea (A section).

◆ *They hear orchestral music as a whole entity*—The child is unable to abstract special sounds from within the whole, so it is inappropriate to ask the child to listen for the special sound of the trumpet when many other instruments are simultaneously playing.

The Four-Year-Old's Behaviors

Imaginative play begins to enter the children's world; however, four-year-olds are still sorting out fantasy and reality, often believing that everything they see is real. These children talk a great deal, exaggerate, boast, tell tall tales, and ask many questions. Often, questions are used as a device to keep the conversation going rather than to seek more information.

Four-year-olds like nonsense words, silly language, rhyming, and new and different words. They interject irrelevant subjects that reveal their inattention to the ongoing activity and their inability to internalize and recall previous experiences. They also love dramatic play, are able pretenders, and readily assume the roles of imaginary and real characters.

Four-year-olds possess good motor control—they can run more smoothly and stand on one foot. Small-muscle coordination is more controlled in these children, as indicated by their ability to cut on a line and handle small objects such as beads and puzzle pieces. Finally, four-year-olds test their power over objects, other children, and adults. They like to see how hard they can throw an object or how safe it is to say "No!" to a parent.

THE FOUR-YEAR-OLD'S MUSICAL PLAY

Children at this age become rather competent musicians. Their increased skills and understandings afford many options for experiencing music. Four-year-olds musically respond in the following ways:

◆ *They demonstrate awareness of beat, tempo (fast-slow), volume (loud-soft), pitch (high-low), and form (same and different phrases)*—The child can accurately create the sounds of a moving train on sandpaper blocks to accompany a song such as "Little Red Caboose."

◆ *They enjoy singing a wide variety of songs*—The child likes silly songs, game songs, lullabies, finger-play and body identification songs, and songs about nature and mechanical things.

◆ *They perform best when songs are within their singing range*—Typically, the four-year-old's most usable song range is from D (immediately above middle C) to A. This child can also successfully sing songs that have a few pitches in a more extended range (middle C—d' above second space c'). A song within the D–A range is "Mary Had a Little Lamb"; a song within the extended range (C–d') is "She'll Be Comin' 'Round the Mountain."

◆ *They have difficulty accurately singing pop tune–type songs due to the many words and complex melodic/rhythmic lines*—The child can frequently master the more complicated words to the latest Disney songs (which are in the pop tune style), but often does not sing the melody or rhythm correctly. The child should not be discouraged from enjoying and performing these songs.

However, it is important that this music not be the only literature the child is offered due to its complexity.

◆ *They continue to make up their own songs/instrumental pieces but are more critical of their own efforts; they now demand a more traditional musical structure in their own improvised songs*—The child is aware of how songs in his culture are performed. He hears equal-length phrases in traditional songs and so attempts to create equal-length phrases in his own improvisations. The child sings about his grandpa, stretching out each phrase to make them equal, then abruptly ends the song:

> I love pa-pa so mu-u-uch
> He is so ni-i-ice.
> He likes me, too-oo-oo.
> That's the end!

◆ *They demonstrate awareness of tonal center when they make up a song while hearing a recorded ostinati pattern (short, repeated pitch sequence such as C-G-A-G)*—The child sings a rambling tune but returns to C (tonal center) with great frequency, even to the point of ending the song on C.

◆ *They bring more imagination, logic, and story sequence to improvised song making*—Upon seeing a picture of a bird in the rain, standing under a flower, the child sings:

OH, LITTLE BIRDIE

◆ *They demonstrate interest in rhyming when they listen to songs or create their own lyrics.*

> See this kitty cat. He gots a hat.
> He's a fat__ (pause)____ cat! (giggle)

◆ *When guided, they can follow a musical story sequence, such as one involving the size and speed of moving trains*—The teacher uses pictures of various animated trains to guide the child in listening to "The Little Train" from *Once Upon a Time Suite* by H. Donaldson. This is a musical version of the little train that tried. The little train's encounters with the various trains that are reluctant to help are clearly depicted in the music.

- *They can interact with simple, iconic pictures to tap out steady beats of a song*—The child taps sequential pictures of sleeping and awakening faces while singing "Are You Sleeping, Brother John?"

ARE YOU SLEEPING

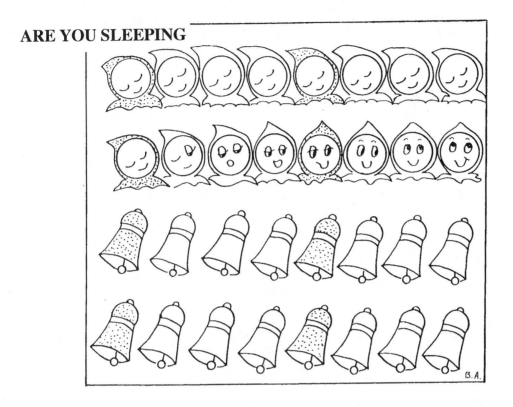

- *They recognize traditional music notation in printed music and are aware that it helps the musician know what to play and sing*—While the child is generally aware of the function of musical symbols, it is not appropriate for her to be encumbered with attempting to read or understand these abstract symbols.

- *They explore sounds of musical instruments with great zeal*—The child will spend long periods of time testing the many ways to create different sounds on instruments, including soft and very loud banging. Multiple sound starters, such as mallets, beaters, or sticks, enhance the play.

- *They begin to play simple accompaniments on instruments that have controlled pitches*—Orff-type bar instruments with preset pitches (only C and G) or a specially tuned guitar (C-G-C-G-C-E) allow the child to strum/strike steady beat harmonic accompaniments.

- *They can identify the shape, size, and sound of classroom and some orchestral instruments*—The child can differentiate between the sound quality (timbre) of grossly different instruments such as a trumpet and a drum, a violin and a sousaphone, or a maraca and a flute.

- *They acquire a larger music vocabulary from the teacher's descriptions and labeling during musical experiences*—This vocabulary includes words that describe sounds: loud-soft, high-low, fast-slow, long-short; words that label musical objects: names of instruments; and words that describe how music makes one feel: go-to-sleep music or laugh-and-jump music.

- *They delight in expressively moving to music*—The child is not yet inhibited or self-conscious about freely participating in group or solo movement play in response to music.

◆ *They use movement to describe distinct ideas heard in the music*—The child taps/claps/walks the beat or shakes her fingers when a contrasting maraca sound is distinctly heard. She responds with a menacing gesture when instruments express the sound of a roaring lion such as in Saint-Saëns' "Royal March of the Lion" from the *Carnival of the Animals*. (The child's ability to isolate a given sound or musical idea within the context of other instruments requires that the adult's recorded examples be very obvious.)

The Five-Year-Old's Behaviors

Five-year-olds strive to use new and larger words and question the meaning of words. They are aware of symbols and ask questions about their meanings. At this stage, children are really seeking information when they ask questions.

In addition, five-year-olds are able to group or classify objects on the basis of similarities, are more attentive to detail, and thus are more aware of differentiation. These children imitate readily but may think it is their own idea. They also think more logically when sequencing story ideas. Finally, five-year-olds use imagination to a great extent in play to increase their skills and sense of power.

THE FIVE-YEAR-OLD'S MUSICAL PLAY

Five-year-olds are increasingly able to accurately perform and understand musical ideas. They are growing in ability to interact with icons and introductory-level musical symbols. Five-year-olds musically respond in these ways:

◆ *They enjoy performing alone as well as in a group*—The child is more able to musically function in group activities due to increased social skills and more competent musicianship. He can sing simple songs with acceptable melodic and rhythmic accuracy, match pitches of others, and participate in song arrangements that call for a solo time and a time for all to join in. He continues to like repetition of favorite songs.

◆ *They acquire a large repertoire of songs*—The child sings many songs learned at school, from the media, and from parents or other caring adults.

◆ *They play instruments alone and in ensemble*—The child's ability to play basic accompaniment patterns involving borduns (patterns built on open fourths or fifths) and ostinatis (short patterns repeated throughout the composition) on xylophone-type instruments and one-chord songs on the autoharp is increasing.

Simple Bordun: (Tonic and Fifth)

Ostinato (Repeated Pattern)

◆ *They demonstrate an increasing ability to play simple melodies on bells*—The child often struggles, but she loves to attempt playing a three-tone melody such as "Hot Cross Buns." She finds it easier to play up- or down-scale songs such as

"This little pig went to market (C), This little pig stayed home (D), This little pig ate roast beef (E), This little pig had none (F), This little pig cried (G) Wee, wee, wee (A), All the way (B) home (c')."

◆ *They continue to move expressively to many different styles of music*—The child enjoys making up simple dances to music from different cultures, such as a fan dance to "Sakura" (Japan) and the hula (Hawaii). Props and costumes are greatly enjoyed.

◆ *They can follow movement directions for simple traditional dances*—The child can perform dance movements, especially when the words of the song provide directions.

CIRCLE AROUND
German Folk Dance

Words by Margaret Lowrey

Cir - cle a - round to the right in a ring,

Then to the left as so gai - ly we sing.

Walk to the mid - dle as close as you can;

Step back in rhy - thm to where you be - gan.

"Circle Around," *The Music Book—Grade 2*, 1984. Holt, Rinehart and Winston. Used by permission.

◆ *They become more competent in responding to the underlying beat or pulse of music*—The child can clap, march, or use other body gestures to indicate an increasingly accurate beat competency.

◆ *They use rhythmic body sounds to accompany songs and chants*—The child can stamp or tap a patterned rhythmic accompaniment while chanting "Hot Cross Buns" or "One, Two Tie My Shoe."

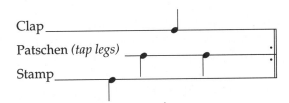

◆ *They begin to read and write musical ideas using icons (topical and generic)*—The older five-year-old may begin to make limited transitions from icons to simple traditional notation.

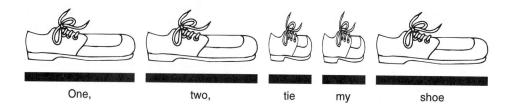

One,　　　　two,　　　　tie　my　　　shoe

◆ *They are able to move from the wholeness of the musical idea to accessing more discrete information within the whole*—The child becomes aware of musical form. He realizes that a given melody may be heard more than once within the song or may alternate with another melody.

◆ *They acquire understandings about basic music concepts: melody, rhythm, timbre, dynamics, articulation, harmony, texture, form, and expression*—The child becomes aware that melodies are made up of pitches that move up and down by steps and skips, and that rhythm is made of combinations of long and shorter sounds.

◆ *They become aware of how these basic music elements are combined into a whole that reflects the origin and use of the music*—The child can identify musical styles such as a march, bugle calls, church music, lullabies, or ballet music.

◆ *They use more music vocabulary with greater understanding*—The child begins to work with more discrete music concepts, thereby acquiring appropriate descriptive vocabulary such as "same," "different," and "similar" as related to musical form.

◆ *They readily express nonmusical ideas through music*—The child sets poems and stories to music and uses music to express sounds or ideas about nature and feelings:

> I thought I saw an old bull frog
> Or was it a dog, hopping on the log?
> I know I saw an old bull frog
> How silly to think it was a dog!

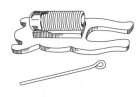

Drum plays hopping sounds; frog guiro plays Brrrrumph!

◆ *They improvise their own songs and instrumental pieces*—The child needs more adult encouragement as she begins to question her own ability to create music that measures up to what she hears performed by others.

◆ *They can improvise within structured parameters*—Strategies can be set within the workable limits of the child's ability. A strategy might be for the child to make up a piece about a star using cymbals and triangles that are sometimes very soft or very loud.

◆ *They can create instrumental and vocal introductions, codas, or endings to phrases*—The teacher sings, "I see a little bug." The child completes the musical phrase, "He lives in a rug."

◆ *They love participating in musical drama*—Singing or using instruments to tell a story is most exciting.

◆ *They are delighted by live musical performances*—The child enjoys live music at school, malls, concert halls, and other performing sites. Special favorites are excerpts from *Peter and the Wolf* (orchestral), *Hansel and Gretel* (opera), and *The Nutcracker* (ballet).

◆ *They can identify various large performing groups such as bands, orchestras, and choirs*—The teacher initially identifies these performing groups both by sight and sound as children listen to the given ensemble's music. After acquiring the group's identifying label the child easily uses it during subsequent listening experiences.

The Six- to Eight-Year-Old's Behaviors

Music programs for primary-level schoolchildren have a long history, dating back to the era of Singing Schools in which one of the primary uses of music was to make the teaching or reading of words more palatable. Grade level music textbook series have been available as resources for teachers for many years. These series have grown in sophistication of content, sequence of information, and quality of age-appropriate musical examples and activities. Text resources now involve pupil books, teacher's guides, large chart books, quality recordings, CD-ROMS, laser disks, and other assorted supplemental materials. The series provide teachers with a comprehensive model of time-tested "doable" experiences for children at each primary grade level. These series address appropriate vocal range, logical sequence for introducing musical understandings, and quality-guided listening and movement experiences.

Children in this age group are able and expected to understand introductory musical concepts about rhythm, melody, timbre, dynamics, articulation, harmony, texture, form, expression, and time and place. They become aware of these ideas as they perform (sing and play instruments), describe (move and verbalize), and create (improvise and compose) music.

An example of the musical understandings and behaviors appropriate for primary-level children might appear as follows in a typical first-grade teacher's guide:

Concept: Musical Form

◆ A musical whole begins, continues, and ends.

◆ A musical whole is a combination of smaller segments.

◆ A musical whole may be made up of same, varied, or contrasting segments.

◆ A series of sounds may form a distinct musical idea within the musical whole.

◆ A musical whole may include an introduction, interludes, and an ending segment.

Predictable Skills/Behaviors

Describe

◆ Show recognition of phrase changes with movement.

◆ Demonstrate awareness of whole-part structure and repetition and contrast.

◆ Organize geometric shapes to indicate understanding of same-different.

Create

◆ Plan a long song by combining short songs.

◆ Develop introductions, interludes, and endings for songs.

Holt Music—Book I, 1988. Holt, Rinehart and Winston. Used by permission.

An appropriate learning experience for first-grade children might be as follows:

◆ *Lesson Focus*

◆ *Musical Understanding: Form*—A musical whole is a combination of smaller segments.

◆ *Child's Behavior*—Describe (move/verbalize/visualize).

◆ *Conceptual Mode*—Iconic (pictures representing each line (phrase) of the song).

The song "Miss Polly" is selected for the lesson because it is attractive and within the singing range of this age group (C–b). Children are introduced to the song

MISS POLLY
Old English Nursery Song

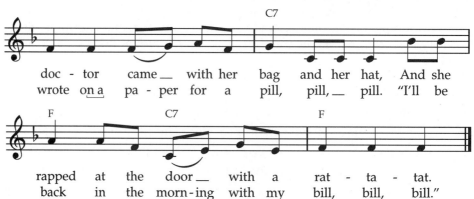

"Miss Polly," *Holt Music—Book I,* 1988. Holt, Rinehart and Winston. Used by permission.

with icons that represent each phrase of the song. Children become aware that the whole song, or form of the music, is made up of eight parts (phrases). Icons used for "Miss Polly" include eight pictures, one for each phrase of the song: a child with a doll, a child talking on the telephone, a doctor walking to a house, a doctor knocking on the door, a doctor examining a doll, a doctor and child putting the doll to bed, a doctor writing a prescription, and a happy doctor leaving the house.

Teachers and care providers should refer to these reliable sources and then adapt the materials and approaches to meet the unique needs of their students and their own ability to communicate musical ideas. An effective series teacher's guide provides step-by-step instruction for helping primary-level children experience music and musical ideas to the fullest.

Six- to eight-year-olds are socially aware and should be involved in many cooperative music play experiences. These years are crucial as children develop a concept of music, gain fundamental performance skills, acquire a sensitivity to musical sounds and their beauty, and use music as an expressive art. Appropriate music-making experiences include large- and small-group activities that involve singing, playing classroom instruments, moving expressively and with precise responses to ideas heard in the music, listening to music from many cultures, and beginning to acquire skills in reading and writing music. Guiding children's musical literacy should continue to be based on developmentally appropriate practices whereby the adult nurtures curiosity and encourages the learner to seek more information.

The Sequential Acquisition of Musical Skills

The following is a brief overview of how children perform music, infant through eight-years of age. These observable behaviors are arranged in an acquisition hierarchy based on the initial responses of the infant or young child to the more complex performance skills of the more mature child.

SINGING

Young children sing in two ways: (1) they improvise their own vocal play and (2) they structure songs of their culture. Improvised songs typically involve voice inflection tunes that have little regard for musical rules. Such tunes tend to musically ramble, disregard logical lyrics, and mix ideas with fragments of traditional songs. Children demonstrate the following developmental sequence as their musical abilities increase: (1) voice inflection play, (2) singing their own rambling tunes, (3) combining rambling tunes with fragments of traditional songs from their culture, (4) singing global properties (most obvious words or melodic patterns) of traditional songs, (5) increased skill in performing lyrics with rhythmic and melodic accuracy.

MOVING

Movement is an important musical response because it is nonverbal and allows the observer to better understand what children are sensing from the music. Early movement activities center on the body (body touch, finger play, song games) and responses to the wholeness of the music. As motor skills develop, children can respond more sensitively to musical ideas. Four- and five-year-old children begin to refine gestures to perform and describe introductory-level musical information such as timbre, expression control, rhythm, melody, and form.

PLAYING MUSICAL INSTRUMENTS

Interest and curiosity are keen in young children as they explore the sights and sounds of musical instruments. It is often enough for the child to just repeatedly ring a bell to savor the delightful sound. Discovering that sounds can be the same, similar, or quite different provides opportunities for auditory discrimination and cognitive problem solving. Instruments can be used in the learning environment to explore shape, size, and sound relationships; organize, order, and classify sounds; use sounds to express musical (wood block to create a loud and soft composition) and nonmusical ideas (wood block for the sound of ponies), or play simple accompaniments for songs or other musical works; and perform rhythmic and melodic ideas.

Playing instruments with rhythmic and melodic accuracy is a developing skill, so it is inappropriate to press young children to attain this goal. However, in-tune sounds can be attained even at the exploratory level when, for example, an adult presets xylophones with removable bars to control pitch choices.

A teacher cannot tell children about musical sounds; they must experience them. Therefore, it is important that the effective learning environment contain many options for exploring the sounds of quality instruments.

READING AND WRITING MUSIC

Three- and four-year-old children are at a concrete level of learning, thus abstract symbols, such as traditional music notation, are meaningless to them. Games in which children are encouraged to jump on staff lines and pretend to be musical notes are not understood by this age group and should be considered inappropriate practice.

Older four-year-olds can be introduced successfully to pointing/tapping pages that depict musical ideas using "pictures of sound" (icons). Iconic pictures for these children are usually topical in nature, representing such ideas as steady beat tapping to accompany chanting/singing. An example of a tapping page appears on the following page.

Five- to eight-year-old children continue to respond to icons but are becoming aware of the meaning and use of traditional musical symbols. To build a true understanding of abstract symbols, continued interplay between icons and symbols must be encouraged throughout children's introductory experiences with music notation.

SUMMARY

Children acquire and demonstrate musical skills and understandings based on their developmental growth. Children cannot be expected to tap a steady beat if their muscles are not prepared to do so; nor can they comprehend the meaning of abstract symbols if they are still at the concrete stage of learning. However, they can hear the steady beat or other musical entities long before they are able to perform them. Common sense dictates that there is truly a time and place to introduce various concepts and a time to expect skillful responses.

A Rhythmic Tapping Page

Jack had a **kit**-ty,   **Jack**   had a   **cat**,

Jack   put **kit**-cats,   **in** his   **hat**!

Creating an environment so that one learning experience generates the next is predicated on knowledge about the child's physical and musical development. One must first know about the child before planning an early childhood music curriculum. The wise teacher is aware that children of the same age function at differing levels of ability. Thus, categorizing musical behaviors based on chronological age provides only a convenient general reminder of how children acquire skills and understandings.

The material in this chapter has attempted to provide a developmental reference point for children's musical behaviors. Such information is important for the teacher who is responsible for planning appropriate musical experiences for young children.

THINGS TO DO

1. Become a child "watcher" for one week. Spend time in places where you are likely to encounter children—a childcare center, mall, restaurant, sports event, church, school, or home. Keep a journal about observed spontaneous musical behaviors exhibited by children. Such behaviors may be brief and fragmented or more deliberate. Use many adjectives and adverbs in your comments to better describe the true nature of the children's experiences. Indicate the length of time you spent observing at each given site.

2.   Review two lessons in a first- or second-grade music series textbook. Note the expected musical learning and predicted responses of children. Evaluate the merits and/or limitations of the lesson on the basis of age appropriateness and your personal ability and interest in presenting the lesson.

Notes

[1]Mechthild Papousek, "The Mother Tongue Method of Music Education: Psychobiologic Roots in Pre-verbal Parent-Infant Communication," in *Papers of the 15th International Conference of the International Society for Music Education,* ed. J. Dobbs (Republic of Singapore: Chin Long Printing Service, 1982), 105–106.

[2]Elayne Metz, "Movement as a Musical Response among Preschool Children," Ed.D. Dissertation, Arizona State University, 1986, 78–85.

[3]Comments from the sections, "Toddler's Behaviors," "Three-Year-Old's Behaviors," "Four-Year-Old's Behaviors," and "Five-Year-Old's Behaviors" are a revision of materials from an earlier work by Barbara Andress et al., *Music in Early Childhood,* published by Music Educators National Conference (MENC), Copyright ©1973 by MENC. Music Educators National Conference, 1806 Robert Fulton Drive, Reston, VA 22091. Used by permission.

3

A Meaning-centered Approach to the Young Child's Musical Play

Current practice in teaching music to preschool children is typically activity oriented. Teachers and care providers present music materials and ideas that are, first, entertaining and, second, educationally effective. Activities may involve singing songs, engaging in musical games, playing instruments, moving, and listening. This random activity approach, although fun, is a fragmented program that lacks a well-defined, organized curriculum plan of guiding young children's musical growth.

An entry-level core of musical knowledge may be presented to very young children encompassing developmentally and individually appropriate activities. A curriculum that attends to basic musical understandings can be playful, yet it must include meaning-centered activities that have the potential to promote a sensitivity for and understanding about music.

The National Association for the Education of Young Children (NAEYC) and National Association of Early Childhood Specialists in State Departments of Education (AECS/SDE) guidelines call for meaning-centered, integrated, "mindful" curriculum, but such curriculum is only achieved if the other perspectives that inform curriculum are activated—child development knowledge, discipline-based knowledge, and knowledge of the individual developmental/learning continuum of each child. [1]

Meaning-centered activities should be planned so that they are easily carried out by novice music teachers or care providers. The teacher uses techniques such as *modeling, describing,* and *suggesting* to impart understandings and to help children interact at their own individual level of mastery.[2] The teacher models a musical sensitivity to qualities heard and performed, such as volume, timbre, and tempo. When appropriate, the teacher introduces labels that describe music and musical ideas. Children are challenged to solve musical problems as the teacher makes suggestions or asks questions during the experience.

39

There are risks associated with implementing a conceptually based or meaning-centered early childhood music curriculum. An overzealous approach that presses the learning of musical elements or the development of performance skills may diminish the child's joyful knowing and playful interaction with musical ideas. However, if lessons are well conceived and implemented in a developmentally appropriate manner, a meaning-centered approach will help teachers become more musical in their presentations and will provide effective guidelines for planning early childhood music experiences that don't detract from the joy of the experience.

Identify and Implement a Meaning-centered Early Childhood Music Program

We first approach music by focusing on the beauty and totality of its whole sound. Children respond joyously by singing, moving, and playing instruments with carefree abandonment, truly responding to the wholeness of the musical effect. A growing awareness of the many musical parts that contribute to that whole provides children with the understandings and skills that empower them to control and more sensitively use music as an expressive tool throughout their lives. We refer to these musical parts as *elements,* from which children learn concepts that are inherent in music. These musical elements are as follows:

◆ *Volume*—gradations of loud and soft in the music

◆ *Tempo*—rate of speed

◆ *Articulation*—packaging or shape of a sound (connected or disconnected)

◆ *Timbre*—quality of sound

◆ *Rhythm*—groupings of long and short musical sounds in relation to the underlying pulse

◆ *Melody*—a succession of pitches having a recognizable musical shape

◆ *Form*—the overall structural organization of the composition

◆ *Style*—the distinctive manner in which the elements of music are organized, reflecting their use throughout various times and places; examples are baroque, gospel, folk, rock, and calypso

The following sections identify a musical idea and then provide examples of exploratory-level play that is developmentally and musically appropriate.

Infants to Eight-Year-Olds Explore the Bank of Musical Knowledge

EXPRESSIVE CONTROLS

Volume

◆ Sounds may be relatively loud or soft.

◆ Sounds may gradually become louder or softer.

Key Music Descriptors—loud, soft, becoming louder, becoming softer
Musical Play

Mommy plays body touch games while she sings, "Pop! Goes the Weasel" to her toddler (see page 108). She sings *softly,* gently rubbing the baby's hands together. The word "Pop" is *loud* and explosive as she claps the baby's hands together, throws his arms open, and laughs.

Daddy faces his child and plays a finger-walking game while a brief recorded excerpt (first 24 measures) of Haydn's *Symphony in G, Second Movement* ("Surprise Symphony") is heard.

This eight-measure musical theme repeats, then changes briefly (four measures) to a new melody that ends as a fragment of the original theme is played (final four measures) much higher.

◆ *Movement Gestures 1*—Daddy holds the child's hand palm up, makes his fingers walk from the palm to the inside of the child's elbow (four steps, two per measure), then moves his fingers back down to the palm (four steps). Next, daddy's fingers walk rhythmically (eight steps) up to the child's shoulder. The first musical idea and gestures are repeated but, the second time, when the fingers walk all the way to the shoulder, the motion ends in a chin tickle as *very loud* surprising sounds are heard.

◆ *Movement Gestures 2*—The music continues briefly (four measures) with a different musical idea (daddy and child sway their heads back and forth).

◆ *Movement Gestures 3*—On the final four measures of the music, a fragment of the first melodic idea is heard. Daddy makes his fingers again walk palm to elbow—four steps; he returns to the palm in four steps. The play ends with daddy kissing or blowing on the child's palm.

The child is at first a bit reluctant to extend his arm, but he trusts daddy. As the play is repeated, the anticipation of the loud, surprising music and tickle makes this an exciting game. The child demands many replays by saying before the music ends, "Again!"

Three-year-old Janey makes up a "put-the-baby-to-sleep song," then she wakes the baby up in a song-shouting manner. The teacher casually describes the sound contrasts by saying, "That song was so *soft,* it really made me sleepy, too. Wow! But you made me wake up with that *loud* sound!" thus helping Janey to expand her music vocabulary.

Four-year-old Robbie is independently reading his own version of the parade story "Thump, Thump Rat-a-tat-tat!" (Baer 1989) after hearing the teacher model the expressive volume changes during a group presentation. His voice begins *softly, becomes louder,* then again *becomes softer* as the illustrations change from one small approaching marching image to increasingly more and larger ones, ending with smaller retreating images (icons).

Later in the year, the teacher again presents the book. This time, no words are used. Children are invited to listen to the music as the pages of the book are turned. The teacher turns the pages in a synchronized manner to the musical selection "Parade" by Morton Gould. This selection is performed by a percussion ensemble, and it musically describes the coming and going of marchers in a parade with *gradually louder* and *gradually softer* sounds. The children are now more able to associate the icon imagery (illustrations in the book) with the musical sounds.

During a second-grade music class, children are invited to create a rainstorm. They begin with a few sounds, then combine many sounds. First they use their fingers for small drops (snapping/tapping); then they slap their hands on their thighs for large raindrops; next they stamp their feet rapidly for rolls of thunder, ending with a loud hand clap. The storm recedes as thigh slapping ceases, then one by one the finger snappers drop out until only one child is snapping, and then silence.

The teacher asks Julio to make a picture of their rainstorm on the blackboard. Julio, the self-designated class artist, draws small to larger raindrops, a large figure holding a lightning bolt, then larger to smaller raindrops to complete the picture. The teacher asks about the figure, and Julio explains that it is a thunder god. Discussion ensues about how the sounds began softly, became louder, and then softer. The teacher draws crescendo and decrescendo marks around Julio's picture, and the class suggests appropriate placement of the volume symbols, *p* = piano (soft) and *f* = forte (loud), to complete the picture.

A RAINSTORM VISUAL

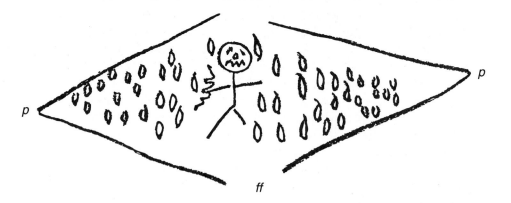

Tempo

◆   Sounds may be relatively faster or slower.

◆   Sounds may gradually become faster or slower.

Key Music Descriptors—fast, slow, becoming faster, becoming slower
Musical Play

Megan, almost four years old, plays an Orff-type xylophone (C, D, E, G, A, c' pentatonic pitches only). The teacher sits on the floor and repeatedly strums a C chord (C, G, C, G, C, E open-string tuning) on the guitar. The teacher asks, "Shall we make a *fast* song or a *slow* song?" Megan replies, "*Fast!*" She then begins to furiously strike the xylophone. The teacher complies and accompanies Megan with rapid strums on the guitar. When the "Concerto Furioso" subsides, the teacher adds, "That was really *fast* music. I didn't know you could play the xylophone that *fast!* Who would like to make *slow* music? . . . Who would like to play sneak-up, then run-away music? . . . " After the teacher leaves the play area, Megan takes over the teacher's role as other children join the play.

First-grade children are exploring music ideas. A box is prepared to look like a castle. Seventeen small trolls (teacher makes paper/cloth or purchased figures) are made available. As a recording of *The Hall of the Mountain King* by Edvard Grieg is played, the children are invited to count from one to eight with the music, clapping their hands on the count of eight. The same pattern is repeated until the children begin to sense the length of the phrase (musical sentence).

Fourth Movement   1   2   3   4   5   6   7   Clap!

You will note that this melodic idea is repeated throughout the entire composition.

Now the fun begins. Small pictures of trolls, troll pillow dolls, or commercially made trolls are distributed to the children. They are invited to sneak up one at a time (move expressively to the music) and drop their troll into the castle (a box). The troll is to be dropped precisely on the count of eight. The children use many different sneaking styles and routes to use up their musical phrase (eight counts). The excitement heightens to a frenzy as the children realize the tempo of the eight counts is increasing and that the trolls must hurry ever more quickly as the music comes to a frantically rushing end.

Articulation

- ◆ Sounds may be smooth and connected (legato) or jagged and disconnected (staccato).

Key Music Descriptors—smooth to jagged
Musical Play

Expressive movement play helps children become aware of differences in the articulation of sounds. The teacher invites the children to move with the sounds of a drum as she rubs the head of a hand drum, creating smooth, sustained sounds. She describes the sliding movements of John, then several other children copy John's motion. The teacher then thumps the hand drum, making short, quick, disconnected sounds. The children respond with jerky, jabbing movements. The teacher alternates between the two sound ideas as children continue the play.

An activity is presented that allows three-year-old children to progress from a *concrete* to an *abstract* experience.

◆ *Step 1*—The children are each given a small paper cup into which the teacher carefully pours about a quarter inch of water. The children are asked to move very carefully with their water while the teacher rubs a continuous sound on a hand drum. Occasionally, verbal comments are added by the teacher such as, "Can you carry your water high?" "Can you carry your water low?" "Can you walk backwards?"

◆ *Step 2*—The children are asked to drink their water and then pretend the water is still in the cup. The movement ideas and accompanying sounds are repeated as the children carefully move with their imaginary water.

◆ *Step 3*—The children are then asked to place the paper cup on the floor. The movement ideas and accompanying sounds are repeated, with the children now pretending to carry a cup of water.

◆ *Step 4*—The teacher warns the group that she will be adding a surprise sound (rapid, repeated sounds on the drum in contrast to smooth, rubbing sounds). The children are encouraged to move any way they like. Their response to the contrasting sounds tends to be either jerky and jabbing or sliding and flowing gestures.

Four- and five-year-old children are playing in the dancing area. The teacher sits at the piano and plays a "Gavotte" by Handel. Children respond to the staccato music with tiptoe steps. Without any comment, the teacher plays the same melody in a sustained legato manner. The children alter their movement, now using flowing, swooping gestures. The teacher alternates between the two ideas as the dancing continues.

"Gavotte," Holt Music, 1988.
Holt, Rinehart and Winston.
Used by permission.

GAVOTTE

by George Frederick Handel

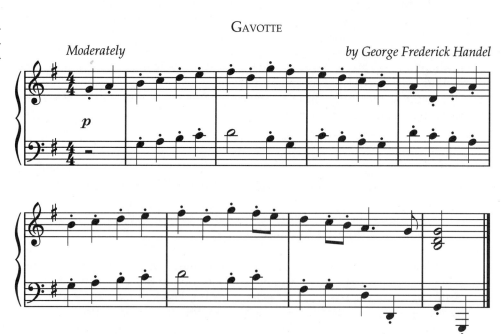

First-grade children form a double line, creating an alley for players to step down. All chant these words as the couple at the top of the alley begins to move down it:

Down came a lady/gentleman,
Struttin' on through
Down came a lady/gentleman,
And she/he was dressed in blue.

(Couple moves after the chant, during the instrumental interlude)

The moving couple is told to listen to the sound of the instrument and move expressively down the alley in response to the sounds. The teacher then plays staccato or legato sounds on various instruments such as wood blocks, drums, tambourines, and triangles. Sometimes she stops, and the strutters freeze in place for a moment. Typically, the strutters tiptoe, glide, slide, and otherwise move in response to the way the sound is articulated. The chant is repeated and the next couple moves down the alley.

Timbre

◆   Voices have distinctive qualities of sound.

◆   Instruments have distinctive qualities of sound.

Key Music Descriptors—ringing, clicking, swishing, clattering
Musical Play

The teacher plays the recorded selection "Ghost Dance" from *Ancient Voices of Children* by G. Crumb. The composer uses two distinct sounds throughout the composition—rattles (staccato) and electronic pitch swoops (legato). The teacher invites the children to move only when they hear the rattling sounds or the electronic pitch swoops. The children respond by shaking their fingers or other body parts when they hear the rattle sounds, and make swishing or sweeping motions with their arms or all of their body when they hear the swooping, connected sounds. The selection is a bit lengthy for young children, so the teacher brings the game to an early end by slowly turning down the volume and allowing the music to fade away.

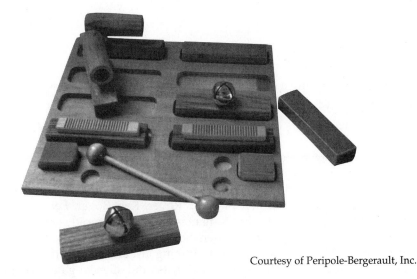

Courtesy of Peripole-Bergerault, Inc.

Three-year-old Robbie and Marie play with distinctive qualities of sound by using a timbre board that has two each of four different sound blocks (a jingle bell, sand block, ratchet block, and wood block). The children play alone or with other friends to match sounds. The matched sounds are placed side-by-side on a puzzle board. The teacher helps describe the sounds by saying, "You found the two ringing sounds . . . clicking sounds . . . swishing sounds. . . ."

STRUCTURED MUSICAL RESPONSES

The musical ideas of tempo, volume, timbre, and articulation discussed earlier are all expressive controls. This means that an idea such as a given melody may be enhanced or better expressed by altering its speed, volume, quality, or way in which the sound is "packaged." Ideas about expressive controls are easily shared with young children because they encounter many of these same concepts in everyday events. For example, loud is loud and soft is soft regardless of what these concepts refer to—a shutting door, a speaking voice, or music. There can also be a wider latitude of what is acceptable or unacceptable as the children apply such contrasts to their performances.

On the other hand, ideas about rhythm and melody in music demand a more structured response and understanding from children. They need to internalize a sense of the underlying beat. Rhythm patterns have a prescribed structure that are meant to be performed in a specific way, and composed melodies include pitch patterns and phrases that are intended to be sung only one way. Now we introduce a definite right or wrong way to perform, so games with rules become an important part of the play experience. Adults need to be aware that a child's ability to successfully perform this more structured response depends on his or her developmental stage. For example, to expect a two- or young three-year-old to imitate a clapped rhythm pattern is probably fruitless, but a four-year-old can begin to respond fairly accurately. This does not mean that young children should be denied exposure to melodic and rhythmic ideas in music; it does mean that we should be aware of their comprehension and performance levels at various stages. Young children should first have many opportunities to play with the broader ideas of rhythm (sound and silence) and melody (pitch contrasts of high and low) before they are introduced to more complex understandings and performance skills.

Rhythm

◆   Music may have moments of sound and silence.
◆   Music moves with a basic underlying pulse/beat.
◆   Sounds may be relatively longer or shorter.
◆   Rhythmic ideas are formed when longer and shorter sounds are combined.

Key Music Descriptors—sound, silence, steady beat, longer/shorter sounds
Musical Play

Three-year-olds Brian, Billy, and Juan are on the playground, standing at the fence ready to play a version of "Red Rover, Red Rover. Let____come over!" The adult calls one of the boy's names and plays rapid sounds on a hand drum. The chosen boy moves when he hears the drum and stops when the sound stops. The boys have great fun running fast and then putting on the breaks when the sound stops. This stop-and-start (sound-silence) game continues until the child reaches the adult, where he playfully makes a loud thump on the drum before running back to the fence.[3]

Young three-year-olds tap their hands on their upper legs while sitting on the floor during circle time. They fairly accurately sing and tap the underlying beat of the song "Hickory-Dickory-Dock." As the song continues, some children weary and lose interest, which results in lagging or totally inaccurate tapping. The adult changes the play, but returns to it during the next day's circle time music activity to provide further practice play in sensing the underlying beat.

Older four-year-olds play with visualizing rhythmic ideas at the iconic level. After becoming familiar with the song "Skip to My Lou," a tapping page is placed in the choice time play environment. Steady beat icons are depicted on the page that reflect the topical lyrics of the song: a skipping boy, little girl, Lou, and valentines. Each image is tapped in sequence (on the boldfaced word) as the song is sung:

Skip, skip, skip to my **Lou**
Skip, skip, skip to my **Lou**
Skip, skip, skip to my **Lou**
Skip to my **Lou** my **dar-ling!**

The use of visual icons is considered a top-level challenge for four-year-olds, and they should be presented to a child only when they are individually appropriate and after the child has had many experiences at the enactive (sensing-doing) level of musical play. Iconic-level activities assume that the child is able to internalize some ideas about sound. In the previous example, a child might have demonstrated that he had internalized the feeling of steady beat by clapping his hands or patting his thighs while singing "Skip to My Lou" and before playing with the iconic tapping page.

An icon is *presymbolic* in that it is a picture of sound that is depicted to look like the sound as much as possible. Hence, the beat of a song can be depicted iconically by the same visual arrangement of repeated topical characters in the song, or it can be illustrated with a more generic visual, such as repeated equally short lines. Relatively longer and shorter topical and generic icons are used later when ideas about longer and shorter sound relationships (rhythm patterns) are visually introduced.

Second-grade children are working in small cooperative play groups. They are manipulating sound blocks that are twice and four times as long as the shortest block (similar to Cuisenaire math blocks). Each block has a ratchet sound affixed to the top. The children are busily determining how to write the rhythm pattern of the song "Yankee Doodle Dandy" by using the blocks to represent the long and short sounds of the words. They determine that the shortest sounds are "Yan-kee Doo-dle went to" and that words such as "town" are twice as long. After the song is completed, the children slide a plastic pick over the blocks to play the rhythm of the melody.

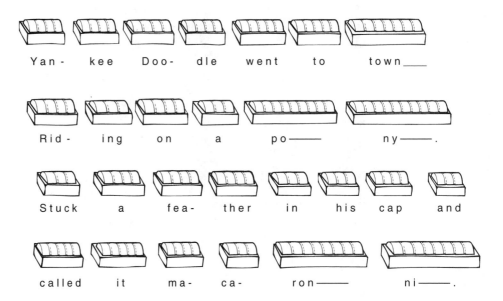

Children complete the play by assigning note values to the blocks as follows: shortest sound block = quarter note; twice as long sound block = half note. The children then transfer the look of the blocks to traditional notation, writing a rhythmic score for "Yankee Doodle Dandy." This activity serves as a transitional experience that represents a move from the enactive, iconic level to the symbolic level.

Melody

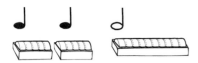

◆ Sounds may be relatively higher or lower.

◆ Melody may remain the same, move upward or downward by steps and skips.

Key Music Descriptors—high, low, moving higher, moving lower, stepping up/down, skipping up/down
Musical Play

While towel drying her 20-month-old grandchild before a mirror in the bathroom, a grandma begins to play a copycat voice inflection game. She makes funny faces and adds silly sounds such as "doo-ky, doo-ky, doo-ky, whoooooooop!" The child delightedly echoes a few sounds before abandoning the game.

During school time, the teacher begins a group improvisational experience, reading a poem about a duck:

> I have a duck
> My duck is soft.
> I have a duck
> My duck is yellow.
> I have a duck
> My duck says, "Quack! Quack!"
> I have a duck
> And I just love my duck.

"I Have a Duck," *Holt Music—Book II,*
1988. Holt, Rinehart and Winston.
Used by permission.

The objective is to help children progress from speaking, to voice inflection games (high-low vocal play), and finally to creating short melodic phrases. The teacher models each sequence of the play, inviting the children to echo her ideas. She begins by speaking each line of the poem blandly, using very little voice inflection: "I have a duck" (children echo) . . . The teacher then performs the poem using a great deal of voice inflection:

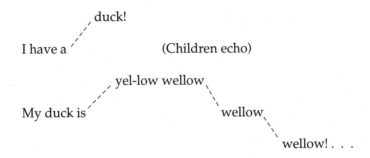

The children are encouraged to be the leader and offer their own ideas for everyone to echo. Finally, the teacher models a simple melodic phrase:

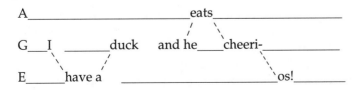

Children echo the teacher's idea, and then they are invited to make up their own melodic ideas about a duck for others to echo. The teacher is sensitive to the children's ability to respond and does not force all children to meet her goal of creating a short melody.

Another time, a "Duck Musical Theater Play" is presented. The teacher helps the children learn to sing a new song about ducks.

SEE LITTLE DUCKLINGS

"See the Little Ducklings," *Holt Music—Book II*, 1988. Holt, Rinehart and Winston. Used by permission.

An overhead projected visual of a black, straight, horizontal strip of construction paper and a duck stick puppet are used as the song is sung. The puppet duck creates a shadow as it swims randomly on the water. On the last phrase of the song, the duck dips its head in the water, leaving only its tail in the air.

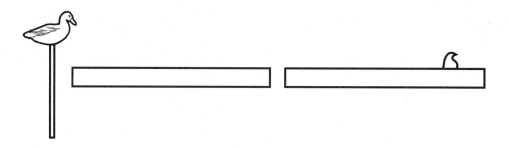

The teacher then exchanges the horizontal water strip with one that is cut like a down-up-down wave.

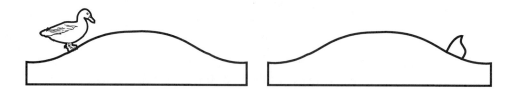

The game is again sung and played. This time, the teacher guides the children's eyes as the duck moves up the wave and the melody becomes higher, and then down the wave as the melody descends. Again, the game ends with the duck's tail in the air. The teacher's use of the puppet provides an experience that involves left to right and up and down in conjunction with the up and down pitches. Even though the teacher is aware that the song began tonally low, moved higher, and then moved back down again, melody is not discussed; the children are simply led in a visual tracking experience that, by the way, also makes a picture of the melodic contour of the song.

To extend the play, the teacher places the paper water, duck puppet, and overhead projector inside a "music theater" play space (a large cardboard appliance box). One inside wall of the box has been prepared as a movie screen (a white piece of paper). The children delight in crawling into the dark theater space and using the overhead projector to sing and create the shadow story.

A group of six-year-old children are playing a body scale game in which specific pitch numbers/labels (one-two-three or do-re-mi) are assigned to various body parts. The body scale play is initiated to provide children with the kinesthetic experience of using large motor movements to sense the upward and downward movement of individual pitches within a melody.

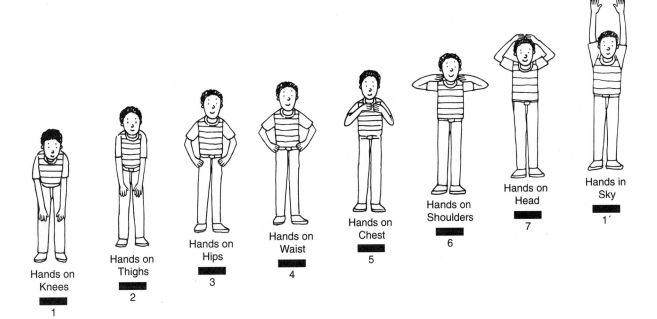

Body scale ideas from *The Music Book*, 1981. Holt, Rinehart and Winston. Used by permission.

The teacher initially uses a body scale game song that contains only three pitches (one-two-three). The song was chosen because the pitches move predictably up and down by steps or repeat the same sounds. Children touch their own assigned body scale parts as the pitches are sung:

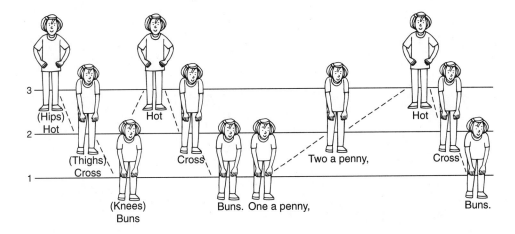

Understanding pitch movement is an abstract idea for young children. The body scale provides a playful, developmentally appropriate, concrete experience that creates a basis for children's growing understanding of how pitches move within a melody. This information will later transfer to how melodies are traditionally notated on a musical staff. Children should not be rushed into responding to traditional music notation.

Visually depicting melodies with contour lines and kinesthetic play to represent melodic direction is a high-level challenge for older four-year-olds and younger five-year-olds. It is appropriate to model such ideas, but all young children in this age group may not be developmentally ready to respond accurately. The adult must always be sensitive to each child's comfort level during such activities and be ready to diffuse any undue stress caused by the play.

Form

◆ Musical ideas may be the same or different.

Key Music Descriptors—same, different, almost the same
Musical Play

Four-year-old Jeremy and his teacher are playing a game using two sets of matching picture disks (pictures glued inside plastic soft-drink cup lids): (1) sleeping John, (2) waking-up John, (3) morning bells, and (4) ding, dong, ding bells.

Use illustrations that depict children of color and both sexes in the game disks so that antibias play is encouraged.

Antibias Considerations: multiracial-gender

The singing game commences by dividing the sets of picture disks so that each player has one set. The teacher begins by placing the first disk on the table while singing "Are You Sleeping?" Jeremy echo sings while placing his matching picture beside the one on the table. The teacher then places the second disk in the row and sings, "Brother John." Jeremy echos the phrase and matches the second disk. The game continues until all matching disks are lined up in rows on the table.

Jeremy has been involved in a song game in which each short phrase of the song is repeated in the same manner. A picture of how the song is organized (form) is created (A, A, B, B, C, C, D, D) with the game disks. The teacher's only comment regarding the form of the music is, "Jeremy, did you know that when I sang about my picture, you sang just like I did?"

Second-grade children are moving in a circle, clapping and stepping the steady beat while singing "Ring around the Rosy." They are asked to turn and reverse their direction at the end of each phrase while continuing to clap and walk:

> Ring a round the Rosy *(Turn)*
> Pocket full of posies *(Turn)*
> Ashes, Ashes we'll *(Turn)*
> All fall down!

The children become aware through this movement play that there are four phrases in the song.

Style

◆ Musical elements (pitch, rhythm, etc.) are combined in different ways to reflect the music of people from many cultures in various times and places.

Key Music Descriptors—name ethnic instruments such as the koto, maracas, and ukulele as they are heard; name performing groups such as a marching band as they are heard

Musical Play

Children know that in the dancing place, a permanent space in front of a large acrylic mirror, music of different cultures is rotated. One day, Aaron and Millie arrive at the center and notice that there are many brightly colored fans and a picture of kimono-clad dancers in the dancing place. A cassette tape is playing a recording of the lovely Japanese folk song "Sakura." The children begin to move with the fans, swishing and waving them high and low. In general, their movements reflect the smooth flow of the music. At times, the children make silly gestures, which indicates that they are more interested in the fans as props or other imaginative toys than as tools for expressing the music.

Another day, the children find paper finger puppets that depict dancing people clad in traditional kimonos. They watch themselves in the mirror as their fingers make the people dance to the music.

Children are delighted to find small American flags on sticks in the dancing place. A Sousa march, "The Stars and Stripes Forever," is playing. The children need no prompting to immediately begin marching, gesturing up and down and swishing the flags side to side. Some children maintain a steady stepping beat with the music; others move in a nonrhythmical fashion. All have an exciting time, responding in their own way to the music.

Second-grade children are playing music from an around-the-world game. The teacher places a large globe or map in front of the room, then plays a tape of short musical examples from various countries. Children are asked to identify the people whose music is performed and to find the country on the globe or map. The teacher first uses only three selections—Japan, Africa, and Mexico—all countries that the children have discussed in social studies units. Later, other countries are added. The children take great delight in finding the countries on the globe.

Musical styles and instruments that are easily identified and associated with their cultures by second graders might be Mexico—mariachi; Hawaii—ukulele; Scotland—bagpipes; Japan—koto; and Africa or Native American—drums/rattles. Music of other cultures may be found on Nonesuch Recordings or in many of the basic textbook series.

Summary

In a conceptually based, meaning-centered early childhood music program, a variety of activity-based experiences are used to help young children become aware that people perform many different kinds of music alone and in groups, and that music is truly an exciting, expressive, and beautiful experience. The meaning-centered approach should be no less playful than an activity-based program. The teacher is just more aware of the musical content of the art and thus better equipped to appropriately incorporate pertinent information when creating environments for musical play. It is important that, in an effective child-centered program, the zeal to teach musical understanding never overshadows the young child's joy of interacting expressively with the music.

Things to Do

1. Prepare a meaning-centered music experience for an age group of your choice.
    a. Identify the age level.
    b. State the music concept/understanding to be explored.
    c. List key music descriptors or vocabulary that might be used.
    d. List materials and equipment needed.
    e. Describe the activity or learning environment.
    f. Project your ideas of how children will respond.
    g. (Optional) Try your activity with one or more children.

Recommended Readings

Andress, Barbara, and Linda Walker, eds. *Readings in Early Childhood Music Education.* Reston, VA: Music Educators National Conference, 1992.

Bredekamp, Sue, ed. *Developmentally Appropriate Practice in Early Childhood Programs Serving Children from Birth through Age 8.* Washington, DC: National Association for the Education of Young Children, 1989.

Brownrigg, Carolyn, and Cindy Olson. *Music and Creative Movement.* In ECE/CDA Training Series. Coolidge, AZ: Central Arizona College, 1990.

Resource

The Timbre Board from Peripole-Bergerault, Inc., 2041 State Street, Salem, OR 97301.

Notes

[1]Sue Bredekamp and Teresa Rosegrant, eds., *Reaching Potentials: Appropriate Curriculum and Assessment for Young Children, Vol. I* (Washington, DC: National Association for the Education of Young Children, 1992), 70.

[2]Elayne Metz, "Movement as a Musical Response among Preschool Children," Ed.D. dissertation, Arizona State University, 1986, 75–85.

[3]Barbara Andress, *Music Experiences in Early Childhood* (New York: Holt, Rinehart and Winston, 1980).

4

Setting the Young Child's Environment for Musical Learning

Previously, we have explored the strength and viability of using meaning-centered music programs for young children rather than relying solely on activity-based programs. Armed with the knowledge of which musical understandings can and should be shared with young children, planners must then determine a comprehensive learning environment in which to deliver this information.

Using music solely as a circle- or group-time activity does not meet the developmental needs of children; we know that musical experiences must be tailored to the unique learning style of each individual child within the group. Our understanding of these unique learning styles is derived from the child's cognitive, physical, social-emotional, and cultural background—in other words, the child's total growth and development package. Such a package includes the child's language acquisition and play level. Mildred Parten proposed a developmental scheme of how children play:[1]

Child plays by just watching (onlooker).

Child plays independently, without reference to what other children are doing (solitary).

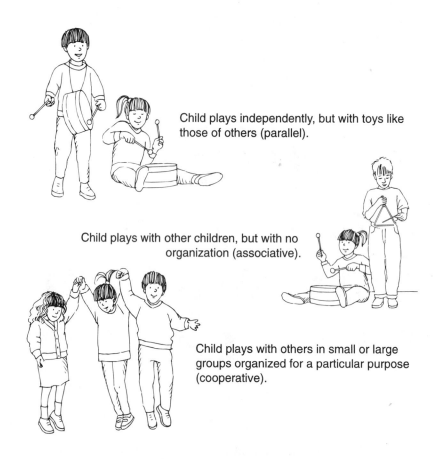

Child plays independently, but with toys like those of others (parallel).

Child plays with other children, but with no organization (associative).

Child plays with others in small or large groups organized for a particular purpose (cooperative).

Because each child's approach to learning is unique, teachers must provide a variety of physical environments in which children can explore, practice, and strive for mastery at their own pace and level of ability.

Combining the many facets of early childhood development with knowledge about children's likely musical behaviors gives us a three-part model for setting music-learning environments.

Permeable Learning Settings

In a permeable learning environment, music permeates, integrates, and enriches children's other daily curriculum experiences. Music is a part of daily play routines such as instruction giving, story time, rest time, construction activities, and topical unit projects. Elkind first introduced the idea of permeable learning in relation to activities that make up a young child's day. Some sample permeable music play settings are described next.[2]

To Market, to Market

Children are learning about good eating habits, so the teacher prepares a game that teaches about nutrition and music. A music play mat is created that depicts a house connected to a supermarket by a path of four dots. The supermarket has picture cards of fruit and vegetables that the child may choose and collect. The child moves a "person" game piece, tapping the dots on the steady beat while chanting about going to the market:

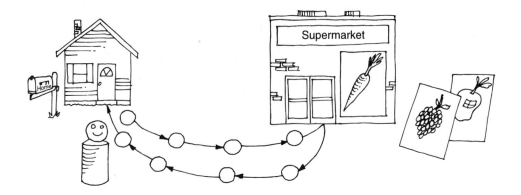

To **mar**-ket, to **mar**-ket to **buy** some good **fruit.**

The child chooses a fruit picture at the market and then chants and rhythmically moves the figure back home:

Home again, **home** again **root**-y, toot, **toot!**

The game is repeated until the child gathers many cards. The play may be ended by chanting:

To **mar**-ket, to **mar**-ket to **buy** some good **spin**-ach.
Home again, **home** again. **Now** we are **fin**-ished!

Transportation Unit Play

The teacher places the following items in the play environment for the children's construction and play: two prepared cardboard boxes (to form the front and rear of a vehicle), five large cake or pizza cardboard disks, smaller disks, glue, and several pillows.

◆ Box 1—square box with an open top
◆ Box 2—square box on its side with one flap extending up to form a window
◆ Small disks for headlights
◆ Large disks for wheels and steering wheel
◆ Pillows for car/bus seats

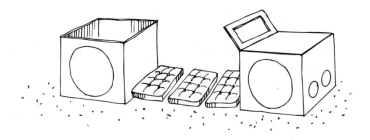

The children assemble the vehicle, adding pillows for seats, then improvise their own songs or sing traditional songs such as "Riding in My Car" by Woody Guthrie, "The Wheels on the Bus," or "Ride a Train" (traditional melody-adapted words, page 173). The teacher places small instruments such as sand blocks, whistles, bells, and bicycle horns in the environment to be used as sounds.

Science Play—Homes for Creatures

The teacher prepares cards that have pictures on them, such as a nest and bird, barn and cow, or rabbit and hole. The cards are scrambled and then matched and arranged, with the "home" card placed over the appropriate "creature" card. One child taps on the top "home" card while singing the song "Hey! Ho! Anybody Home?" The top card is removed, revealing the creature who sings, "Here I am!" or "Go away . . . I'm not home today . . . ." If the cards are not matched correctly, the child improvises, "Hey! I don't live here!"

HEY! HO! ANYBODY HOME?
Early English Round

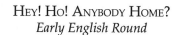

Music and Children's Literature

Many verses in children's books contain words or poetry with a distinct rhythmic flow. The teacher selects one of the rhythm features on an electronic keyboard that appropriately enhances the text. She plays the electronic rhythmic accompaniment as she reads/sings the book. The book *Teddy Bear* (Lawson 1991) becomes a rather jazzy story when it is read to the rhythmic accompaniment.

Special Interest Areas

Special interest areas are areas of prepared topical play settings in which items such as instruments, story characters, and other game pieces are available to be manipulated by the children. The word *interest* indicates that the child is free to choose to play or not to play in this area. Such play might include music play mats, a singing book corner, a musical zoo, or a dancing place. The teacher is responsible for providing and preparing materials for these individual and small-group play areas. Some items may be teacher constructed and consumable; other items may be more sophisticated and of lasting quality so that they can be used repeatedly. For example, singing people (people figures with open singing mouths that can be manipulated) can either be wooden dowel figures that have been purchased, made on a wood worker's lathe, or created from PVC pipe joints, toilet tissue rolls, or broomstick handles. Obviously, commercially prepared and other wooden figures will last longer than paper rolls.

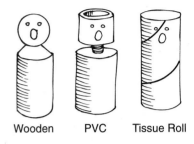

Wooden   PVC   Tissue Roll

The Hokey-Pokey Play Mat

The teacher laminates a large play mat that motivates the child to independently sing a familiar song, match handprints, and rhythmically tap the figures. The child begins singing the "Hokey-Pokey" while placing his left hand on and off the pictured handprint as indicated by the song words: Box 1— ". . . left hand in . . . out . . . shake about." On the last two phrases of the verse, the child taps each figure in the box with his pointer finger on the rhythmic accent Do . . . Hok-. . .; his voice elongates and exaggerates the word "turn" as his finger slides along the circled/twisted character. The play continues with the child singing additional verses involving his right hand, then both hands.

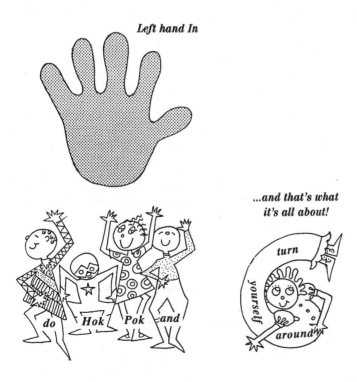

Left hand In

...and that's what it's all about!

do   Hok   Pok   and

turn   yourself   around

B. Andress, *The Hokey-Pokey Play Mat*. Andress ©1991. First printed in *You, Your Children and Music,* Vol. I, Issue 8. Arizona Early Childhood Music Collaborative Project. Permission to enlarge and otherwise reproduce this play mat is granted for the personal use only of users of this textbook.

Spiders

The teacher prepares a place to act out spider songs. Materials needed are:

◆   1 12-inch length of white 2-inch PVC pipe

◆   1 2-inch PVC pipe cap

◆   1 plastic spider

- 1 short length of fishing line
- 1 constructed wooden box/shelf
- 1 girl cone puppet

The teacher constructs a box with an upright board back for the spider play area. For the "Eency Weency Spider" drama, the teacher uses PVC pipe. He cuts a view gap in one lower end of the pipe, drills a hole in the middle of the cap, and places it on the top of the pipe. He attaches the pipe to the wood backing and drills a small hole in the wood backing just above the cap. He then ties a spider on the end of fishing line, threads the spider line up the pipe, through the cap and back hole. He ties a handle at the end of the line, which may be pulled to make the spider enter and disappear or reappear out of the pipe as the song is sung.

For "Little Miss Muffet," the teacher drills two holes in the shelves to accommodate a girl cone puppet. (Cone puppets may be purchased at toy stores or craft fairs.) The puppet is inserted in the holes and one child manipulates it up or down as the spider comes out of the pipe to "frighten Miss Muffet away."

Note: You may wish to clamp the spider play to a table so it won't tip over during use.

Hickory Dickory Dock

The teacher prepares a manipulative play puzzle that motivates the child to sing the familiar nursery tune with wood block and bell accompaniment while playing a counting game. The teacher places the wood block grandfather clock, mouse mallet, and assorted paper clock faces in the play environment. The child selects a clock face that has the hour highlighted (for children who may recognize numbers but cannot yet tell time) and places it in the proper place on the puzzle. The mouse mallet is used to tap the ticking sounds as the song is sung. The child may gesture up or down the clock with the mouse mallet in response to song words. After the child plays the game several times, the desk bell is added to the puzzle over the clock face circle. The child now taps the ticking sounds on the wood block and adds the chime of the clock after the hour is sung in the lyrics, "The clock struck 'three'" (three bell sounds).

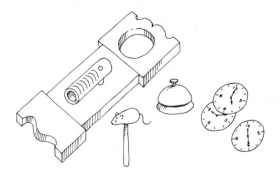

When preparing a program that uses special interest area plays, the teacher should acquire and/or create 10 to 15 kits as a starter set. Complete early childhood music play kits or parts for kits may be purchased commercially or collected by the teacher. Many musical instruments, sounds, or topical manipulative items can be found in usual and unusual places. The usual resources are commercial music vendors or the school music room, where quality in-tune instruments such as xylophones, finger cymbals, drums, and guitars can be found. Toy instruments are rarely tonally accurate enough in pitch to be used to accompany a song or play in an instrumental ensemble, but they may be acceptable for sound effects in stories. More unusual places to find pieces for music play kits are bookstores, school libraries (illustrated children's songs), yard sales, or swap meets, where one may find a variety of brass bells, maracas, guitars, or toy figures. The number of prepared kits will quickly increase as the teacher becomes more aware of the play possibilities of found sounds and objects.

Various play materials need to be organized for easy storage and retrieval so that each kit does not have to be recompiled each time it is used. Plastic bags can be used to hold small game pieces, play mats can be placed in chart racks or in large tagboard folders, and instruments may be stored on shelves. Extra-large plastic zipper-type bags can be obtained that hold both an 11-by-17-inch play mat and the required game pieces.

Guided Group Play

A third music setting is guided group play in which the teacher directs large-group interactive activities. Many centers refer to this activity as "circle time." Traditionally, guided group play has been used for music making, guided listening, and expressive or directed movement experiences. The children interact with others in the group to create, perform, listen to, and describe music. The group setting is important because children need to know that music is a shared art both at the performance and consumer levels. Group sessions provide practice time for associative and cooperative play, as well as time for enhancing children's music performance skills. It is a time for children to sing and play instruments together, thereby learning to match the pitch and the rhythmic flow of others. It is also a time to be introduced to new ideas and musical examples and a time to fantasize and joyfully play with others.

MODEL FOR A GUIDED GROUP LESSON

Many lesson formats are available for planning group music sessions. The following is a model for a song-focused lesson approach.

Select an invitational song that can be used routinely to call children to "circle time" for music play. Such songs may include "Hello Everybody" (Charity Bailey), "The More We Get Together" (traditional), or a parody song to a familiar tune such as "Hey There Betty Martin" (traditional melody, see page 65).

Next, sing something familiar, a beloved tune that the children know well such as "Old MacDonald," "This Old Man," or "If You're Happy and You Know It."

EVERYBODY COME NOW
Variation on "Hey There Betty Martin"

B. Andress

1. Ev' - ry - bo - dy   come now,   come now,   come now.

Ev' - ry - bo - dy   come now,   sing   with   me!

2. I see Megan come now, come now, come now.
    I see Megan come now to sing with me.

Now introduce a new musical idea. Planning this segment of the lesson should begin by first establishing what the learning goals are for the activity. For example,

Musical understanding—Sounds may be relatively loud or soft.

Materials—Two duck puppets or soft toys or duck guiro with metal sound starter

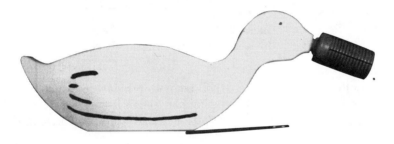

Photo courtesy of Peripole-Bergerault, Inc.

Procedure—Introduce the song by singing and manipulating the duck puppets (baby and mother), then invite the children to sing along. After the song, briefly discuss how the mommy duck changed her voice (quacked loudly) to make the baby duck come back (see page 66).

Play a loud-soft game using the duck guiro. Identify the duck guiro as the mommy duck. Explain to the children that when the duck softly quacks, they are to take tiny tiptoe steps away from the duck (the teacher initially holds the duck and plays the sounds), but when the duck quacks loudly, they must come running back and stand very close to the duck. When appropriate, invite a child to be the mommy duck and play the instrument. Play the duck guiro and use a chant to calm the children after this boisterous activity, then segue into the next activity.

The mommy duck says, "Quack! Quack! Hop! Hop! Hop!" *(Very loud)*
The mommy duck says, "Quack! Quack! Stop! Stop! Stop!" *(Medium loud)*
The mommy duck says, "Quack! Quack! Turn around!" *(Speak slower and softer)*

The mommy duck says, "Quack! Quack! Sit gently down." *(Speak much slower and very softly)*
The mommy duck says, "Sh! Sh! I cannot speak."
The mommy duck says, "Sh! Sh! I'm going to sleep!" *(Cradle duck in arms)*

ONE LITTLE DUCK
Traditional

One lit - tle duck went out to play

O - ver the hill and far a - way, but the

Mom - my duck said, "Quack! Quack! Quack!"

That lit - tle duck did not come back!
That lit - tle duck came run - ning back!

Pause briefly for pretend sleep, then begin a familiar tune such as "Are You Sleeping?" Or, sing a familiar finger-play song such as "Where Is Thumbkin?" (which uses the same melody as "Are You Sleeping?"). End the circle time session

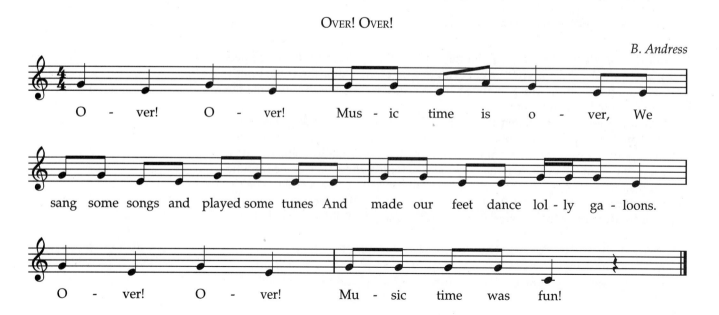

OVER! OVER!

B. Andress

O - ver! O - ver! Mus - ic time is o - ver, We

sang some songs and played some tunes And made our feet dance lol - ly ga - loons.

O - ver! O - ver! Mu - sic time was fun!

with a routine song that signals group music play is over. "Goodbye Everybody" (Charity Bailey) or a two-three tone chant (pitches G, E, A) such as "Over! Over!" may be sung.

Which of the three learning environments to use will shift depending on the age of the children. Very young toddlers tend to participate more effectively in special interest areas because of their level of social-emotional development. Adults can enter other play settings (permeable learning), but children often withdraw if the adults appear in any way threatening. Toddlers can participate in group time, but they often do not abide by the rules (want to dance rather than sit and sing), or they wander off.

More mature children—older four- to eight-year-olds—are increasingly capable of cooperative play, thus sharing, planning, and abiding by simple rules become more tolerable and useful in each of the learning environments. Exploratory play and independent problem solving can be a part of the special interest play environment, while group time is a wonderful time to be with and do things with friends.

Implementing Music Learning Environments in Early Childhood Classrooms

Young children are nurtured in a variety of classroom settings with numerous music learning activities. A typical childcare center or kindergarten classroom contains child-size furniture, a wet or dry table, and designated areas for painting, housekeeping, reading, wheel toy/construction play, and large-group activities. Some schools have large spaces for many play areas while other schools barely have enough space for the children.

Children enter the classroom, hang their coats in their "cubbies," and begin their day by freely choosing from among prepared activities. At specified times, all children are called into the large-group space for story time, music, or some other guided interaction. After scheduled outdoor play, the children may be served snacks. The outdoor play area is a valuable learning space where children have special areas for large wheel toys, sand boxes, and other play equipment.

An early childhood center is usually staffed by a lead teacher and one or more teaching assistants. The program is designed so that teachers interact with children on an individual basis, although they also work with children in small and larger groups. The general teacher or care provider is usually responsible for guiding musical experiences with occasional assistance from an itinerant music professional.

Numbers of young children enrolled often have a way of growing in some of these settings, often overwhelming the allocated space. Even though assistant care providers may be added to comply with adult-child ratios, the size and variety of the learning settings may still be compromised. Ideally, an early childhood classroom should be large enough to allow for children's personal space as well as multiple learning settings.

First- and second-grade children tend to be placed in more structured classrooms that do not have enough space for free-choice exploratory play centers. Many educators decry the prevailing concept that these children no longer need an interactive play environment. Sometimes, children go to a special room for music, but the general classroom teacher has the option of planning additional musical experiences by designing and implementing activities within the home-room space.

Another option is for the music teachers to prepare centers in the music room that are available during certain weeks of the year so that, in addition to large group activities, children have the opportunity to explore the specially prepared centers on their own. During this time, the classroom teacher or teaching assistants may be asked to remain with the music teacher and provide necessary small-group assistance.

Can a three-part model for early childhood musical experiences be implemented in such disparate settings? The answer is yes. If care providers wait for everything to be perfect, they will never implement a program. Those who wait for a larger room so children can dance will never dance; those who wait for space to prepare a center will never enable children to independently explore.

SUMMARY

Young children are predominantly at the concrete stage of learning, so it is crucial that their learning environments include independent play with hands-on, manip-ulative materials. Musical instruments certainly should be used, as well as game pieces and song play mats, to effectively motivate musical play.

Because each child is individually unique in learning style and developmen-tal stage, it is important that three approaches to daily musical interaction be used: (1) permeable learning, (2) special interest areas, and (3) guided group play. The planned availability of the multiple systems for delivering music allows for individual differences in how each child best processes learning. These learning environments allow children of different ages to use the same setting at their own level of ability and sophistication.

The three music learning environments are as important for school-age chil-dren as they are for younger children in care centers. Independent exploratory play, using music to enhance lessons in other areas, and performing within groups are important for all children. Providing such a program requires adminis-trators to rethink staff responsibilities. A collaborative effort among the classroom teacher, the teaching assistants, and the music teacher is necessary.

Effective learning environments pique children's interest and curiosity and create the desire to be part of the musical play. Adult leaders are most important in the environment because, through their careful implementation of settings and personal modeling, exhibited both by performance and attitude toward music, they put a stamp of approval on the experience. Young children are avid copycats and imitate and take ownership of behavior that is valued by the adults they love and respect.

THINGS TO DO

1.   Plan an experience for young children in one of the following music learning environments: permeable learning; special interest areas; or guided group play.

2.   Create a setting or activity within your chosen environment that will arouse the child's curiosity, reflect the developmental stage of the child, involve a hands-on activity, and have musical validity (meaning-centered).

3.   Be prepared to share your ideas and materials with classmates.

RESOURCES

Andress, Barbara. "Hokey-Pokey." *You, Your Children and Music,* Vol. I, Issue 4. Arizona Early Childhood Music Collaborative Project, 1991.

Early Childhood Music Play Kits available from Peripole-Bergerault, Inc., 2041 State Street, Salem, OR 97301, 1-800-443-3592.

The suggested songs listed below may be found in most basic elementary music texts, Grades K–2. (New York: Macmillan Publishing Co; Morristown, NJ: Silver Burdett & Ginn). They may also be found in other children's song collections such as the *Wee Sing Series.* Los Angeles: Price/Stern/Sloan Publishers.

"The Hokey-Pokey," "Hello Everybody," "The More We Get Together," "Old MacDonald," "This Old Man," "If You're Happy and You Know It," "Are You Sleeping?," "Where Is Thumpkin?," "Hickory Dickory Dock," "Little Miss Muffet," "Eency Weency Spider," "The Wheels on the Bus," "Riding in My Car."

NOTES

[1]Mildred Parten, "Social Participation among Preschool Children," *Journal of Abnormal and Social Psychology* 23 (1930): 243–269.

[2]David Elkind, *Miseducation: Preschoolers at Risk* (New York: Alfred A. Knopf, 1987), 167.

5

The Teacher's Role

Master teachers must certainly have a great love for young children and possess seemingly boundless energy and patience. The awesome challenges in effectively guiding this age group are to be informed and willing to invest time in preparation and planning. Teachers must be tirelessly dedicated to the importance of early childhood education, because much of the teaching work takes place long before the children arrive. Even though teachers often stay late to plan and arrive early to set up the learning environment for each day's activities, they must somehow maintain an upbeat mood throughout the day while using many personal coping skills to help their young charges interact with materials and peers. Do such paragons of perfect teaching exist? The answer, thankfully, is a resounding yes.

Teachers/care providers of young children are found in both the certified and noncertified ranks. Certified teachers, who have a minimum four-year education degree, have been steeped in child development, communication methods, and appropriate materials. Certified teachers are often directors of childcare centers, advisors/instructors for care providers, or teach in public school programs. Noncertified adults are usually care providers or teacher assistants who work at childcare centers, Head Start programs, or as aides in kindergarten through second-grade classrooms. Noncertified care providers' education ranges from little formal training to on-site training and some formal coursework. Many workers in the childcare provider field hold a Child Development Associate Certificate (CDA), which is granted after they complete a certain amount of training, preferably at a community college. Both certification approaches—training or earned college credit—involve daily on-site involvement with young children.

It has been established that teachers/care providers need to know (1) how young children develop; (2) what their predictable musical behaviors are; (3) the focus of curriculum content (musical concepts and ideas); and (4) how to teach within the three learning environments. The many roles teachers must play and how they implement effective programs are the focus of this chapter.

The Teacher as Curriculum Designer

In most of today's early childhood classrooms, teachers follow an activity-based music curriculum, and the quality of the curriculum depends on the competence of the planner. Even when individual activity-based sessions appear to be effective, teachers tend to use a "shot-gun" approach in delivering music to young children. They may scatter ideas and activities randomly throughout the year, using music to fill a daily time allotment or meet goals for social-emotional experiences, often with little regard for continuity between experiences. Such a casual approach reflects a lack of knowledge about the integrative nature of the program and conveys a cavalier attitude about the power of one learning experience to generate new learnings.

Historically, curriculum development for public school–age children involved an activity-based approach in which teachers planned events for the entire year or used textbooks that taught children to learn 100 songs each year, 10 of which were to be patriotic, 30 holiday, and the remaining folk songs with or without dances. Materials were often arranged into topical units, such as songs about community helpers, cowboys, or the westward movement. Classical music selections were intermittently presented, and a thread of music theory was inserted, often in isolation from the musical context. Performance goals were in-tune singing, playing classroom instruments, and sight reading.

With increased knowledge about how children learn and what of music they can understand and demonstrate at each stage, national organization, state department, district, and local planners for school-age children now construct curriculum guides that take the learner through a logical sequence of musical understandings. These understandings are packaged in attractive music materials and activities.

Music curriculum for two- to four-year-olds does not have the history that public school curriculums do. Only in recent years have we begun to truly look at developing such programs. We can learn from earlier planners that we should not be satisfied with activity-based or overly structured programs. It is appropriate that curriculum for two- to four-year-olds be based on a meaning-centered model if planners hope to maintain a sensitivity to the developmentally appropriate behaviors of the learners.

When planning meaning-centered lessons, teachers believe that one learning generates another learning. Thus, planning involves recording what has already been presented (entry-level information), identifying what must currently be communicated about an idea (lesson goal), and deciding what will be needed for tomorrow (reinforcement and extension of goal). Teachers should reflect on all of these aspects as they plan each session. In this way, children are not left on their own to make connections between day-to-day content, but are guided in the synthesis process and helped to more logically transfer one learning to the next learning.

The following flowchart is a framework for establishing curriculum from which specific lessons may be planned.[1] The flowchart is a synthesis of the findings of psychologists and early childhood educators. Readers will recognize the obvious influence of Piaget in the "Mode of Learning" section. The section on "Understandings and Behaviors" is a music curriculum refinement of Lilian Katz's work in the area of categorizing learning,[2] and the term "Permeable Learning," as coined by David Elkind,[3] refers to integrating music in the many projects that make up a child's day.

Using this framework, teachers identify the child's developmental level and mode of learning (see Chapters 1 and 2), select an entry-level musical understanding (see Chapter 3), make decisions about what the interactive play will entail (predictable responses of the child), consider the child's performance level (observable musical behaviors), ponder the aesthetic qualities of the experience (feelings and dispositions), and set an attractive environment for the child's musical interaction (see Chapter 4).

An Early Childhood Music Curriculum Framework

DEVELOPMENTAL STAGES

Level 1   Level 2   Level 3   Level 4

MODE OF LEARNING: INTERACTIVE PLAY

The Child:
◆ Senses (hears, sees, feels)
◆ Does (manipulates, performs)

In Order to:
◆ Assimilate
◆ Accommodate
◆ Discriminate
◆ Classify

UNDERSTANDINGS AND BEHAVIORS

Knowledge
◆ Information, ideas, facts, regarding basic musical understandings: loud-soft, fast-slow, quality of sound, melody, rhythm, form, style

Observable Musical Behaviors
◆ Sing, play, listen, move, read, write

Dispositions
◆ Lifelong interest in, curiosity about, and feelings for music

DELIVERED THROUGH THREE LEARNING ENVIRONMENTS

◆ Permeable Learning
◆ Special Interest Areas
◆ Guided Group Play

The Teacher as Evaluator

Evaluating the effectiveness of a music program and the individual progress of young children is an important responsibility for teachers. Teachers often feel overwhelmed when they are confronted with assessing students on an individual basis, as time and attention to others in the class become a major factor. However, only through systematic notation of each child's responses can we be assured that effective methods, materials, and musical growth are in place. Therefore, some doable, credible form of evaluation is truly necessary.

Because very young children are limited in their ability to verbalize, teachers must base their teaching on what they know about the age group and a certain amount of faith; that is, faith based on knowledge that the enriched learning environments and early interaction with music they have implemented are indeed making a difference and that some form of understanding is taking place. Fortunately, teachers have some instant feedback that indicates children's attitudinal responses, such as uninhibited glee and joy during an experience. Because music is a performing art, teachers are also immediately aware of how well children sing, play, or move. Sometimes, though, a teacher remains in the dark when, for example, a child does not participate within the group but independently performs elsewhere, thus leaving the teacher with questions about the child's real abilities.

Formal evaluation that involves various forms of individual assessment, such as verbal questioning, using pictures or colors to elicit a yes or no response, or determining the ability to match pitches or rhythm patterns, has questionable validity when it is applied to very young children. Teachers cannot determine if a child's responses reflect a lack of musicianship, limited language development, or a fear of the stranger administering the test or the unique environment. Thus, keeping a record of observable behaviors is a more reliable way to formulate a profile of each child's musical progress.

Promising Practices for Evaluating Musical Progress

Creating a Portfolio

Teachers can establish a portfolio for each child that contains information about the child's musical responses and progress. Contents of a portfolio may include anecdotal notes based on observations of the child at play or in guided group settings. Such observations may come from parents, teachers, aides, other caring adults, or even peers. Observers are encouraged to use as much descriptive terminology as possible, including many adjectives and adverbs. For example, the sentence "Jamie joyfully jumped, stamped feet, and whirled high and low while singing only a few words of the song 'Jump Jim Joe'" is more useful than "Jamie moved while singing a song."

The portfolio may also include formal evaluation reports that are planned and administered throughout the year. Such reports might contain minimal single-focus information, such as the child's approach tendencies to the music play area. The teacher plans a time to observe the child, then tabulates the child's time on task, frequency of returns to the task, and level of participation. Such teacher observations would include noting the child as an active, nearby watcher, distant observer, or his delayed response. Form should be kept simple, with a goal of gathering minimal information.

The teacher may want to include in the portfolio a recording of the child's singing or playing. Every three to six months, the teacher records the child singing his own improvised song or one he has learned or performed on an instrument. This activity takes place in a music play environment, so the teacher should not hover or direct the recording session other than to change the tape as new children participate.

Art, iconic, or notational representations that result from the child's music play may also be inserted into the portfolio. For example: The child creates a music score for the song "Jingle Bells." She randomly draws many bells on a piece of paper and then studiously pretends to read them while singing the song.

Young children are aware of the look of traditional music notation. Although they understand little about the meaning of the symbols, they realize one sings or plays an instrument while looking at the little balls with sticks. Pictures of the child's version of musical notes may appear in her artwork. These pictures provide information about the child's awareness that people read music, as well as words, in storybooks.

Evaluating the Individual within the Large Group Setting

One approach to tracking individual children within the larger group is to plan a lesson or series of lessons that include a built-in evaluation format. In this way, assessment becomes integrated throughout each lesson. This type of evaluation focuses on tracking the level of learning at which the child is expected to perform while interacting within the large group. Learning levels might be knowledge, analysis, synthesis, and judgment. Children are involved in activities that progress from lower levels of learning, such as minimal knowledge acquisition, to increasingly higher levels of analysis, synthesis, and judgment.

When a child makes musical decisions or judgments, she is operating at the highest level of learning. Musical experiences that involve only parroting (learning words of traditional songs) or labeling (naming instruments) are the lowest level of knowledge acquisition. Though this form of knowledge acquisition is critical, in the hierarchy of learning levels, it is only a beginning and thus considered to be a low- or entry-level experience. Very young children frequently operate at this low level as they acquire a repertoire of songs, establish music vocabulary, name instruments, and describe sounds in instrumental play.

Higher levels of learning enter the instructional scheme when teachers encourage children to improvise with instruments, create their own songs, construct their own music machine, or assemble a ringing tree. These activities require the child to draw upon acquired knowledge and analysis findings (what rings and what does not ring); synthesize other learnings (create his own song perhaps similar to one he has heard in the culture); and make musical decisions when discussing musical ideas or instructing playmates about what they should do during cooperative playtime. (While looking at pictures of a marching band, the child says to a friend: "You don' sing loud here cause the band is going away!" Or another time: "You be the daddy and I be the mommy and this is baby. Daddy, you sing soft to baby.")

THE EVALUATION PROCESS

The teacher first evaluates the total group experience based on the functioning level of learning. The evaluator can see at a glance the overall quality of the children's experience by identifying observable behaviors and the levels in which they fall.[4]

LEVELS OF LEARNING	OBSERVABLE BEHAVIORS
Knowledge	Naming, labeling, listing,
Analysis	Discriminating, differentiating, classifying, ordering
Synthesis	Improvising, composing
Decision making	Judging, liking, disliking

Next, the teacher observes the individual within this group, considering the following questions. When given the opportunity, does the individual

◆ involve himself in decision-making play?

◆ participate in creative musical play?

◆ transfer ideas previously heard or learned into his own spontaneous play?

- ◆ use descriptive musical vocabulary during play such as loud-soft or fast-slow?
- ◆ exhibit curiosity about the play?
- ◆ remain at a task or return to the music play area frequently?

The strength of this combined instructional and evaluation approach becomes obvious. The teacher first looks at the total group experience, knowing that the quality of the experience will strongly influence the level of the individual child's response. If the teacher only presents a song or names an instrument, the child automatically functions minimally. If the teacher organizes environments that motivate improvisation and decision making, the child is involved in higher levels of learning. The teacher who utilizes each level of learning in a cyclical fashion has a built-in tracking format. This cyclical sequence ensures that the child will regularly return to the knowledge level to acquire new information for use at higher levels. An overall evaluation can be made at a glance as the teacher sees the group involved at various levels of learning, such as synthesis or analysis. A closer look at the individual's role within the group setting provides more definitive information for the child's personal profile.

Overemphasis on testing or gathering progress reports can skew the activities so that performance goals become more important than the child. If a child does not function at the synthesis level or sing for the portfolio recording, does that mean he or she has failed music? Of course not! Again, developmental concerns guide a child's readiness for specific activities. The teacher will find that appropriate, well-planned activities inherently contain many opportunities for monitoring progress. Special evaluation activities that interrupt the flow of the musical experience or are administered out of the musical context add little to the portfolio information and may well be a waste of young children's (and evaluators') time.

The Teacher as Materials Seeker

We said earlier that instructional resources that fully support a music program are readily available for school-age children. Children less than five years old are not as adequately served. There is no organized basic music textbook series with recordings for very young children; however, there are many diverse, if rather scattered, materials on the market such as recordings, song collections, and classroom instruments. Teachers of children under five, for the most part, must fend for themselves, compiling materials from their own music repertoire, selecting from among commercially prepared music collections of varying qualities, attending in-service workshops/coursework to gather ideas and handouts, visiting conference exhibits, and, most important, relying on the generous sharing of colleagues. With the exception of in-service and coursework resources, the available materials make little attempt to provide sequential instructional guidelines, so teachers must depend on their own knowledge about developmentally appropriate usage. This approach to obtaining viable resources for a music program is far from ideal, because it places responsibility for the quality of the collection and development of materials on the busy teacher. The following sections discuss some suggestions for teachers as they search and invest in their music classroom materials.

BASIC TEXTBOOK SERIES

Many songs and recordings in current K–2 basic music textbook series are available for publishers or are owned by public schools. Appoint a liaison to make contact with the music or classroom teacher in a public school or seek out a local college music education library to review these materials. The teaching suggestions they contain may need to be adapted to younger children's needs, but selected examples from the song literature, listening, and movement recordings will be applicable. After determining their usability, the teacher can order the materials from the publisher. Be aware that the adoption of a textbook series in a local school district is for approximately five years. A childcare center may obtain some of the materials that have been replaced through a cooperative arrangement with the neighborhood school or district office. Publishers currently marketing basic textbook series are Silver Burdett & Ginn and Macmillan. Addresses of publishers' representatives are usually available from the public school administration office.

COMMERCIAL SONG COLLECTIONS

Most available early childhood song material is recorded on audiocassette or compact disks. These recordings may or may not have accompanying song sheets (words only) and/or a music book. Many recording artists create their own music and lyrics that typically center on children's interests. Many songs are cute, jazzy, and otherwise attractive, but they may be difficult for children to sing. If the goal is to entertain children, these recordings may be useful. If the goal is for children to sing along, then a careful analysis of the selections should be made.

For example, teachers should ask the following questions: Are the songs in a singable range? They should be neither too high nor low (C–d'). Is the melody overly complicated with wide intervalic jumps? Are there too many words involving a long, detailed story? Is there some predictable repetition of words and melodic ideas? Is the style of music based only on the pop/rock form? Does the song have musical merit, or is it used only to teach about such concerns as the environment or self-image? A well-composed song can have merit as well as teach about extra-musical ideas. Sadly, many contrived songs on today's market do not meet this criteria.

Some enjoyable and singable commercial recordings and music books are also available. These collections contain wonderfully entertaining, newly composed songs and arrangements of traditional songs that children have loved through the ages. Good examples of these types of materials are the *Wee Sing Series* and recordings by performers such as Raffi, The King's Singers, Ella Jenkins, Greg and Steve, and Sharon, Lois & Bram. These recordings are available in the children's section of most record shops and local music vendors.

CLASSICAL RECORDINGS FOR CHILDREN

Children listen to classical music for many reasons: as background music to set the mood for arriving at school, as a topical/art project, or for rest time. A more musically focused approach is to have children move expressively, participate in a directed listening lesson, or play with a hands-on activity related to a classical selection. A few examples of this music include the following:

◆ *Rest Time*—"Dreams" by Tchaikovsky; "Lullaby" (cradle song) by Brahms; "Dreams" from *Scenes from Childhood* by Schumann; "Evening Prayer" from *Hansel and Gretel* by Humperdinck

◆ *Trains (topical)*—"Little Train" from *Once Upon a Time Suite* by Donaldson; "The Little Train of Caipira" by Villa-Lobos

◆ *Things That Swim and Fly (topical)*—"The Flight of the Bumblebee" by Rimsky-Korsakov; "Aquarium" and "The Cuckoo in the Woods" from *The Carnival of the Animals* by Saint-Saëns; "Dance of the Mosquito" by Liadov

◆ *Imaginative Play*—"Ballet of the Unhatched Chicks" and "Bydlo" from *Pictures at an Exhibition* by Mussorgsky; "Hall of the Mountain King" from *Peer Gynt Suite* by Grieg; "Royal March of the Lion" from *Carnival of the Animals*; "Viennese Musical Clock" from *Hary Janos Suite* by Kodaly

◆ *Dances*—"Sleeping Beauty Waltz" from *Sleeping Beauty Ballet* by Tchaikovsky; "The Emperor Waltz" by Strauss; "Jesusita en Chihuahua," Mexican folk; "Music Box Waltz" by Shostakovich; "Walking Song" from *Acadian Songs and Dances* by Thomson

◆ *Marches*—"Stars and Stripes Forever" by Sousa; *Pomp and Circumstance No. 1* by Elgar; "March of the Toreador" from *Carmen* by Bizet; "Children's March" by E. F. Goldman; "March of the Toys" from *Babes in Toyland* by Herbert; "March" from *The Comedians* by Kabalevsky

◆ *Majestic Music*—"The Great Gate of Kiev" from *Pictures at an Exhibition* by Mussorgsky

◆ *Suites*—The following larger works contain many selections that are appropriate for young children and that should be in every classroom music library: *The Carnival of the Animals* by Saint-Saëns; *The Nutcracker Suite* by Tchaikovsky; *Pictures at an Exhibition* by Mussorgsky; *Peter and the Wolf* by Prokofiev; and *Hansel and Gretel* by Humperdinck

Many of the nation's finest orchestras have recorded classical music especially for young listeners. The Boston Pops Orchestra is notable among these groups. Purchasing one of these collections is a more economical way to acquire a listening library than to seek individual pieces. However, sometimes it is worth it to acquire a recording that contains only one useful selection. After purchasing recordings, the teacher may still need to alter the material by excerpting themes from those selections that are overly long, by gently fading out the music as the children's interest wanes, or by ignoring selections that may not be developmentally appropriate for young children, such as "The Witch's Dance" from *Hansel and Gretel*.

It is important to have quality recordings that are readily accessible. A teacher rarely has time to engage in a hunting expedition when quiet-time music is needed. A small, basic library of recorded music should be maintained in every early childhood classroom as standard equipment. Plan to supplement the classroom recordings with less frequently used selections from a public library or make additional purchases for the center's central resource room.

CLASSROOM INSTRUMENTS

Many classroom instruments may be purchased from local music vendors or from catalog firms. Instruments range from small percussion to the more expensive xylophones, autoharps, and pianos. Instruments should be acquired through a consistent purchase plan that includes replacement or repair of damaged items.

Instruments from toy stores should be carefully screened because they often do not have high-quality sound. Toys should not be considered as the basic music-making instruments in the classroom, but they are acceptable as additional resources for improvisational music play. Investing in high-quality instruments is economically wise because most of them are quite sturdy and remain in service for many years.

Basic Instrumentation/Equipment for the Classroom

Acquiring the following instruments and equipment should be a goal for every classroom:

◆ *Small percussion*—Jingle bells, jingle clogs, triangles, large cymbals, finger cymbals, gongs, sticks, ratchets, claves, rattles, maracas, guiros, bongo drums, tub drums, tunable hand drums, tambourines, resonator bells, step bells

- ◆ *String instruments*—Autoharp, guitar, ukulele, cello (specially tuned)
- ◆ *Keyboards*—Piano, electronic keyboard
- ◆ *Orff-type instruments*—Xylophones (bass-alto-soprano), metallophones (bass-alto-soprano), glockenspiels (alto-soprano), timpani drums (two pair, different pitches)
- ◆ *Recording equipment*—Audiocassette player, compact disk player

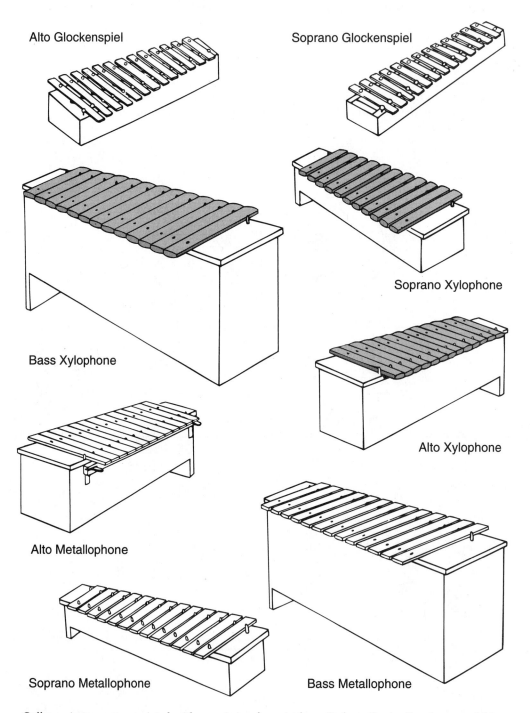

Orff-type instruments reprinted with permission from Andress, Barbara, Eunice Boardman, and Mary Pautz, *Holt Music Grade 1,* Holt, Rinehart, and Winston, 1988.

Hints for Purchasing Instruments

When purchasing small percussion instruments, consider their usefulness in matching games. Thus, buy two instruments of the same size (e.g., two identical 7-inch triangles, two 10-inch hand drums).

The same instrument in assorted sizes will help children explore indefinite pitches as well as the timbral quality of sound. For example, purchase individual cymbals that range in size from 6 to 10 inches. Exploratory play can involve dangling different-sized cymbals by their leather straps on a wooden rod that is placed securely between two chair backs. Children then use soft beaters to explore the sounds of a cymbal carillon. (Weather permitting, the teacher may wish to set up the carillon outside; it promises to be sound intense.)

Hand drums are available in many different sizes and may have all-weather heads (plastic) that are slick or rough. Select a rough-textured drum head so that swishing sounds as well as thumping can be made on the instrument. Drum heads may be nailed to the drum shell or attached with tuning keys. The drums with tuning keys are more expensive, but they have the additional option of changing pitch. Sound starters are very important because one instrument may have many different timbres depending on with what it is struck. Drum sounds may be initiated by using beaters, sticks, or brushes. Plan to include a variety of sound starters in your purchases.

String instruments such as guitars and cellos can be specially tuned for the use of young children, which makes these instruments appropriate for a classroom collection. Open-string tuning from low to high is C, G, C, G, c, e (guitar) and C, G, c, e (cello).

Damaged and discarded instruments may be available for the asking from music vendor repair shops. They may donate a piano with an open case so that children can see and touch hammers, a severely cracked bass fiddle, or a bass or snare drum with only one usable head. These less-than-perfect instruments are good for exploratory play because children will poke, strike, pluck, and pretend play with them.

Sponsor a "clean out the attic/basement day." Encourage parents and caring individuals in the community to contribute instruments. You may be surprised how many dusty gongs, maracas, or brass bells from India you will acquire. You will also inherit some dated clarinets and trumpets. As these wind instruments may not be sanitary enough for children to blow on, place them in a "Meet the Instruments" kit where they will be used for display, exploration of valves and keys, or pretend play. A kit may include, for example, one trumpet with a recorded example of its sound, pictures of its placement in a symphony orchestra or combo, a picture of a noted performer such as Satchmo, and a book about an inner-city African-American child who wants to play trumpet more than anything else in the world (*Ben's Trumpet* by Rachel Isadora). Encourage children to touch valves or march around the room while holding the instrument in playing position but away from their mouths. Children will probably insist on putting the mouthpiece in their mouths. If this becomes a problem, have the children take turns so that you can thoroughly sterilize the mouthpiece between players.

Remember that setting the environment for musical play requires a rich variety of quality sounds available for children's exploration. Teachers need to be instrument purchasers and scavengers, never passing up the acquisition of an instrument for the classroom. Gently used or discarded instruments often can be found at flea markets, yard sales, or acquired through donations from individuals in the community. An important caution is that any instrument to be used must be child-safe, with no sharp edges or parts that can be easily removed and swallowed.

The Teacher as Facilitator

Teachers of public school–age children are usually responsible for working with large groups of children. They must cleverly plan for cooperative play groups or other small-group activities to narrow the teacher-child ratio within the classroom. Even so, these teachers continue to be responsible for large numbers of children throughout the day. Their opportunity to interact with individual children may be limited, but it is still possible.

When a system is properly administered, teacher/care providers of two- to four-year-old children have the luxury of working with individuals, pairs, and small groups. If the class load follows recommended ratios for children in this age range, it should not exceed 10 to 12 students per teacher (with the additional assistance of an aide). Teaching at this level affords many opportunities for the adult to interact one-on-one or with only a few children at a time.

Interacting with the young child in the learning setting enables the teacher to model, motivate, clarify, or redirect while recognizing and valuing the child's offerings. The teacher becomes a play partner in the musical exploration or game. The teacher must be aware of the tenuousness of the play, realizing that forcing structure, rules, or logic on the experience may discourage the child. Following are a few suggestions for the adult who engages the child in musical play.

The teacher should not expect or demand that every child actively participate in the play. Many children are content to be far-off observers and take pleasure from what they see others do. As they begin to feel safer, they will join the play.

A delayed response is typical in young children. If the teacher elicits no response from a child after presenting ideas or music, the teacher may become frustrated or feel she has failed to reach the child. However, days later, the child's parent or another adult may report that the child sang, talked about, or demonstrated general awareness of the experience, thereby reaffirming that he or she did not miss the presentation.

If the teacher is seated on the floor, a child may attempt to sit on his or her lap. The child should take this initiative rather than the adult placing the child in this position. Of course, sharing teacher's lap is not possible for all children at once, and concepts of fairness and sharing may become a problem for the children.

The teacher should not tower over children. When possible, he should kneel down or sit so that he is at their level during play. Also, the teacher shouldn't pick up or carry the child. The child's feet should remain on the floor to give the child a sense of self-control.

The teacher should look at the child during presentations and individual play to give her a signal that she is important. However, be aware that direct, lingering eye contact can become overwhelming and even threatening to the young child. If the child begins to withdraw or appear fearful, the teacher should quickly avert his eyes or address comments to another more receptive child or adult in the area.

Young children are very curious about the intriguing sounds and shapes of classroom and orchestral instruments. They rarely need encouragement to gather around the presenter to hear and create their own sounds on the instrument. To encourage this play, the presenter simply needs to find a place on the rug and make sounds on the instrument. Children respond like bees to honey, immediately rushing to be near the performer. Excited children ask questions and attempt to touch the instrument. Soon, other more hesitant children may join the crowd.

The teacher should not leave fragile instruments such as guitars and drums unsupervised. Damaging an instrument can be a very sad experience for the child, as well as an unfortunate loss of equipment. Rule of thumb: If the teacher doesn't want a child to handle an instrument or game piece, she should place it out of sight.

The teacher needs to tell children what *to do* rather than what *not to do*. For example, the wrong approach is as follows: The child is tugging on a guitar string. The adult says, "Don't touch the string, it will break!" The child tends not to hear the word "Don't," but does hear "touch the string." Thus, the child does just the opposite of the adult's instruction. A better approach is: "Touch right here." (Adult gently points to a string on the guitar) If the child continues to abuse the instrument and redirecting fails, the instrument is removed from the play.

Young children often do not share well; turn-taking is still a developing social skill. Persuading the child to give another child a turn should involve preparation for what will be happening. For example, the teacher says, "You will need to play one more time, then it will be Robin's turn." The teacher should help children anticipate when their turn is coming: "Robbie is playing now, then Maria will play, and then it will be Brian's turn." The teacher can set up expected behavior by saying, "I like the way Megan is waiting for her turn. She is carefully watching so she will know what to do when it is her turn."

The teacher should not use a confrontational approach by forcibly or abruptly taking an instrument or mallet from the child's hand. Instead, she should instruct the child to freely give the object to another. For example, "Johnny, now you can put the mallet in Wayne's hand and he will be ready to play." The teacher praises the child for sharing by saying, "I really like how David gave the mallet to Gretchen. He is a good turn-taker!"

The teacher can reduce the threat when interacting with a timid child by working through a third person. He may hand a mallet or cello bow to a care provider, parent, or sibling with whom the child is more comfortable, suggesting, "Daddy, would you like to play the drum?" "Daddy, I bet you could show Mark how to play the drum." "Daddy, would you like to give Mark the mallet?" "Daddy, could you play right here?" (Point to an xylophone bar) or "Daddy, could you make sounds on the cello? Maybe Mark would like to hold the bow."

The Teacher as Continuous Learner

Inherent in the profession of education is that educators never complete their schooling. Remaining on the cutting edge of evolving curriculum, methodology, materials, and personal skills entails continual participation in local, state, and national conferences; in-service activities; college courses; and reading professional journals and publications. Most early childhood educators are members of the National Association of Education for Young Children (NAEYC) or other similar organizations. Through the national and state affiliates of these organizations, educators have ample access to the best minds in the country.

The Music Educators National Conference (MENC) and its state affiliates are the professional organization of music specialists. This organization, which performs similar functions as NAEYC, is designed to meet the needs of music education in the nation, preschool through higher education. The organization encompasses all areas of music education: instrumental, choral, and general music. National conferences are held biannually, with state groups meeting annually. MENC has a strong commitment to music in early childhood as evidenced by its many publications and special conference sessions.

Educators are strongly urged to collaborate with organizations that share mutual educational concerns. It is important that early childhood generalists and music educators take advantage of the expertise that these organizations offer. Early childhood educators need to know that they are welcome to participate in the many music education activities and that national, and some state, groups include special early childhood days or events during their major conferences. Through the professional stimulation organizations offer, teachers can stay current and well informed to meet the needs of the children.

SUMMARY

We ask much of early childhood teachers and provide little time for them to develop program and materials. It is gratifying to see that, in spite of these drawbacks, they rise to the challenge and strive to provide quality programs for children. A curriculum design is a constantly evolving plan, changing and being refined yearly. It is important that a framework exist or the logic of the learning may be lost. Teachers must adapt ideas and design a curriculum to fit the specific needs of the children in their charge. A curriculum model from which this adaptation can evolve is an important springboard for initiating the process.

Understanding how to interact with preschool children in a learning setting is critical, for this age group plays in order to better know their world and the objects and people in it. Skills for effectively guiding and playing with young children are acquired by care providers and teachers throughout their careers.

Knowing whether or not we "did the job we thought we did" is important, so some system should be instituted for evaluating programs and children's progress. Many assessment models must be surveyed and one, or a combination of several, selected to form a systematic approach that works within the teacher's time frame and ability to implement it.

The challenge of reviewing and compiling materials for the classroom remains the teacher's responsibility. This means the teacher must seek information from professional experts about where to find resources, if these resources are developmentally and musically appropriate, and what the most effective means of delivering the ideas to children are. It is highly recommended that the teacher use the expertise and resources of national and state-affiliated professional organizations that are concerned with music and early childhood education.

THINGS TO DO

1. Develop an assessment file for one child. Determine a time line for your assessment, then record the musical behaviors/responses/progress of the child. Initiate a music portfolio and describe the nature of the content you will be including and how you will go about obtaining this information.

2. Review a children's song book. Select four songs (words and music) that you think are musically appropriate and worthy of use in your classroom. Justify your choice of songs.

3. Attend a workshop sponsored by a state affiliate of either NAEYC or MENC. Write a summary of one presentation and describe one activity that you feel was especially effective.

Resources

Music Textbooks

Palmer, M., M. Reilly, and C. Scott. *The World of Music.* Morristown, NJ: Silver Burdett & Ginn, 1991.

Staton, B., M. Staton, M. Davidson, and S. Snyder. *Music and You.* New York: Macmillan & Company, 1988.

Classroom Instruments

Magna Music, Inc.
10370 Page Industrial Blvd.
St. Louis, MO 63132
1-314-427-5660

Peripole-Bergerault, Inc.
2041 State Street
Salem, OR 97301
1-800-443-3592

Rhythm Band Instruments
P.O. Box 126
Fort Worth, TX 76101-0126
1-817-332-5654

Suzuki Musical Instrument Corp.
P.O. Box 261030
San Diego, CA 92196-9877
1-800-854-1594

Professional Organizations

National Association for the Education of Young Children
1509 16th Street, N.W.
Washington, DC 20036-1426

Music Educators National Conference
1902 Association Drive
Reston, VA 22091

Notes

[1] Barbara Andress, "Music for Every Stage. How Much? What Kind? How Soon?" *Music Educators Journal* (October 1989): 22–27.

[2] Lilian Katz, "Early Education: What Should Young Children Be Doing?" in *Early Schooling: The National Debate,* eds. L. Kagna and E. Zigler (New Haven, CT: Yale University Press, 1987), 156.

[3] David Elkind, *Miseducation: Preschoolers at Risk* (New York: Alfred A. Knopf, 1987), 143–147.

[4] Barbara Andress, *Music Experiences in Early Childhood* (New York: Holt, Rinehart and Winston, 1980), 54–55.

6

~~~~~~

Models, Materials, and Methods: Singing

The voice is the child's most constant musical instrument. He uses it deliberately and spontaneously in play at home, school, in the car, or at a restaurant. A young child has no qualms about bursting into playful singing while clinging to mother's skirt as they wait for the elevator or to relieve boredom when all the adults continue to eat a lengthy meal at the restaurant. His voice is at all times a readily available toy. The child in the restaurant is seen rolling eyes upward and wiggling in the confines of the chair while creating a wonderfully random song. The lyrics of the song are quite illogical from the adults' viewpoint.

Being able to appreciate a child's original, unstructured version of a song is one of the unique advantages of working with preschoolers. At no other time do people sing in such an uninhibited manner, free from the dictates of conventional song form. The child certainly does not question the musical validity of what he is singing. It is truly a time of heartfelt musical expression.

Sound educational practice promotes starting at the child's level and then guiding his or her progress along the learning continuum. Entering children's musical world means that teachers also must value the singsong play, even to the point of modeling similar songs. When care providers relax and more freely sing childlike song dialogues and singsong stories, the play takes on a developmentally appropriate stance; that is, the care providers are at the children's level.

Being at the child's level means that the teacher should include improvised song play as well as introduce songs that are a part of the culture. Traditional heritage songs are good models for teaching children how music permeates their world. Children are not too young to hear all music, they are merely too young to perform all music. From birth on, children hear a variety of vocal music performances such as choirs, solos, pop, rock, opera, and songs of many cultures. Children are not yet prejudiced against certain musical styles, so this is the ideal time to expose them to all vocal musics.

The following sections discuss song and voice play suggestions that are appropriate for vocal interaction with young children at early stages of development.

Improvised Song Play

Although children spontaneously create songs during their play, teachers may at first find it a bit awkward to become a part of such play. The following suggestions may help teachers initiate improvised song play with children.

◆   The teacher models singsong conversations that initially may be rather one-sided because children do a great deal of just listening. The teacher often plays *alongside* the child, manipulating a singing character without seeming to play with the child.

(Teacher's rambling tune) "This is Raggedy Ann and she is going to the party. (To the child) Does she have a pretty party dress? (No answer) I think this red dress is very pretty. Time to go to (child's name) party. Who is coming to this party with Raggedy Ann? Maybe Jenny . . . and Alex . . . and Becky . . . and (pauses for child to enter the play)." (Child looks interested but does not sing)

◆   The teacher tries to elicit responses from a child by singing questions or leaving out anticipated words in the phrase for the child to complete.

(Teacher and Megan hold identical clown dolls. Teacher sings) "I see a red nose, I see two eyes, I see one . . ." (points to clown's mouth) (Megan sings) "Mouth." (Teacher continues) "This clown says, 'Hello, Megan.'" (Megan answers) "Hello, clown." (Teacher assumes voice of the clown) "I like you, Megan." (Megan) "I like you, too." (Clown) "I'm going to the circus." (Megan) "Me, too!"

◆   The teacher should know that children readily sing answers to musical questions that involve simple information about colors, time, or names of family members.

◆   Singing while simultaneously pointing to concrete objects such as a picture or a toy provides many ideas for things to sing about.

The adult and child are sharing a Dr. Seuss book. They linger on one page, pointing and singing about characters on the page. "This a kitty cat . . . he gots a funny big hat . . . see his big eyes and long tail!" Soon the child runs out of ideas for singing, so he turns a clump of pages, mindless of the story sequence that might have occurred had he gone from page to page. Now songs are made up about the new characters and pictures.

◆   Children love to catch adults' mistakes. The adult sings, "This clown's nose is green!" The child grins and says, "No, it's red!" The teacher feigns great remorse at his silly error.

◆   For large-group improvisations, the action should be planned so that the group gives a fixed response as various individuals create the improvised ideas. In this way, the majority of children are involved throughout the activity rather than sitting idly by until it is their turn to create a song idea. The group sings one verse of "The Wheels on the Bus," using it as a repeated topical response throughout the song. Between verses, the teacher sings questions to elicit sung responses from individuals. When ideas wane, the teacher indicates that all should again sing the verse. Then a new set of questions triggers additional responses from the improvisers.

The people on the bus go up and down,
Up and down, Up and down,
The people on the bus go up and down
All through the town.

(Teacher's singing question) "Where are the people going, Megan?" (Megan sings) "Down to the town." (Teacher) "Is this town Phoenix?" (Megan) "Yes." (Teacher indicates that all children again sing the verse. Teacher asks) "Who is riding on this bus?" (Children randomly offer names, some by singing, others by speaking) (Teacher) "What are they going to buy at the store?" (Children randomly offer names of vegetables, toys, etc.)

◆   Improvised song play is not only for the very young, but should remain with people to some extent throughout adulthood. Young children create loosely organized songs, older children apply more musical knowledge and verbal structure to their original songs, and adults make up whistling tunes and original songs (perhaps only in the shower) or maybe enjoy hearing and experimenting with skat singing.

SUGGESTED IMPROVISED SONG PLAY ACTIVITIES

Finger-people Props

Parents or other adults can entertain children during tedious waiting or traveling times with finger-people song play. They can draw the eyes, nose, and mouth of a character on the fleshy end of one or more fingers. Then they play out song conversations, story ideas, or sing a traditional song such as "Where Is Thumpkin?" popping up each finger person from a closed fist as the song progresses.

WHERE IS THUMPKIN?
(Tune: "Are You Sleeping?")

Where is Thumpkin, Where is Thumpkin
Here I am, here I am
How are you today, sir? Very well, I thank you.
Run away! Run away!

The adult can also invite the child to have his own finger person. If the child is agreeable, the adult draws a face on one or more of the child's fingers, and the play continues. Children love to anticipate a surprised, silly, or scary face on their fingers as a part of the song play.

Another finger-people game is the adult draws faces on his own fingers, one of which looks scary or silly. The play begins with the adult's fingers closed. New words are sung to the melody of "Are You Sleeping?" The child lifts the adult's fingers one by one, looking for the special face:

Where is big bad (silly) John?
Where is big bad (silly) John?
He's not here!
He's not here!
Where can he be hiding?
Where can he be hiding?
Here he is!
Here he is! (Spoken)
. . . and he's going to get you/tickle you!

(Optional idea: Where is pretty Anne . . . and she's going to kiss your toes/nose/ear/ eye . . .)

The game is played out on the child's own fingers, with the adult finding the scary or silly face.

Entering the Child's Play

Jenny is swinging and begs for someone to give her a push. The adult obliges and begins to make up a swing song: "Jenny goes high . . . Jenny goes low . . . see her up high in the sky!"

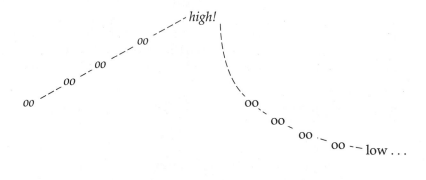

The adult encourages Jenny to join in the up-and-down voice inflection sound play. The play continues as Jenny and the adult begin to make up songs about other children who are also playing on the swings: "Nam Hee swings high . . . high in the sky; Billy's feet touch the ground. Billy is silly . . . he twists around!"

Improvising a Song in Relation to a Tonal Accompaniment

The teacher prepares the play environment by recording instruments that are performing an ostinati accompaniment, such as a simple one-measure pattern repeated continuously. Each ostinato lasts for about three minutes, then a new accompaniment ensues. The tape player and tape recording, along with a picture book, are placed in the play area. The teacher models "how to play" by singing about the pictures as the accompaniment tape plays. The children, who are older three-year-olds, soon take over the play and make up countless musical stories.

The teacher may use this musical play to assess a child's progress. An additional tape recorder is placed in the area with a microphone to record a child's song responses. A spot check of the tapes demonstrates that many children are influenced by the accompaniment, indicated by their in-tuneness and a sense of tonality in common with the music they are hearing. The tapes are ultimately placed in the child's progress folder.

Embellishing Nursery Rhymes

Young children enjoy embellishing favorite nursery rhymes. During group time, they sing a familiar nursery rhyme such as "Sing a Song of Sixpence." The teacher interrupts the traditional melody at any time to musically ask a question or allow the children to create special sounds. (This song is difficult for this age group to sing. The teacher sings the traditional song and the children improvise the story variation.)

(Adult begins singing)

Sing a song of sixpence,
A pocket full of rye,
Four and twenty *kitty-cats*
Baked in a pie.
When the pie was opened
They all began to sing

(Children make up kitty cat songs: Meow, Mew, Phist, Purr)

(Adult continues)

Now wasn't that a dainty dish
To set before the King?
Do you think the King wanted kitty cats in his pie?

(Children continue the play by singsonging about what the king and others might have said)

The angry king sings: "Who put kitty cats in my pie? Bring me the cook at once! Why did you put kitty cats in my pie?"

The frightened cook sings: "I didn't do it, they must have jumped into the pie when I wasn't looking."

The kitty cats sing: "We didn't mean to be in the pie. We just fell in when we were running too fast, and then someone put a lid on us. It was very dark and scary inside the pie . . ."

Mommy cat: "Where are my kittens? I've lost my kittens!" etc.

The book *Four & Twenty Dinosaurs* (Most 1990) is a takeoff on Mother Goose rhymes. After the teacher reads it to the children, they may wish to "Sing a Song of Sixpence" with dinosaurs in the pie. What would the king think about a tyrannosaurus in his pie?

Group Improvisational Play

The following sequence is recommended for leading children from a simple response such as speaking to one that involves more responsibility for a performed musical idea. The sequence is: (1) echo the spoken sentence, (2) make up a spoken sentence, (3) echo a musical phrase, (4) make up a musical phrase.

The children are invited to walk around randomly while the teacher leads a rhythmic chant.

◆ *Step 1*—The teacher chants,

When **I** was **walk**-ing **down** the **street**
A **fun**-ny **man** I **chanced** to **meet.**

(Walking and rhythmic chant stop as teacher expressively says)

He had fifty-two cats!

(Children echo) He had fifty-two cats!

The chant is repeated several times with other exaggerated statements to be echoed.

◆ *Step 2*—The teacher points to a child and all say,

When **he** was walk-ing down the street
A fun-ny man **he** chanced to meet.

(Child says) He wore a great big hat!
(All echo) He wore a great big hat!

The chant is repeated so that many children are given a chance to say something about the funny man as the group echoes each idea.

◆   *Step 3*—The teacher improvises a melody for the silly statement. The children echo the silly melodic statement, then the teacher and the children begin to sing the chant.

◆   *Step 4*—The teacher points to a child and all sing,

> When **he** was walking down the street
> A funny man **he** chanced to meet.

The child sings a funny statement for others to echo.

As I Was Walking Down the Street

B. Andress

As   I   was walk-ing   down the street, a   fun - ny man   I   chanced to meet.

"As I Was Walking Down the Street," *Holt Music—Grade 2*, 1988. Holt, Rinehart and Winston. Used by permission.

Rhyming Play

The teacher sings a three-tone "I see" game. She sings a short phrase, leaving children to supply the final rhyming word.

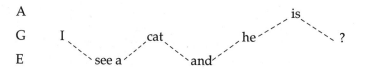

Include models of nonsense rhyming words:

> I see a gurple and he is (purple).
> I see a toad and he is (poad).

The teacher invites a child to sing what he sees, and the teacher adds the final rhyming word.

A Singing Jack-in-the-Box

The teacher prepares a large cardboard box in the style of a jack-in-the-box that has a flap lid covering the top. Inside the box is a pretend microphone. The box is placed in the play environment, and the children are invited to take turns squatting down in the box to become the singing jack-in-the box. The game rules are that each singer can sing only when someone lifts the box lid. The singer then stands up with the microphone and sings an improvised or familiar song. When the lid is closed, the music stops.

Toddler Songs

Children are rapidly acquiring vocabulary during the early years. Phillippe Muller pointed out that the acquisition of language is indicative of emerging thought. "Initially, the child's vocabulary is limited to an average of three words at one year old, 272 words at age two, 1,540 at three, and 3,562 at six years old."[1]

Toddlers have a growing vocabulary, but they often are overwhelmed when attempting to sing songs with lengthy, meaningless lyrics. Toddlers listen and move to such songs, but rarely do they sing along for obvious reasons. Teachers should create or find songs with limited vocabulary, then anticipate that the toddlers may sing during the play or have a delayed response in another setting.

"Kitty Cat"

A teacher can make a four-page booklet consisting of the song (page 1), the tiger cat (page 2), the fluffy cat (page 3), and the real fur cat (page 4) (cut out a faux fur cat and glue it to the page). The teacher sings the song, encouraging children to join in when they are ready, and points to and rhythmically taps the tiger cat while the song is sung. The same motion is repeated as children view the fluffy cat. The song is sung once more and, as the last page is turned, the teacher says, "Would you like to pet my kitty cat?" Children eagerly reach out to pet the soft fur, then demand many repetitions of the song. The activity involves a song with limited words and the anticipation of the culminating tactile play in touching the soft fur.

SONGS FOR TODDLERS

PAGE 2

PAGE 3

PAGE 4

First printed in B. Andress, "Song-Making Experiences for Two–Four-Year-Olds," *The Orff Echo* (Winter 1984), American Orff-Schulwerk Association, Cleveland, OH.

This same melody and booklet idea can be used to create songs about other creatures such as dogs, rabbits, or birds. The final doggy and bunny pictures are again made of fur; the bird has one beautiful feather for "special touching" on its tail. A one-word song book is created by using magazine pictures of heavy road construction equipment. The children point to the pictures and sing, "Diggers, diggers, diggers . . ."

PAGE 1

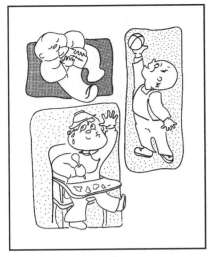

PAGE 2

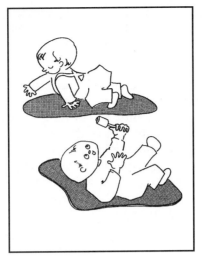

PAGE 3

. . . **this little baby I love-ee-love.**
PAGE 4

First printed in B. Andress, "Music for Every Stage," *Music Educators Journal* (October 1989). Used by permission.

"The teacher can use baby pictures for a "pointing" song game. The teacher sings the song, inviting the child to point at a picture of one baby to love (pages 2 and 3). She repeats the song several times asking, "Now which baby shall we love?" The child selects a different baby picture. She ends the song by turning to the last page, pointing to the child's own snapshot, and saying, "This little baby I love-ee-love!"

"Tree, Tree, Tree"

Appropriate songs can be found in the literature. Toddlers enjoy the repetition in "Tree, Tree, Tree" by Fred Rogers. The teacher can make up additional verses such as when the child arrives at school proudly wearing new shoes, and all celebrate by singing "Shoes, Shoes, Shoes."

© "Tree, Tree, Tree," 1967, Fred M. Rogers. Used by permission.

Easy-to-Perform Songs

Young children do not need a lot of songs in their repertoire because they like to repeat favorite familiar tunes. Top songs on preschoolers' hit parade are "Jingle Bells" and "Happy Birthday to You." Why are these songs so popular? They are certainly singable, they have the same word idea repeated many times, they are musically short and simple, and they represent exciting memorable occasions. In short, they have passed all the child's tests for best-loved songs. Children joyfully sing these songs out of season or without benefit of a need to celebrate. Many other songs in the literature fit this same criteria. The following tunes represent typical songs that can be performed successfully and enjoyed by very young children.

"Clap Your Hands"

This simple song provides clear instructions that precisely match the movements to be used. The teacher may add other movements such as "Touch, touch, touch your nose" or "Tap, tap, tap your elbow."

CLAP YOUR HANDS
Traditional

1. Clap, clap, clap your hands, Clap your hands to-geth-er,
2. Stamp, stamp, stamp your feet, Stamp your feet to-geth-er,

Clap, clap, clap your hands, Clap your hands to-geth-er.
Stamp, stamp, stamp your feet, Stamp your feet to-geth-er.

Tra-la-la-la, etc.

"Clap Your Hands," *Music Experiences in Early Childhood.* Holt, Rinehart and Winston, 1980. Used by permission.

"Teddy Bear"

This song is a traditional favorite of children and uses simple movement directions. Initially, the teacher may want to pause at the end of each phrase to allow children time to complete their motion.

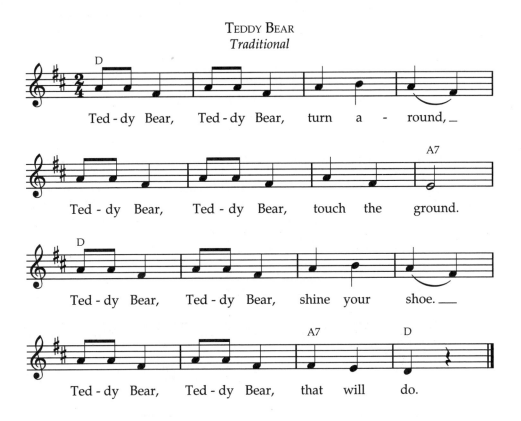

"Bye Low, Baby-O"

This brief lullaby has limited pitches and words that can be sung over and over. Children may pretend to rock their doll while singing.

Brown Bear, Brown Bear, What Do You See?

"Sing" the book *Brown Bear, Brown Bear, What Do You See?* (Martin 1970). The following pitched sequence may be used for the words on most pages in the book:

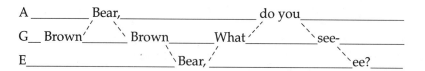

The final page, on which all animals are reviewed, may be "sung" using only two pitches:

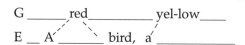

"Charlie Over the Ocean"

Each musical idea in this song is sung twice, which makes it an easy echo song for children to perform. The teacher sings the first idea, and the children repeat exactly what was sung. The teacher can personalize the song by using the names of children in the classroom in place of "Charlie."

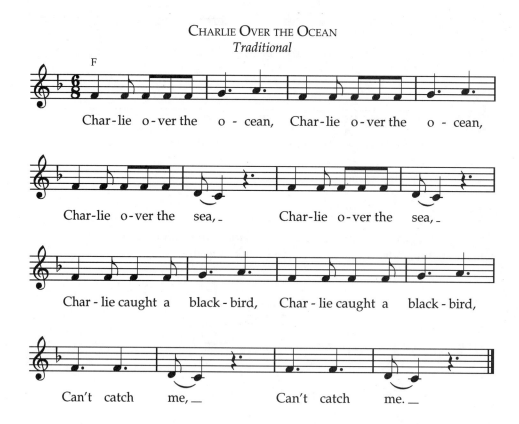

"Love Somebody?"

The teacher asks the question, "Love somebody?" and each time the child answers, "Yes, I do." The teacher sings the fourth phrase, "Love somebody and it must be . . ."; the child supplies the final word, indicating who or what is to be loved.

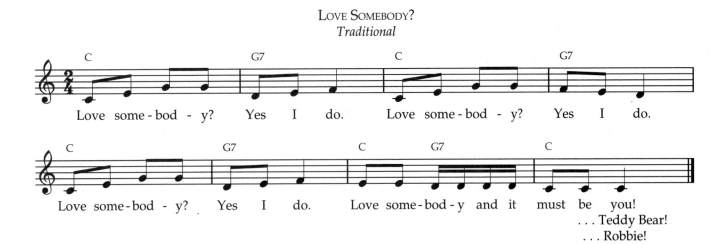

LOVE SOMEBODY?
Traditional

Love some-bod-y? Yes I do. Love some-bod-y? Yes I do.

Love some-bod-y? Yes I do. Love some-bod-y and it must be you!
   . . . Teddy Bear!
   . . . Robbie!

Song Stories

Children love to listen to, sing, or otherwise become a part of unfolding dramas that are depicted in many narrative-type songs. Such song stories are often lengthy, contain many words, or involve cumulative play, where the children must recall a sequence of characters and events. Pictures, storyboards, and play mats are but a few of the visual aids that can guide the children as they perform these songs.

"She'll Be Comin' 'Round the Mountain"

The teacher invites children to sing this familiar song with a new twist—a music play mat. He may use these fun sounds and comments at the end of each phrase or make up his own:

> She'll be comin' 'round the mountain when she comes. Toot! Toot!
> She'll be drivin' six white horses when she comes. Neigh.
> We will catch the old red rooster when she comes.
> *(Rooster's emphatic comment)* W-r-o-n-g!
> We will have chicken and dumplin's when she comes.
> *(Chick says)* No way, Jose!
> We will have to go get pizza when she comes. Yum! Yum!
> She will have to sleep with grandma when she comes. *(Snore)* Huh-Phew!

The teacher prepares for play by enlarging and laminating the game board play mat. He reproduces it then cuts out the circle game pieces. Musical play is a rhythmic tapping game. The child begins in the lower left-hand corner of the game board. The song is sung as the child taps each picture of the train engines and tooting whistles.

The children place the circle game pieces on the play mat as they sing the remaining verses of the song. They may know other verses that are not included in this game. The teacher can invite them to draw their own circle pictures that depict known verses or illustrate ideas they have created for the song. She will have to watch cartoons when she comes . . . She will have to play with dinosaurs when she comes . . . She will wear Power Ranger sneakers when she comes . . .

Rhythmically touch pictures on mat.

She'll be <u>com</u> - in' 'round the <u>moun</u> - tain when she <u>comes</u>, <u>Toot</u>! <u>Toot</u>!

Cut out circle game pieces to place on playmat.

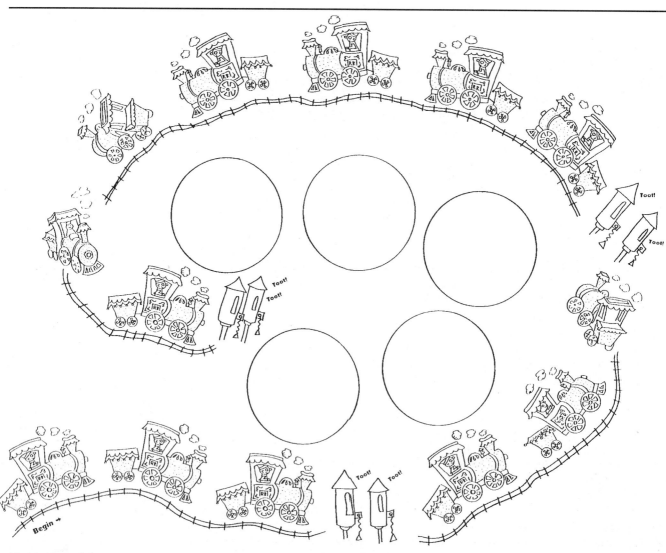

"Comin' 'Round the Mountain," reprint from *You, Your Children and Music*, Vol. IV, Issue 3. Arizona Early Childhood Music Collaborative Project. Used by permission. Permission to reproduce this page for personal use only is granted to users of this textbook.

"My Goose"

Singing a cumulative song (a song that combines and sings ideas in reverse after each new verse is sung) is a difficult task for young children because they often have difficulty recalling information. The teacher uses pictorial reminders with pages that unfold to reveal each new character to be included in the song play.

To prepare for play, the teacher copies and then cuts the pictures along the dotted line. She tapes the two pieces together to form a long song strip chart, folds the pictures so that initially only the goose is visible, and then unwraps the chart to reveal the other animals.

MY GOOSE
Traditional

Why does-n't my goose Sing as well as your goose,

When I paid for my goose Twice as much as you?

VERSE I — THE GOOSE

Honk!   Honk!   Honk!   Honk!

The teacher sings Verse 1 about the goose, after which the children rhythmically make honking sounds. The teacher sings the song again, substituting the word *cat* for *goose*. She points to the cat while the children sing cat sounds, then returns to the goose picture as the children make honking sounds.

VERSE II — THE CAT

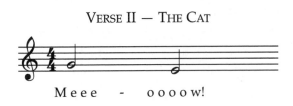

M e e e - o o o o w!

The play continues with each new verse substituting the name and sound of the next animal. The teacher points to the unfolded pictures as the animal sounds are cumulatively sung in reverse at the end of each verse.

VERSE III — THE HEN

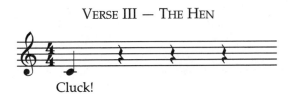

Cluck!

VERSE IV — THE COW

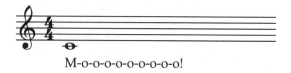

M-o-o-o-o-o-o-o-o-o!

VERSE V — THE PIG

Oink!   Oink!   Oink!   Oink!

"My Goose," chart reprint from *You, Your Children and Music,* Vol. II, Issue 4. Arizona Early Childhood Music Collaborative Project. Used by permission. Permission to reproduce this page for personal use only is granted to users of this textbook.

"Elephants"

Sitting together, the child and teacher sing and point to storyboard pictures displayed in a sequence. The child sings and is involved in dialogue play.

Ideas for song story play include the following:

1. and 2.   The child makes "zu-zu-zu" sounds of a busy spider spinning a web.

3. The song begins, "One elephant went out to play, out on a spider's web one day."

4. "He had such enormous fun, he called for another elephant to come."

5. The teacher calls a new elephant by rhythmically chanting, "Ellie Lou Mae . . . come out and play!" The child pretends to be Ellie Lou Mae, saying, "Who, Me?" Teacher answers, "Yes, you!"

6. Sing, "Two elephants went out to play, out on a spider's web one day."

7. "They had such enormous fun, they called for another elephant to come." The teacher may wish to point out the increasing concern the spider has for the safety of his web.

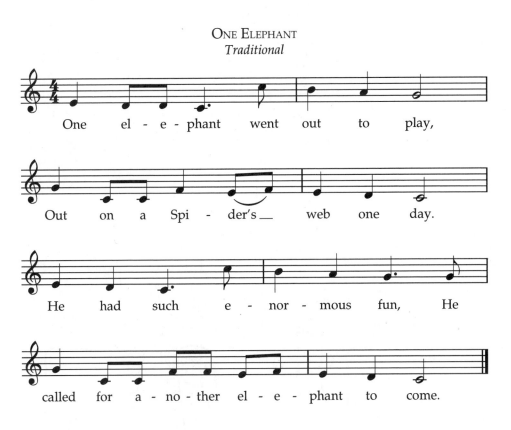

ONE ELEPHANT
Traditional

One   el - e - phant   went   out   to   play,

Out   on   a   Spi - der's __   web   one   day.

He   had   such   e - nor - mous   fun,   He

called   for   a - no - ther   el - e - phant   to   come.

8. The teacher says, "Jim Jumbo Jay . . . come out and play." The child pretends to be Jim Jumbo Jay, saying, "Who, me?" Teacher answers, "Yes, you!"

9. Sing, "Three elephants went out to play, out on a spider's web one day."

10. "They had such enormous fun, they called for another elephant . . ." (Stop before singing the final word)

11. Crash! Pow! Boom! resounds as the elephants all fall into the broken spider web. By this time, the poor little spider is really upset because his beautiful web is all broken down.

"Elephants," reprint from *You, Your Children and Music*, Vol. I, Issue 4. Arizona Early Childhood Music Collaborative Project. Used by permission. Permission to reproduce this page for personal use only is granted to users of this textbook.

12. The disgusted spider begins to spin a new web: "Zu-Zu-Zu."

13. The child may make the tapping sound of the hammer as the spider posts his warning signs. The child ends the play by firmly saying, "Keep off! No Elephants allowed!"

Older Children Read and Sing

First- and second-grade children are able to perform more complicated melodies and are capable of using a textbook to learn their songs. In preparation, children begin to play with ideas of how music "looks" without the use of the book. They simultaneously hear the music and describe melodies by moving their hands/body to indicate the overall up, down, and sameness of the melody. As they become more able, they draw pictures of melodies and gradually begin to understand the look of traditional melodic notation.

Building understandings about and acquiring the skills to use and communicate melodic information verbally or in written form takes place through a series of developmentally appropriate experiences. Young children begin with simple awareness of highness and lowness of sounds that they hear. They begin to acquire some means of describing this concept through body movement, words, or visual representations. A typical transitional sequence begins with general awareness of pitch differences of a melody.

In the enactive stage, children gradually are able to describe the most obvious high-low pitch contrasts with large body movement gestures and descriptive vocabulary and describe overall melodic direction with large body movements.

In the iconic stage, they are able to describe overall melodic direction by drawing contour lines in the sky or on paper (melodic contour is a general sense of how the melody moves, but does not reflect specific pitch information) and differentiate among up-down-sameness of pitches within the melody. They also use specifically assigned gestures and numbers or syllables to describe simple stepwise pitches as heard in the melody (body scale). These children explore through body touch and a sense of spatial awareness the relationship of pitches within a melody (whole and half steps and skips) and use visual icons that reflect more specific pitch relationships, such as hand signs and stairstep visuals.

In the symbolic stage, children transfer understandings from hand signs and stairstep icons to the up-down-sameness of written traditional notation symbols.

Models for Reading and Writing Music

ENACTIVE-LEVEL PLAY

"See-Saw Sacradown"

Children enjoy singing this song. During group time, they move expressively, reaching up and down as they pretend to travel to London Town. The teacher makes a picture in the sky of the melody by using a puppet to help the children follow the up-down-same movements of the melody. The song is sung as the puppet travels to London Town (a previously prepared box castle). Children play independently with the puppet, traveling to London Town many times.

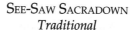

SEE-SAW SACRADOWN
Traditional

See - saw,   sa - cra - down,   Which is the

way to Lon - don Town?   One foot   up   and   one   foot

down.   This   is   the   way   to   Lon - don   Town.

"See-Saw Sacradown," *Holt Music—Grade 2*, 1988. Holt, Rinehart and Winston. Used by permission.

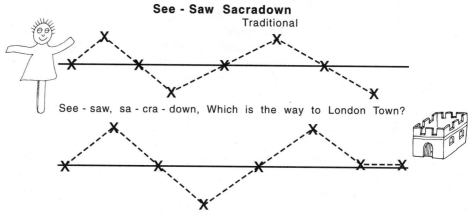

See - Saw Sacradown
Traditional

See - saw, sa - cra - down, Which is the way to London Town?

One foot up and one foot down, This is the way to London Town.

ICONIC-LEVEL PLAY— MELODIC CONTOUR

"Hawaiian Rainbows"

Children draw a rainbow in the sky while singing the first and third phrase of the song. The arch of the rainbow matches the low-high-low movement of the melody. The teacher might say, "Your picture of a rainbow looks just like the melody sounds."

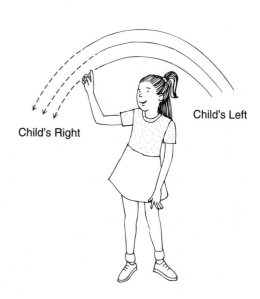

Child's Right   Child's Left

HAWAIIAN RAINBOWS
Hawaiian Folk Song

"Hawaiian Rainbows," *Exploring Music—Grade 3*, 1975. Holt, Rinehart and Winston. Used by permission.

"Pop! Goes the Weasel"

Game shared by Mary Pautz, The University of Wisconsin—Milwaukee. Used by permission.

The teacher introduces the song, choosing different motions, such as a loud clap, throwing hands up in the air, or tongue clicking, in place of the word *pop*. The teacher can also help children become aware of the melodic contour of this melody by using a play mat.

To prepare for play, the teacher enlarges and laminates the play mat. She creates a pop-rattle box with an empty plastic audiocassette tape box. She places a small amount of popcorn kernels inside the box, seals it, and wraps it with opaque contact paper.

After children are familiar with the song, the teacher introduces the play mat that shows the approximate melodic contour of the tune. Children use their index finger to trace the up-and-down path as the song describes the chase. The teacher

POP! GOES THE WEASEL

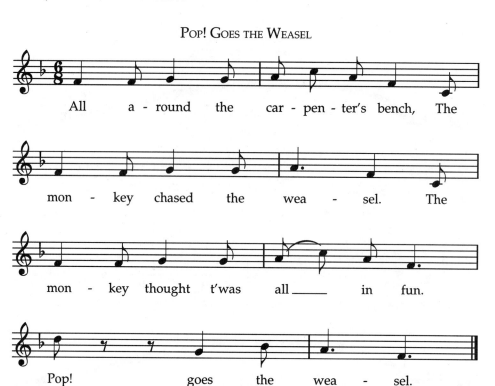

All a - round the car - pen - ter's bench, The
mon - key chased the wea - sel. The
mon - key thought t'was all _____ in fun.
Pop! goes the wea - sel.

shouldn't worry if the children are not moving their fingers along the path accurately. This is a time for achieving a general sense of direction. When the "Pop" comes in the song, children may tap the pop-rattle box with a finger, then continue tracing the trail to end the song.

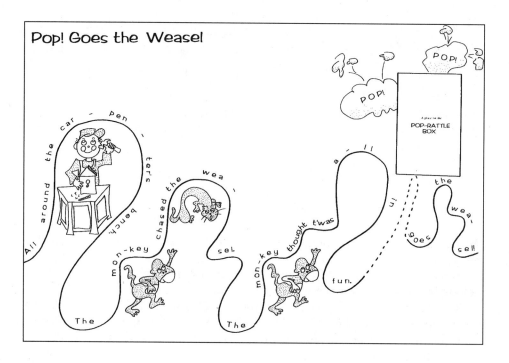

M. Pautz, "Pop! Goes the Weasel," *You, Your Children and Music,* Vol. II, Issue 5. Arizona Early Childhood Music Collaborative Project. Used by permission. Permission to reproduce this play mat for personal use only is granted to users of this textbook.

"Old Man, Old Man, Where Do You Go?

This song also provides opportunities for children to understand relationships of melodic pitches by touching identified body parts that represent steps in the scale.

The teacher introduces the body scale by singing and identifying each body part either with a number (1, 2, 3, 4, 5, 6, 7, 1') or with syllables (do, re, mi, fa, sol, la, ti, do'). He uses the body scale to help children sense the relationships between pitches as they sing this song.

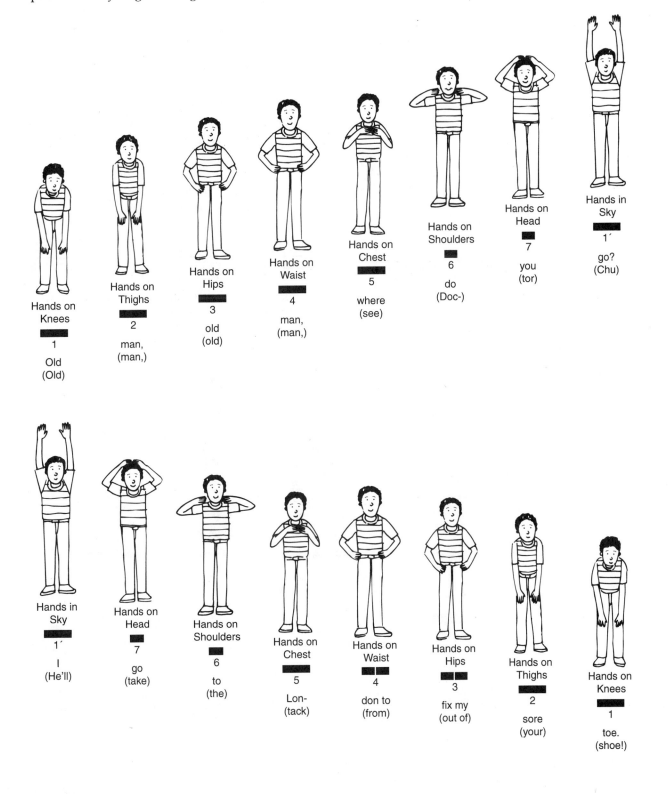

Body scale games should use only a few pitches. For example, children echo the pitches and movement: 3, 2, 1 (echo) 3, 2, 1 (echo) 1, 1, 1, 1, 2, 2, 2, 2 (echo) 3, 2, 1 (echo). Teacher and child perform the song together using numbers: 3, 2, 1,___; 3, 2, 1,___; 1, 1, 1, 1, 2, 2, 2, 2; 3, 2, 1,___. Children may recognize they have been singing "Hot Cross Buns." (Solfege syllables may be substituted for numbers: D, R, M.)

"Gretel, Pastetel"

The body scale can be used to help children sense skips and stepwise melodic motion as they sing this song.

GRETEL, PASTETEL
German Folk Song

1. Gret - el, Pas - tet - el, oh where is your goose?
2. Gret - el, Pas - tet - el, oh where is your hen?
3. Gret - el, Pas - tet - el, oh where is your cow?

She sits in the wa - ter, oh who turned her loose?
She sits on her nest and lays eggs when she can.
She stays in her stall but I can't milk her now.

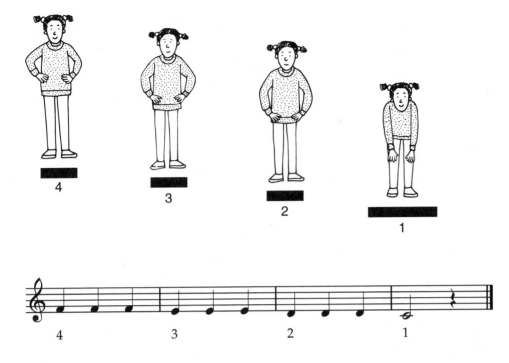

"Gretel, Pastetel," *The Holt Music Book—Grade 3*, 1981. Holt, Rinehart and Winston. Used by permission.

SYMBOLIC-LEVEL PLAY

It is important for children to function at the symbolic level of learning because the use of symbols is the most expeditious way to communicate musical ideas. There are many approaches to introducing children to traditional melodic symbols. Some methods recommend first using only two tones and excerpted patterns from songs. Typical of this approach are the Orff and Kodaly methods, where children begin to read notated sol-mi syllables and then progress through various steps that help them read more pitches. The literature for these limited-pitch songs includes chants, some traditional melodies, and some contrived songs—songs written to accommodate the desired pitches. The approach involves much practice of certain patterns, such as sol-mi and sol-mi-la, before the child progresses to the use of additional pitches. Some proponents believe that children should not be encumbered with other songs until they master each level in the process. Others who use this method include typical children's songs in their curriculum while teaching limited-pitch patterns.

A second approach to teaching children to read melodic notation involves introducing the whole song rather than a specific pattern within the song. Proponents teach pitch differences, directions, and intervals within the context of a whole song while drawing attention to the patterns within. Teachers who use this approach argue that children do not always recognize the relationship between fragmented patterns and the song from which they came, so it is more musical and effective to use the whole song.

These two approaches reflect contrasting beliefs: a holistic (Gestalt) approach to learning as opposed to an approach that begins with the smallest unit and builds toward the whole. Whichever approach is used, the main purpose of notating music is to help readers independently discover how a song sounds when there is no one to sing it for them. The goal of reading music is learner independence. Written melodic notation should be visually clear, contain very obvious melodic information, and be presented in the most musical way possible. Literature may be selected that has limited pitches or obvious up-and-down progressions. In either case, the song should have musical value.

Children may look at musical notation for clues about how the song *generally* will sound: The notes go down so our voice goes down (becomes lower). The notes go up so our voice goes up (becomes higher). The children may sing the song "Charley Warley" to see if this is indeed what happens. Another time, children may view the whole song "Ring around the Rosy" for *specific* pitch information. They see that the song uses only three pitches (S, M, L) until the very last note (D).

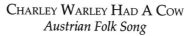

CHARLEY WARLEY HAD A COW
Austrian Folk Song

Adapted Nursery Rhyme by B. Andress

Children transfer knowledge gained from enactive- and iconic-level play and apply it to the written page. As they become more skillful, they are able to discover discrete information about the composition of songs such as specific pitches, repeated patterns, and phrases.

Pitches
Used:

S   M   L   D
(5) (3) (6) (1)

RING AROUND THE ROSY
Traditional

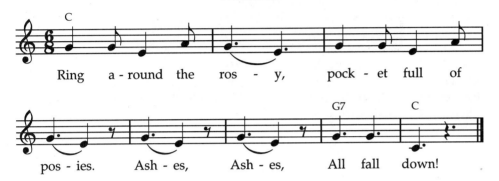

Ring   a - round   the   ros - y,   pock - et   full   of

pos - ies.   Ash - es,   Ash - es,   All   fall   down!

How to Teach a Song

A variety of techniques can be used to help children learn to sing songs. Teachers may depend on a recording to teach a song and serve as accompaniment or they themselves may sing or instrumentally accompany the tune.

Following are some suggestions for using a recording to teach a song.

◆ Voices on commercial recordings may be that of men, women, or children. The performers are usually professional, thus the quality of the musical model should be good. Learners will probably have a reliable, in-tune model.

◆ The voice quality and range of the singer(s) should be replicated easily by the children. Young children can successfully sing with a lower adult male voice by intuitively seeking their own comfort level an octave higher. The octave higher should, however, be within the children's range.

◆ Recorded songs usually have an instrumental introduction, so the teacher does not have to supply a beginning song pitch or establish tonality.

◆ A recording doesn't wait for or correct mistakes; it continues on with or without the performing child.

◆ The recorded selection should be played at random times during the week before it is taught.

◆ Teaching with a recording is a whole-song method. Children hear the entire song and then, through many repetitions, acquire the ability to sing along.

◆ The tempo (speed) of the song has been recorded at a performance level, thus it is often too fast for children during the learning stage. The teacher needs to depend on repeated hearings, introduce the song by singing it himself at a slower tempo, or at least more slowly chant the words.

Following are suggestions for using voice to introduce a song.

Beginning Pitch

When singing with children, teachers often begin the song without warning except to announce the title of the song. Children vainly try to join in, half speaking-singing the words, but usually matching the correct pitches only after they are well into the song. It is important to provide "starting and singing together" information to children before they begin the song.

Share the starting pitch of the song by (1) humming the beginning pitch; (2) giving instructions with your voice by singing on the beginning pitch (e.g., "Here we go" or "Ready now"); (3) playing the beginning pitch on an instrument such as a bell, piano, or pitch pipe.

An even more musical way to start a song is to provide the beginning pitch, but also place it within the harmonic structure of the music. For example, "Merrily We Roll Along" is written in the key of C and begins on the pitch of E. The teacher sings the C major triad on a neutral syllable, then returns to the beginning pitch of E for the first word of the song:

Children now have a sense of the song's tonality, as well as the beginning pitch (E). The first syllable of the first word, **Mer**-ri-ly, begins on E.

Whole-Song Method

Introduce a song by using the whole-song method. Slowly sing the whole song. Children first listen several times and then join in.

> Eency weency spider went up the water spout!
> Down came the rain and washed the spider out.
> Out came the sun and dried up all the rain
> So eency weency spider went up the spout again.

Song Phrase Method

Songs can be introduced with the phrase method. Children hear the total song, then begin to learn it one phrase at a time. The advantage of the phrase method is that it allows the teacher to catch children's musical mistakes before they continue on to new phrases. For example, the teacher sings, "Eency weency spider went up the water spout!" (Children echo) Teacher sings, "Down came the rain and . . ." (Children echo) This process continues until, one by one, all phrases are sung and echoed. Then the teacher sings two phrases:

> Eency weency spider went up the water spout!
> Down came the rain and washed the spider out.
>
> *(Children echo two phrases)*
>
> Out came the sun and dried up all the rain
> So, eency weency spider went up the spout again.
>
> *(Children echo)*

The teacher combines phrases until the children are singing the entire song.

There are many ways to help children learn a song, and no one way is used exclusively. In addition to the methods just discussed, older children learn by discovering such things as musical form, melodic, and rhythmic patterns within the context of a song. This analytical approach provides skills for independently unlocking new song literature and need not be odious or tedious. Guided properly, the search becomes an exciting challenge of discovering same and different ideas and how they interact within the musical whole.

Additional Instruction Information

THE ORFF PROCESS

The Orff process is a comprehensive program based on the use of song, speech, body rhythms, movement, and specially designed instruments. The process involves imitation, exploration, and creation, which lead to sensitive music making. Children acquire music literacy by responding to stick notes, hand signs, and traditional notation.

Orff proponents suggest that children begin singing with limited pitches that evolve from the minor third and gradually increase to the five pentatonic pitches (key of C: C, D, E, G, A). Half steps are initially ignored because they are more difficult for children to sing.

In the Orff process, body percussion, such as stamping, clapping, tapping, patschening (patting upper thigh), is used to accompany speech such as chants of nursery rhymes and poems. Mastering body rhythms is a precursor to playing mallet-struck instruments. Movement is structured for specific responses to beat and rhythm patterns as well as for creative and expression purposes.

Specially designed mallet-struck xylophone-type and other percussion instruments are played in ensemble. Much of the music is taught to performers by the rote technique. The range of instruments used and the teaching process provide unique opportunities for young novice performers to function with a high degree of musicianship in an ensemble.

The American Orff-Schulwerk Association is a national group with state affiliates. Its conferences and special coursework provide in-depth insight about this process and can be most useful for curious teachers who wish to further explore this approach.

THE KODALY METHOD

The Kodaly method focuses primarily on developing children's vocal and reading skills. Children are introduced to in-tune singing with solfege, beginning with sol-mi, sol-la, and so on, until five pitches (do, re, mi, sol, la) are included. Ultimately, all chromatic (12 tones) pitches are used. Hand signs are attributed to each pitch and children sign the syllables (do, re, mi, fa, sol, la, ti, do) as they sing. The "look" of traditional rhythmic notation begins with stick notation; note heads are added and written in isolation from the staff. Rhythm syllables are assigned to various note values such as "Ta" (quarter note) and "Ti-ti" (two eighth notes). The complete notes are later placed on the staff and read holistically. The intent of the approach is for children to use folk literature of the culture to master various pitches. Currently, the Kodaly method and the Orff process are often combined into one instructional practice. Proponents of this practice function nationally and locally and provide in-service opportunities for teachers.

SUMMARY

It should now be apparent that the vocal experiences of children involve more than just singing a familiar song. Children play with their voices in many ways: voice inflection games, spontaneous and deliberate original song making, story ideas, and folk and composed songs that exist within their culture. Teachers are responsible for acquiring developmentally and musically appropriate song literature and setting an environment that encourages children to experiment vocally and perfect their singing skills with others. Such exploration takes place in independent play as well as in large-group settings.

There are many tips and time-tested methods for helping children feel confident, free to express their own ideas, and perfect the singing of familiar tunes. Teachers will want to collect information about these approaches by reading the literature, discussing effective techniques with colleagues, and attending many in-service sessions that focus on existing and emerging methodology. Through careful examination of many suggestions, teachers should adopt an approach that is uniquely suited to their own personal use.

Reading and writing music is a natural evolution of song-making experiences that occur throughout a child's early years. Communicating music with written icons and symbols is a developmental process involving maturation and a well-thought-out learning sequence. The models discussed in this chapter are examples of typical literature that may be used to affect such a learning sequence. Children need many experiences at each level to effectively build a basic understanding of how melodies look and function.

We educate children so that they can acquire enough skills to be independent of their teachers. To that end, we must involve children in more than just song singing; we must teach them to understand how melodies are composed and shared with others. This knowledge base begins in early childhood.

THINGS TO DO

1. Describe two ways you would initiate musical song play with children in each of the following settings: in the car, during bath time, when telling a story, and in the classroom.

2. Select an appropriate children's song. Prepare a chart-size page that uses rhythmic and/or melodic icons to communicate the song effectively to young children.

3. Teach one song to the class using the whole-song method and teach another song using the phrase method.

RESOURCES

Andress, B. "Music for Every Stage." *Music Educators Journal* (October 1989): 22–27. Music Educators National Conference, Reston, VA.

Andress, B. Play Mat Reprints, *You, Your Children and Music,* Vol. I, Issue 4; Vol. II, Issue 4; Vol. IV, Issue 3. Arizona Early Childhood Music Collaborative Project, Arizona Department of Education, Phoenix, AZ.

Andress, B. "Song-Making Experiences for Two–Four-Year-Olds." *The Orff Echo* (Winter 1984): 1–3. The American Orff-Schulwerk Association, Cleveland State University, Department of Music, Cleveland, OH 44115.

Boardman, E., and B. Andress, *The Music Book—Grade 3*. New York: Holt, Rinehart and Winston, 1988.

Boardman, E., B. Andress, M. Pautz, and F. Willman, *Holt Music—Grade 2*. New York: Holt, Rinehart and Winston, 1988.

Boardman, E., et al. *Exploring Music—Grade 3*. New York: Holt, Rinehart and Winston, 1975.

Daniel, Katinka Scipiades. *Kodaly in Kindergarten*. Champaign, IL: Mark Foster, 1981.

Regner, Hermann, ed. *Music for Children, Orff-Schulwerk*. American ed. Vol. I—Preschool Based on Carl Orff-Gunild Keetman Music fur Kinder, Schoot, London.

NOTE

[1]Phillippe Muller, *The Tasks of Childhood* (New York: McGraw-Hill, 1971), 179–181.

7

Models, Materials, and Methods: Instruments

The children are greeted at the door by their teacher as they arrive at the center one morning. After hanging up their coats, they notice the visiting music teacher, who sits on a rug in the middle of a masking tape circle and holds a guitar in vertical position. The teacher is softly strumming the specially tuned open strings of the guitar. The children make a wide circle around this "different thing" in their classroom, seeking a familiar play area while continuing to cast watchful eyes on the musician. Soon, a bold, curious child, backed up by two less venturesome followers, approaches the teacher saying, "Whatcha doin'?"

The teacher gestures to the masking tape outline on the floor and replies, "I'm just sitting in this circle playing this guitar. Would you like to play my guitar?" The children enter the circle and, with minimal encouragement, begin to strum the guitar. The two followers also reach to touch the instrument. The teacher allows time for exploration, redirecting any overexuberant strumming-plucking by the trio as they vie for playing position. One child is having difficulty strumming, so the teacher alters the position of the guitar so that his fingers can easily cross the strings. The teacher begins to sing an improvised chant using the children's names and describing how they are playing the guitar. "Eric, Eric, plays so fine. I hear strumming on his guitar . . ." Other curious children now join the group. The teacher is often mobbed by too many fingers and pressing bodies, so play is stopped as the teacher holds the guitar high out of reach. She suggests that the children take turns or that only three children can be in the playing circle at one time. The teacher makes up a "Knock at the Door" song. The children gently knock on the guitar and then strum as the teacher sings. The game is extended by singing questions and answers: "Who's knocking at this door? Why are you at my house?"

KNOCK! KNOCK!

B. Andress

Knock! Knock!   Peek in!   O-pen the door and walk in.

119

Traditional musical instruments and other sound-making objects are high-interest objects in the classroom. Children readily gravitate to the play area to explore each newly introduced instrument, drawn by the beauty or uniqueness of the sounds. As described in the previous guitar activity, children progress from exploratory play to performing music or otherwise using sounds to interpret non-musical ideas. Instruments provide children with wonderful nonverbal tools to express and embellish ideas they wish to communicate; that is, instruments supply a whole new method of communication. An environment rich in sound sources offers many opportunities for exploratory and mastery play whereby young children acquire knowledge and make decisions. Instruments can be played alone or as a part of an exciting cooperative play unit. Young children should have many hands-on opportunities to interact with high-quality instrumental sounds.

Setting a Safe Instrumental Play Environment

Musical instruments are not toys. They should not be tossed into a toy box to be bumped, scratched, and otherwise broken and abused. They should be placed on a music shelf that is readily available for the children's use. High-quality musical instruments are conscientiously constructed by manufacturers that know the instruments will be used by young children, thus every precaution is taken to create safe, user-friendly equipment. The very nature of an instrument's construction and sound mechanism requires the use of small parts that can loosen or come apart. The teacher must assume responsibility for adequate maintenance of instruments so that they will continue to produce high-quality sounds and not be a hazard to young users. The teacher should remain a play partner or keep a watchful eye on the play to safeguard both the children and the instruments throughout the activity.

REMINDERS FOR EQUIPMENT CHECKS

A mallet used to strike xylophones or drums consists of a ball and a wooden dowel. A broken dowel can have sharp, splintered ends. Also, if children repeatedly place the ball head of a mallet in their mouths, the glue may loosen over time and the small ball may fall off. The teacher needs to remove any broken mallets immediately from the play area and repair them for future use.

The tone bars and jingles on instruments such as resonator bells, small xylophones, and jingle clogs are attached to a wood block with long nails. The nails are usually serrated so that they will not easily come out, but these instruments should be periodically checked for any loose parts.

Maracas may be made from natural gourds, turned wood, or plastic. Natural gourds split easily, losing the pellets inside, so they are not recommended for young children. Wood or quality plastic maracas are better.

All painted instruments and equipment should have nontoxic finishes because young children explore by tasting.

Drum heads can break but pose no problem, other than the child's disappointment. Plastic drum heads are more durable than skin heads. Some drums are constructed with broad-headed tacks around the rim. Although these tacks rarely loosen, they should be checked from time to time.

Stringed instruments such as autoharps and guitars have wire with sharp ends that are usually tucked out of harm's way, but an injury from one can be painful. Also, if a child plays with the tuning pegs, he or she may overly stretch the guitar string to its breaking point. This is a real safety concern. Young children should not be allowed to manipulate the tuning pegs on any string instrument. If this becomes a major control problem, the teacher may hide the pegs in a small cloth drawstring bag that has a funny face drawn on it. After the instrument is tuned, the teacher ties the bag over the head of the guitar, thus hiding the pegs from view during play time.

Rhythm sticks and claves are not easily broken. Children should not use them for sword play or other poking and jabbing actions.

Orff-type barred instruments are constructed with removable bars on a sound box. Children often cannot resist removing the bars. If not done properly, the rubberized spacer nails in the sound box can bend and loosen. There are times when children are encouraged to manipulate the bars on the instrument, so they should be taught to lift the bars with one hand at each end of the bar, lifting them straight up rather than at an angle. Any loosened nail should be immediately repaired.

Cymbals, gongs, and triangles are sturdy, durable instruments. However, brass instruments can dent if they are dropped, which affects their sound quality.

The use of any homemade or found objects must always be considered from a safety perspective. Sometimes the object is acceptable but should be used only in supervised play. If corn, beans, or rice in plastic bottles are used, lids must be securely glued shut so that young children cannot open them and swallow the kernels. Also, rubber band violins or harps can break, snap, or be swallowed. Play with rubber bands should always be supervised.

Most quality jingle bells are now securely riveted to straps or sticks, so there is not much that can damage this instrument or the children who use it.

Paramount to preparing instruments is the safety of the children. Furthermore, a damaged instrument is neither musically useful nor aesthetically satisfying. Caring teachers periodically maintain and supervise the use of classroom instrumental equipment.

Exploratory Play

Entry-level exploratory instrumental play involves touching and hearing to assimilate the many musical sounds that abound. Children then begin to manipulate the sounds, forming schemes about similarities and differences in timbre (quality of sounds) and pitch (same-high-lower). During play, children use a variety of motions and sound starters (e.g., mallets, sticks, beaters, picks, fingers), causing sounds to become faster or slower, louder or softer, shorter or longer, and connected or disconnected. Children become aware of the function of instruments as the teacher uses them to accompany songs or otherwise express musical and nonmusical ideas. Some examples of awareness-level play are described next.

My Sound

The teacher provides a single instrument for the child's pleasure such as a resonator bell with mallet or a double-tone wood block that may be tapped repeatedly. During this play, children may be overheard saying, "This is my very own sound."

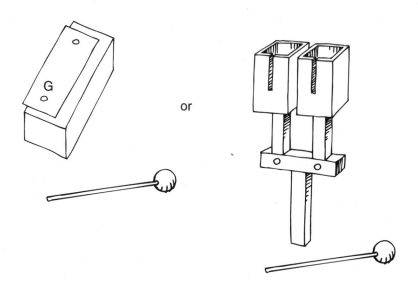

or

Clicking Circle

The teacher places a hula hoop flat on the rug to create a "clicking circle" and sets only clicking instruments in the space (e.g., wood blocks, tone blocks, sticks, claves, temple blocks). He tells children this is a special place where only clicking/ticking sounds can be heard. One at a time, each child sits in the circle and explores the various clicking/ticking sounds. The teacher may wish to enter the play by singing "Hickory, Dickory Dock."

Swishing House

A large, sturdy cardboard box with large cement blocks inside for stability is used for this play. Two of the box flaps are angled and taped together to form the roof of the house. All or part of the house's exterior is wallpapered with various grades of sandpaper. The teacher then places small sound starters (e.g., sand blocks) in the area and invites the children to use the blocks to explore loud and soft swishing sounds on the house.

A Trip to Ringing Town

The teacher plans a special trip to "Ringing Town." She prepares jingle bell anklets for each child and explains that each time he steps, everybody will hear his ringing-jingling sounds. The teacher allows stepping-around time.

An area in the room is designated as "Ringing Town." The teacher hides a variety of jingle bells and a few wood blocks or rhythm sticks in the area and then provides a bell-gathering basket. The children are instructed to gather only the ringing sounds that match their anklets and bring them back for the teacher to hear. The teacher meticulously tests each collected instrument to see if it matches the child's anklets.

Autoharp

The teacher places an autoharp and sound starters such as a pick, rubber door stop, or soft rubber-headed mallet on the floor. He invites the child to explore the sounds of a stringed instrument. The child may strum or lightly tap on the strings while another adult or child presses different buttons to change harmonies.

Another time, the teacher places different topical stickers on autoharp picks (e.g., of a bee, fairy, frog, or flower). The child selects one of the picks for strumming as she makes up a song about a bee or fairy flying high and low (low-high-low strumming); a flower swaying in the breeze (repeated strumming back and forth); or a jumping frog (mallet bouncing on strings).

Note that tuning a string instrument such as an autoharp, guitar, or cello is often rather difficult for nonmusically skilled teachers because their ears are not used to matching pitches. These teachers should seek out the area music specialist or a string performer for help with tuning. Teachers should be aware that these instruments readily slip out of tune and need frequent touch-ups. Music specialists are usually more than willing to provide frequent tuning services.

Humpty-Dumpty Box Puzzle

The teacher purchases six identical, unmarked, 12-inch boxes (the post office is a good source for light-colored unmarked boxes), assembles the boxes, then places the following "sounds" inside the boxes: two with a large handful of rice; two with a sleigh-size jingle bell; two with a few marbles. The teacher seals all edges of each box and places the matching boxes side by side. Using a felt pen, she draws a portion of Humpty-Dumpty on each box. The box puzzle is correctly assembled in the beginning. Next, the teacher chants,

"Humpty-Dumpty sat on a wall, Humpty-Dumpty had a great fall." (Teacher bumps the boxes, which all fall down with a great clatter.) She looks mortified and says, "Oh, no! Poor Humpty is all broken up." (She continues the rhyme.) "All the King's horses, and all the King's men couldn't put Humpty together again." (Aside to the children) "I guess we will have to be the ones to put him together again. Who can help?"

The children stack and assemble the boxes to put Humpty-Dumpty together again. They have both a visual clue and the matching sounds to identify which pieces of Humpty go side by side and on top of one another. Even though the picture is assembled correctly, the teacher checks the final puzzle by shaking the boxes and saying, "Yes, You're right! That sounds like two ringing/rattling/swishing sounds to me."

Jingle Phone

Spoons are tied on the ends of a string so that they loosely touch. The teacher wraps the children's index fingers around the string in the middle and places their fingers at their ears. The children then sway to make the spoons gently clang. A lovely ringing sound is transmitted through the string to the children's ears. The teacher then shows children how to wrap the string themselves. The teacher may reenter the play asking, "Can I hear your ringing sounds?" Each child places his or her wrapped fingers to the teacher's ears.

Jingle Bell Play

A commercially prepared Jingle Bell Play is available that consists of nine jingle bell sticks, three each of three different-sized bells. Each bell is mounted on the end of a color-coded handle. Three matching color containers are included. This play is very successful even with young two-year-olds. The challenge for the child is to explore the sounds, and sort and classify the bells by size, color, and sound into the appropriate colored container. The teacher makes comments using descriptive vocabulary such as large-loud-low bell; small-soft-higher bell. Children are also encouraged to sing as they play with the bells ("Jingle Bells") or use the bells, one in each hand, as a dancing prop.

Triangle Play

Seated in a circle, each child is given a triangle beater. The teacher moves among the circle holding two triangles, one on each extended index finger. (A straight finger supports the triangle better than a triangle loop knob.) An extended finger will not diminish the ringing sound of the triangle if it is not curled around the instrument. The teacher sings "Mary, Mary Quite Contrary" while moving in front of the seated children. The triangles are extended to two players on the words, "with silver bells and cockle shells and pretty maids all in a row." The song is repeated until all have made silver bell sounds. (The children's own names may be substituted for "Mary" in this song.)

MARY, MARY, QUITE CONTRARY
Traditional

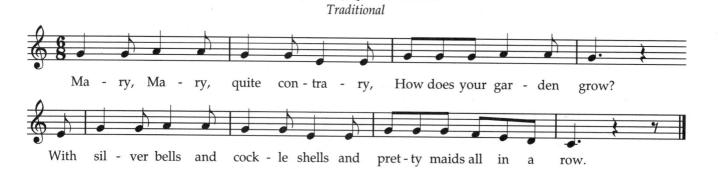

Playing the Cello

The cello strings should be tuned from lowest to highest: C, G, c', e'. The teacher provides an inexpensive or old bow because young children's playing position requires that they touch the hair of the bow on each end. (It is usually recommended that oil from fingers not come in contact with the hair of a bow.) The teacher holds the cello in an upright position facing the child and invites the child to grip the bow on each end, face the instrument, and sway side to side while bowing (rubbing) across the strings. The teacher should adjust the position of the cello to help the child touch her bow to the strings. The teacher may sing a G, E, A chant about how well Merissa is playing the cello or "z-z-z-z, I hear a little bee

buzzing . . . buzzing . . . I guess she's singing a song." Rosin should be applied frequently to the bow. Children will readily do this and will become quite ritualistic about it. In fact, rubbing rosin on the bow often becomes more fun than playing the instrument.

A Drum Wall

Exploratory play with drums can become sound intense. Children also may use a raucous hammering action that needs to be supervised for the safety of the drum head. These concerns aside, drums are obviously high-interest items for children. Creating and playing a drum wall is an exciting construction project. The teacher and children prepare drum blocks by

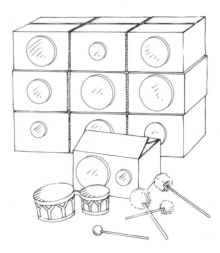

- obtaining one cardboard box for each drum to be used.
- tracing each drum on a side of the box.
- cutting out the circle created by tracing the drum rim.
- inserting and taping the drums from the inside into the opening.

The box is then sealed and ready to be used as a drum wall building block. (If the weight of the drums causes the box to be unstable, a small brick can be placed in the box before sealing it.) The sounds will be more intriguing if different-size drums are used. The children arrange the drum box blocks by stacking them against a wall. Different sound sequences can be created by rearranging the drums in the wall. Drum beaters and brushes are placed in the environment to be used as sound starters. Children play at the wall, randomly striking at it or moving in a left-to-right progression.

Timpani Tables

The teacher turns prepared drum blocks into timpani tables by pairing a large drum with a small drum and placing them heads up, side by side on the floor. He places each pair a small distance from the other pairs. One player uses two mallets for each pair of timpani tables. The children use their pair of drums to play a sound-sending game by taking turns playing sounds or rhythms. Older children can play question-and-answer games that involve rules; for example, rhythmic patterns are echoed or the length of the rhythmic phrases must be the same.

Drum Play

Often there are not enough drums for all children to use at the same time. This problem can be solved with round cake cardboard disks from a craft store. These disks are used as drum pads. The teacher seats the children on the floor with a cardboard disk in front of each of them and tells them this is their drum. The teacher rhythmically chants the rhyme "Rum Puddle" while the children pantomime with picking/giving/pointing motions and rhythmically pat the drum pad with both open palms on the"Rum puddle" phrase

RUM PUDDLE
B. Andress

Pick a little blue bird
Pick a little a star
Rum puddle, Rum puddle, Biff, Boom Bam!
Give it to Peter
Give it to Pam
Rum puddle, Rum puddle, Biff, Boom Bam!
Point to the east
Point to the west
Rum puddle, Rum puddle, *You're the best!*

The teacher can place a few real drums on the cardboard drum pads and repeat the chant several times, moving the real drums around so that each child can use them.

Rattle Boxes

In this game, empty audiocassette tape cases are used as tapping boxes. The teacher

◆ places a small quantity of corn or BB pellets in each box.
◆ securely seals the box.
◆ covers the box with opaque, plastic adhesive paper.
◆ cuts and places two strips of soft foam weather stripping on the bottom of each box and places the box on a table with weather-strip side down.

The child uses a finger or a small soft-headed mallet to bounce the rattles inside the box. Echo games or rhythmic accompaniments can be played. The box may also be handheld and used as a shaker or maraca.

Maracas

In this movement game, the teacher assigns an instrument sound to be played by each child when these words are spoken in the chant: "knees" (large maraca), "toes" (smallest maraca), "nose" (bicycle bulb horn).

> Well, shake my *knees*
> And rattle my *toes*
> Where oh where is my shiny *nose*?

All children move as the chant suggests. After the chant is spoken, children assume and hold an unusual "looking-for-their-nose" position such as under their foot, on their back or elbow, or under an armpit. The teacher draws attention to funny positions by saying, "Oh, Matthew, you are so silly, your nose is not in your pocket." The chant is repeated three times and ends with all children indicating the lost has been found by placing a finger on their nose.

Same Instrument, Different Sizes

The teacher places various sizes of small percussion instruments in a play area. Children will soon discover differences in the sounds. For example, three sizes of maracas can be used that have the following labels:

1. Large—Bass maracas
2. Medium—Soprano maracas
3. Small—Sopranino maracas

Now the teacher may introduce "A Time to Play, A Time Not To Play" game. She asks the bass maraca performer to play when she holds up one finger, the soprano maraca performer to play when she holds up two fingers, and the sopranino maraca performer to play when she holds up three fingers. The teacher guides the performers, indicating when to play and when not to play, as they listen to the Mexican folk dance, "La Raspa."

Using Instruments to Help Express Story/Poetic Ideas

Expressing the sound of thunder or the ponderous stomp of a giant's feet by using drums is an exciting way to help tell a story or enhance a poem. Children easily can use instruments to simulate the sounds of nature, industry, or any idea to be expressed. The following suggested activities are models for such story telling.

THE DANCING WIND
B. Andress

The wind danced high . . . high in the sky
Rustling the trees as it went by! (High sounds)
The wind danced low . . . low near my toe,

It swirled o'er the grass and turned just so. (Low sounds)
The wind played games on my window pane,
It made me think it was going to rain. (Middle sounds)
The wind was pink. That's what I think!
It hid behind a rainbow, as quick as a wink. (Low-middle-
    high-middle-low sounds)

Rain Makes Applesauce

Many children's storybooks are more fun when they are accompanied by instruments. In this play, the teacher uses several small bell-like xylophones or finger cymbals and an assortment of noise makers such as ratchets, slide whistles, bicycle bulb horns, kazoos, or Halloween horns/rattles to accompany a book such as *Rain Makes Applesauce* (Scheer and Bileck 1964). The text begins with the line, "The stars are of lemon juice" and ends with "and rain makes applesauce." Every time the teacher reads the line, "rain makes applesauce," she invites the children to play rain sounds on the xylophones and finger cymbals. The line, "Oh, you're just talking silly talk!" calls for loud, noisy sounds (a prearranged signal needs to be determined for stopping these sounds). There are many opportunities during the story for the children to make rain and silly sounds.

Playing Instruments within the Rules of Musical Structure

The purpose of awareness-level play is to familiarize children with the sights and sounds of various instruments. Few rules are attached to this exploratory play. Children progress to a level where they can understand introductory information about how music is organized, so their instrumental play should include activities that involve ordering, classifying, improvising, and composing. Although their sense of freely enjoying and making their own music is never lost, children become more aware that music of their culture has some prescribed rules of organization. Children become quite able to play cooperatively with instruments and perform more musically demanding material with a friend or in small ensembles. The nature of the experience continues to be predicated on developmentally appropriate practice.

STEP BELLS

Children become aware of the stepwise pitch relationship that is inherent in the eight-tone major scale as they manipulate pitched bells in stairstep play. Two types of step bells are available from music instrument vendors: (1) bell bars permanently affixed to an eight-step wooden frame and (2) stairstep wooden frames that are separated and designed to hold individual resonator bell blocks. Both types are useful. The permanently affixed steps serve as a model for the correct ordering of pitches from low-high or high-low. The separated pieces allow for construction play and problem solving.

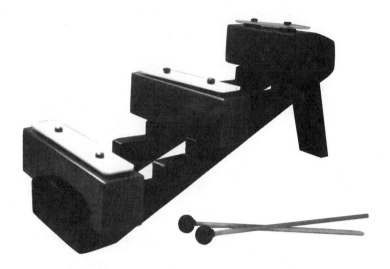

PLAYING WITH STEP BELLS

Games can be played that use descriptive vocabulary to musically express up-and-down movements such as hill or stair climbing. The teacher provides mallets to several children and then initiates small-group play by saying, "Who can go up these steps? Who can come down these steps? Who can find a very funny way to go up these steps? Who can copy my way of going down steps? Who can make stepping-up sounds? Who can make stepping-down sounds? Who can make a big jump up these steps? Who can go up by playing step-step-step-jump? Who can go down by playing step-step-step-fall down?" (Musical concept: Pitches may remain the same, or move up or down by steps and skips.)

Up-and-Down Rhymes

Step bells may be used to help express these rhymes:

CINDERELLA
B. Andress

Cinderella dressed in yellow
Went to find her bow.
She went upstairs to curl her hair, (Step up)
Then came back down below. (Step down)

DOWN WITH THE LAMBS
Nursery Rhyme

Down with the lambs (Step down)
Up with the lark (Step up)
Run to bed children
Before it gets dark.

Scale Songs

The teacher invites children to play the bells as they sing a scale song. They begin on the first step of the scale.

I SAW A SHIP A-SAILING
Nursery Rhyme adapted by B. Andress

```
                                             me!  Ap-
                          pretty things for      ples,
                         bring-ing,                 cin-na-
                       Oh! It was a-                   mon,
                   sea, And                              pep-per-
                sailing on the                              mint,
              sailing, A-                                      gold
          I saw a ship a-                                        rings.
```

Construction Play with Step Bells

The teacher places eight resonator bells (major scale) with two mallets and the stairstep frame in the play area. He invites the children to place the bells on the steps and then play the sounds. The bells will probably be placed in random fashion, thus many mixed-up sequences will be created. He then challenges the children to place the resonator bells on the step frame from lowest (biggest) to highest (smallest), which creates tones like the major scale. The teacher may add a song as a child plays down the scale.

HIGH ON A HILL
B. Andress

```
      High on a
           hill, a
                bird sat
                     still, He
                          made not a
                               sound, but
                                    flew to the
                                         ground.
```

A Sound Story: The Frog Prince

The teacher uses instruments and high and low vocal glides to retell the Brothers Grimm story of *The Frog Prince*. She guides the story sequence by using the following musical/story cue cards, step bells, a frog guiro, and two sizes of wooden tone blocks. An extended play would include the reading of this story as told by Tarcov (1974).

THE STORY. (1) Once upon a time, a beautiful princess was playing in a forest with a golden ball.

She tossed the ball up (voice) ⌒ and down ↘ and up ⌒ and down! ↘

(2) But one time she didn't catch the ball and it fell

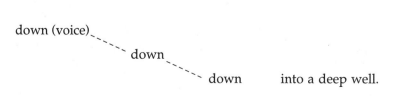

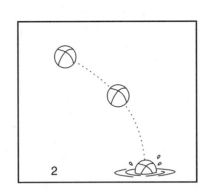

The princess was so sad about losing her golden ball that she cried and cried.

(3) A slimy, slippery, old green frog with a crown upon his head hopped up beside her and said, "I will fetch your golden ball if you will promise to love me, let me eat from your golden plate, and sleep on your royal satin pillow."

The princess doubted that he could find her ball, so she carelessly said, "I will let you do all those things if you find my golden ball."

(4) The green frog dove down (voice)
down
down   into the deep well.

And sure enough, he found the ball. "Here is your golden ball," he said to the beautiful princess. "Now you must keep your promise to me."

The princess was so happy that she didn't even thank the frog . . . she just ran back to her castle.

(5) The next day, when the princess was eating her dinner, she heard hop-hop-hop and a low croak at the door.

> Beautiful princess I'm out in your hall,
> You promised to love me if I found your ball.
> I'll eat from your plate, on your pillow I'll sleep
> For your promise is a promise you really must keep.

The princess thought, "Oh, yuck! I don't want to love a slimy, old, green frog." But she decided she better keep her promise. The frog came in and ate from

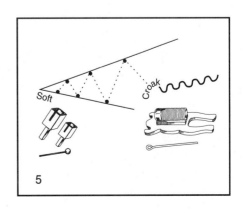

the princess's golden plate, then yawned and said, "Carry me to your room and I will sleep on the royal satin pillow."

Reluctantly, the princess led the frog up the stairs (6) and put him on the golden pillow (7). The frog slept all night, then early next morning woke up, hopped down the stairs, (8) and off into the forest. (9)

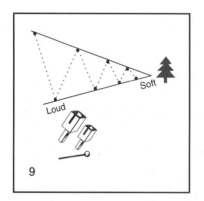

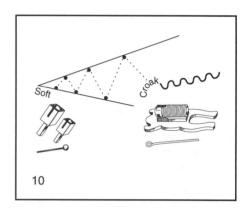

[The story continues with the frog returning to the castle two more days, thus the up-and-down step sequence is repeated as pictorially indicated The princess becomes more fond of the frog each time; she carries him by the toe on Day 2, and tenderly in arms on Day 3. On the third day, the frog does not come down the stairs and returns to the forest. He is gone.]

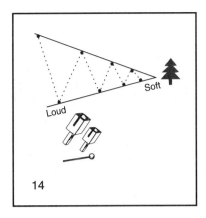

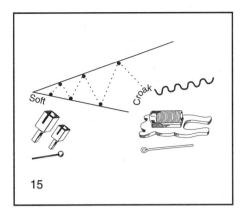

(17–18) The princess cried and said, "Where is my beautiful frog . . . he is lost . . . I will never see him again!" Instead of a croak she heard a gentle voice say, "Here I am." (19) Suddenly, a handsome prince appeared saying, "I am no longer a frog, for your love has freed me from the wicked witch's spell. I am a prince just like I used to be."

(20) The princess smiled and said, "Oh, my handsome frog prince, I'll love you forever and ever." And they lived happily ever after.

Jeremiah Blow the Fire

This play uses only three pitches from the major scale. The teacher invites the children to use step bells, resonator bells, or other barred instruments to play a three-tone pattern (the last phrase) as they sing "Jeremiah Blow the Fire." The children sing the song and play the bell sequence E, D, C to accompany the words, "Puff! Puff! Puff!" The teacher asks, "Can you arrange/play the bells in a different way to blow out the candle?" The children have many choices: C, D, E; C, C, C; C, C, D; E, C, D. The teacher describes what was performed. "I like the way you used the same sound to puff out the candle" or "I heard your sounds go higher as you blew out the candle."

JEREMIAH

British Folk Song

Je - re - mi - ah, blow the fire. _ Puff! Puff! Puff!

"Jeremiah," *Holt Music—K,* 1988. Holt, Rinehart and Winston. Used by permission.

Cooperative Play: The Instrumental Ensemble

Orff-type instruments are especially useful with young children because the bars can be removed or added to accommodate a child's performance level. These instruments may be arranged in certain pitch sets that allow for great harmonic freedom; thus, play on another instrument tuned in like manner can be accomplished even by a two-year-old or a musically unskilled adult play partner. The various ranges and timbres of the instruments provide exciting ensemble sounds because some instruments are very low (bass), others lie in the middle range (alto), and the remaining are high (soprano). The quality of sounds varies: short sounds of wooden xylophone bars, deep chimes of metallophones, and tinkling sounds of glockenspiels. In a full ensemble, tuned drums, cellos, guitars, and many small percussion instruments are used.

The commonly used diatonic (eight tones of the major scale only) Orff-type instruments include extended ranges of the C major scale bars: C, D, E, F, G, A, B, c'. Two additional pitches are provided (F♯ and B♭) to enable music to be played in the keys of G and F.

The most useful pitch set for improvisation and simple accompaniments is the pentatonic scale (five-tone scale). The teacher merely places all bars marked C, D, E, G, and A on the instrument(s). Using these pitches, duos, trios, and large ensembles can play together without producing harmonically conflicting sounds.

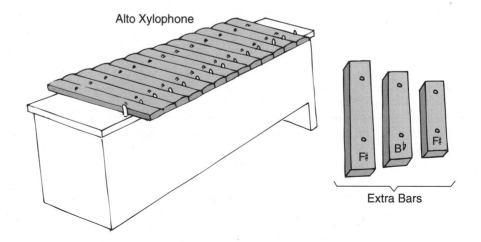

Alto Xylophone

Extra Bars

Children can randomly play any pentatonic pitch while the teacher sings or plays a recorder or other instrument using the same pitches. The following are examples of songs suitable for ensemble play.

IT'S RAINING

"It's Raining," *Exploring Music—Book 1*, 1966, Holt, Rinehart and Winston. Used by permission.

SALLY GO ROUND THE SUN
Traditional

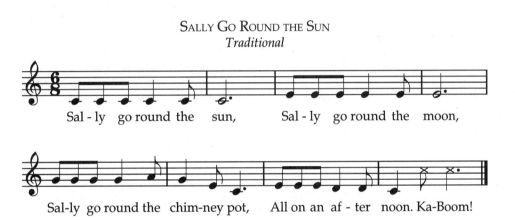

MISS MARY JANE

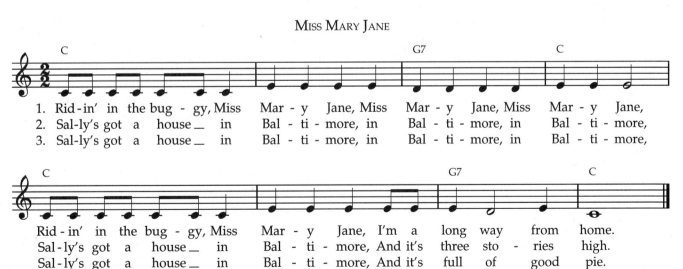

"Miss Mary Jane," *The Music Book—1*, 1981. Holt, Rinehart and Winston. Used by permission.

The familiar tune "Ring around the Rosie" (key of C) is a pentatonic song that is easily accompanied by any of the C-pentatonic pitches.

Introducing the Instrumental Ensemble

The instrumental ensemble is usually just one of many special interest area activities occurring simultaneously in the classroom. Children freely flow in and out of the area, exploring briefly or remaining for extended periods of time. The instruments to be used in the ensemble should be introduced one at a time and over a period of days to avoid confusing and overly exciting the children. The following sections describe the steps a teacher takes to introduce ensemble play.

Step 1

A viable approach to introducing ensembles is to place an unassembled alto xylophone sound box, all bars except F♯ and B♭, and several mallets in an area on the rug. The children's job is to place the bars on the instrument and then explore the sounds. The teacher should supervise this activity so that the instrument is not abused during assembly. (Orff-type instruments are a substantial investment for the care center, so the teacher should always try to prevent unnecessary damage to the instruments.) Children initially place the bars in disarray; this is part of the learning process and the teacher should accept their arrangement at this point. The teacher can further the game by pointing to a bar and saying, "Who can make a soft sound right here?" Pointing to another bar he says, "Who can make a loud sound right here?"

Step 2

Another day, only the pentatonic pitches (C, D, E, G, A) are available for construction play. Again, these bars are assembled by the children in random order. Children will likely comment that there are not enough bars. The teacher agrees that there are fewer sounds to play with today. Though the bars are not in sequence, limited-pitch songs and chants can be sung as the children tap the bars. Children are delighted if the teacher plays a recorder along with their music.

Step 3

Next, the teacher introduces the guitar (tuned from low to high: C, G, C, G, c', e'). He invites a child to strum as others sing any of the songs mentioned in the previous section such as "Jeremiah" or "It's Raining, It's Pouring."

Step 4

The guitar and alto xylophone with pentatonic scale are properly arranged on the xylophone for use in duet play. If children notice gaps between the bars, the teacher may answer, "Yes, that step in the scale is missing. We will not need it for our music today." At this point, the children probably won't ask for an explanation of what a scale is, yet it is good to use accurate descriptive music language.) Interaction with the children in this setting requires the teacher's watchful guidance as well as improvised songs; for example, "We are making music, listen to our sounds." "Shall we make fast or slow music?" "Who has an idea for a song?" or "Let's make a song/music about firetrucks."

Step 5

The teacher gradually adds other instruments to the ensemble but doesn't exceed three or four at any given time. Appropriate additions might be another alto xylophone, an alto glockenspiel, or a bass xylophone. Some independent, unsupervised play with the barred instruments can be allowed when the children better understand the instruments' care and appropriate use. Stringed instruments play in the ensemble, however, always requires supervision.

Teachers should be cautioned that children in introductory ensemble play are not performing specially arranged music, so they tend to strike the instruments with great frequency, producing many sounds. The use of many ringing instruments in the exploratory play ensemble such as metallophones and glockenspiels can create a chaotic sound due to their sustaining quality. Solutions to this problem might be to use softer mallets on glockenspiels or metallophones or to use only one ringing-type instrument in the ensemble.

Step 6

Multiple instruments may be used in guided group play. First, the teacher presents sound stories or some other more freely performed musical selections. Then, the teacher announces a "time to play and a time not to play," using music such as "Old John the Rabbit." Before they can use the instruments, the children are asked to sing only the words "Oh, yes!" The teacher instructs them to hold their hands in the sky on all words except for "Oh, yes!" at which times they tap their hands on the floor.

Using instruments with only C and G pitches, the children hold mallets high in the sky on all words except for "Oh, yes!" at which times they strike the bars with their mallets.

OLD JOHN THE RABBIT
Traditional

Old John the rab-bit, Oh, yes! Old John the rab-bit, Oh, yes! Had a

ve-ry bad hab-it, Oh, yes! Of go-ing to my gar-den, Oh, yes! And

eat-ing up my peas, Oh, yes! And eat-ing my to-ma-toes, Oh, yes! And . . .

Children may add other vegetables that a rabbit might eat such as cabbage, broccoli, carrots, or lettuce.

The song ends with:

And if I live,   Oh, yes!   To   see next fall,   Oh, yes!

I won't plant,   Oh, yes!   A   gar-den for that rab-bit at   all!

Step 7

Using barred instruments with only pitches C and G, the children maintain a steady beat while singing songs mentioned earlier: "Jeremiah," "Sally Go Round the Sun," "Ring around the Rosie," "It's Raining," and "Miss Mary Jane." The children may strike both bars simultaneously, alternate between the two sounds, or create repeated patterns such as ¾ meter, C, G, G; or ¼ meter, C, G, C, rest.

Step 8

Older children may play simple melodies such as "One, Two, Tie My Shoe" using only the E and G bars on the instruments. The melody begins on G. Once children have mastered the melody, another instrument such as a bass xylophone may be set with C and G bars. The child who is playing the bass xylophone accompanies the melody, playing a steady beat accompaniment.

As discussed above, there are many simple melodies and accompaniments that school-age children can perform. With little effort, each child can perform a different part on an instrument, contributing to a musically satisfying whole. In order to do this, children progress through a learning sequence that involves singing, chanting, and body percussion such as clapping, stamping, snapping, and patschening. Such rhythmic activities prepare the children to play instruments in ensemble. The American Orff-Schulwerk Association regularly presents local and national workshops involving movement, singing, playing instruments, and reading notation.

Introducing Keyboard Play

Mom sits on the bench and begins to play a lovely melody on the piano. Three-year-old Tiffany immediately drops her dolly, runs to the bench, and eagerly attempts to climb up. Mom continues to play with one hand, reaching out with her free hand to give Tiffany a boost up, and soon they are both settled in place at the keyboard. As mom plays, Tiffany gently uses her fingers on the keyboard, adding her own out-of-tune sounds. Tiffany looks upward, totally involved and enraptured in her music making, quite oblivious to the dissonant sounds she is contributing to her mom's music.

Whether it is in the home or at school, a piano is a major focal point for children. They delight in touching it, pressing the keys, and exploring its wide range of sounds. It seems that all children tediously play each piano key in sequence from low to high for the length of the piano. Typically, children play the piano with a degree of control only so long, and then their enthusiastic exploration degenerates into banging. This raucous behavior is noisy and somewhat abusive to the piano. Distraught adults often respond by closing the lid of the piano and declaring it off limits. There are, of course, more positive ways to redirect the actions so that children are reinforced rather than made to feel rejected. The following sections discuss some suggestions for interacting with a child during piano play.

HANDLING ENTHUSIASM

◆ Children should not be allowed to use their fists on the piano keyboard. The adult may modify the behavior by saying, "Fingers. I need to hear your fingers playing" or "Our fingers want to play the piano keys."

◆ There are times when the piano is off limits and its lid is closed, but these instances should occur as normal "playing and not playing" times rather than as punishments. Fun signs that show a sleeping or awake face can be placed on the piano, providing a signal as to when the piano can or cannot be played.

◆ Exploratory piano play within the classroom, when several children want to play at the same time, is more successful if the adult interacts in the play. The adult can model, suggest, and describe (see the next section) the various sounds and reinforce and redirect the children's musical behavior.

◆ The number of children at the keyboard should be limited to eliminate congestion, too many fingers, and too many loud sounds. The adult can create a half circle in front of the keyboard and bench with masking tape and explain that only three children may be in the space at one time. Other children may stand close by as listeners and singers, but they know they must wait their turn to play the piano. This is a difficult rule to enforce, but it can be effective if children do not have to wait too long for a turn.

◆ The teacher may wish to set a special time for each child to play the piano by placing a poster with a photo of the child on the music holder. The poster might read, "Susy's Time to Play All By Herself."

THE ADULT MODELS, DESCRIBES, AND SUGGESTS

A favorite time shared by four-year-old Josh, his mother, and older sister is playing and singing "Tomorrow" from the musical Annie. *Mom plays the introduction, then sister and Josh begin to sing, "The sun will come out . . ." Josh is able to perform the song with some accuracy and often requests that they do it again. During one playtime, Josh declares, "Now I will do it all by myself." Mom begins to play the piano, but Josh quickly stops her and emphatically says, "No, all by myself!" Mom says, "OK. You do it." After a very long pause, Josh, looking very intent, still has not begun to sing. Finally, mom says, "OK, Josh, go ahead." Josh's indignant reply is, "I am, I'm waiting for the introduction to be over." (Note: This is a good example of the child's ability to inner hear, or internalize, the music.)*

The adult who can *model* piano play is a wonderful musical playmate for children. Children love to just sit, listen, move, and sing while the adult plays composed and improvised music or uses the piano as a sound source to help tell a story. Such times often provide insight as to how a child is perceiving music.

The adult may also model by telling a sound story about two creatures whose movements are quite different and then inviting the child to play the piano part. Some examples are:

THE SNAIL
(Spoken very slowly)

I saw a snail.
He sure moved slow.
He'd scrunch together
and s-t-r-e-t-c-h w—a—y out.
Yep! That's the way he'd go!

(Move one hand slowly up the keyboard; play sound ideas by stretching out fingers to indicate wide-apart sounds, then close them up to indicate side-by-side sounds)

THE MOUSE
(Spoken very quickly)

there,
I saw a mouse run   and   and there!
                                         there,
He ran down the clock and into a hole
That was under a crack in the stair.

(Use fast, short, scurrying sounds to represent the running mouse)

The adult can improvise or play a variety of waltzes and marches so that the child can whirl, twirl, and high-step around the room. An exciting, creative, interactive play can also occur when the adult suggests that the child perform a "step, point-your-toe dance." The adult performs a rhythm pattern consisting of four stepping sounds and one long point-your-toe sound:

Step, Step, Step, Step,   Point

Music that accompanies dance is usually harmonically and traditionally organized, but sometimes it should include random chord clusters that just "happen" under the adult's fingers, typical of what a child might play. The adult *suggests* movement by saying, "Step, step, step, step, point" or *describes* the child's lovely movement: "I like the way you pointed and held your hands for a long time." The accompaniment should have frequent pauses for applause. The child's bow indicates the end of the dance. After the child dances, the adult invites the child to be the pianist and the adult becomes the dancer. The adult moves to the same rhythm pattern. The child plays random sounds on the piano while watching the dancer. The adult's consistent movement helps the child to rhythmically play the pattern. The adult might reinforce the pattern by softly singing, "Play, play, play, play, hold."

THE ADULT AND CHILD PLAY DUETS

Young children are capable of performing harmonically with an adult who is playing a familiar traditional song. To accomplish this, the piano should be preset with a sticker or note that indicates which piano key should be played repeatedly throughout the song. The stickers could show faces that in some way resemble the character in the song such as Lou in "Skip to My Lou." (Note: Though small, round gummed labels are perfect for this activity, they tend to be difficult to remove from the piano key. Instead, make a sticker from a sticky notepad that can be easily removed or replaced.)

The adult, surrounded by several children, sings and plays a two-chord song. The children use one finger to play their note, the fifth step of the scale, throughout the song. They can play their part by pressing the key with the beat or intermittently at will. ("Skip to My Lou" is in the key of G, thus the fifth step of the scale would be G, A, B, C, **D,** E, F♯, g'.) Stickers are placed on many of the Ds on the piano. Each participating child finds one of the sticker faces to play. The adult sings a new second verse to the song such as "Go to sleep Lou, Lou-ly, Lou-ly Lou . . ." Notice how the children musically respond. Do they reflect tempo changes by playing slower? Softer?

Another song to accompany is "Little Red Caboose." The adult draws a train engine on stickers and places them on many of the As on the keyboard. This two-chord song is in the key of D, so the fifth step of the scale is D, E, F♯, G, **A,** B, C♯, d'. As before, the adult plays/sings the melody while the child taps the train picture. After several repetitions, the adult tells the children that they will make up a special introduction and ending to the song. The adult initially improvises the sounds of the starting and stopping train; later, the children also create these train sounds.

The musical arrangement:

Accelerando

Ch–ch–ch–ch–ch . . .

Ritardando

. . . ch– ch– ch– ch– ch.

LITTLE RED CABOOSE

Lit-tle red ca - boose, Lit-tle red ca - boose,

Lit-tle red ca - boose be - hind the train. _____

Smoke-stack on its back, rum-blin' down the track,

Lit-tle red ca - boose be - hind the train. _____

"Little Red Caboose," *The Music Book—II*, 1981. Holt, Rinehart and Winston. Used by permission.

A Repertoire of Playable Duets

Children can play a C on the piano to accompany all of the two-chord songs listed below. The melody must be sung or played in the key of F.

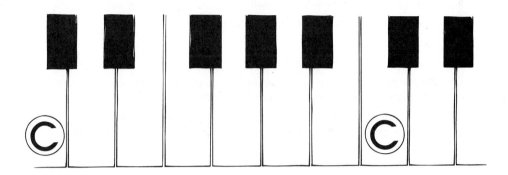

BEGINNING SONG PITCH	SONG TITLE
c'	"This Old Man"
F	"Clap Your Hands"
F	"The Paw Paw Patch"
A	"Go Tell Aunt Rhodie"
F	"Polly Wolly Doodle"
F	"Frere Jacques"
c'	"He's Got the Whole World in His Hands"
A	"Merrily We Roll Along"
A	"Mary Had a Little Lamb"

Two-chord songs abound in children's literature. They are not all necessarily sung in the key of F, which may be too high or low for comfortable singing. Teachers should not hesitate to use music written in other keys such as C, D, or G, but should remember that the child plays only the fifth step in any key chosen.

Summary

The opportunity for children to hear, touch, and manipulate classroom and orchestral instruments is critical to their understanding of how people experience music. They can have early rewarding and successful experiences in making music at their own levels of interest and ability. Preschoolers are not expected to perform on the violin or piano unless they are truly gifted. There are, however, many activities for preschoolers that pique their curiosity and satisfy their feeling of successful instrumental performance. The teacher who is truly concerned about developmentally appropriate experiences will guide children in exploratory-awareness level activities on all available instruments, as well as challenge them to perform simple melodies and accompaniments when they are ready.

An important part of children's instrumental experience is hearing many aspiring and fine musicians perform on instruments. These musicians become models, helping the children understand that people enjoy and use instruments to perform. Such models may also help a child think that he or she, too, can become a musician or, at least, an avid consumer of instrumental music.

THINGS TO DO

1. Plan an interactive setting in which children deal with classroom/orchestral instrument(s) at the exploratory-awareness level. Include:

    a. Educational reasons for the play

    b. Cautions for a safe learning environment

    c. Music vocabulary that might enter the play

    d. Teacher's interactive role

    e. Children's possible behavior during play

    Try out your plan with one or more children. Note differences between your plan and what actually happened during the implementation session.

2. Play a duet with a child on a keyboard instrument using only the black notes. To do this, play a repeated pattern in 3/4 meter using the pitches F♯, C♯, and D♯. The child may use any of the black keys to make up a melody.

RESOURCE

Jingle Bell Play, Frog Guiro, and Step Bells. Peripole-Bergerault, Inc., 2041 State Street, Salem, OR 97301.

8

~~~~~~~~~~

Models, Materials, and Methods: Movement

Young children respond to music with many different kinds of movements. Infants enjoy simple body touch in song play, toddlers move spontaneously to music they hear on television, four-year-olds expressively whirl and twirl in creative dance, and older children dance to traditional musical games. Children's *movements* reflect their level of motor development; their *movement responses* to music reflect their ability to sense and express ideas heard in the music.

Much has been written about children's physical development. We know that a child begins with gross motor movements and gradually develops fine-motor skills. Sensing and describing through movement what is happening in the music is also a gradually developing skill. A two-year-old probably does not have a great sense of rhythm or the motor skills to display it; however, an older four- to eight-year-old is increasingly able to respond with movements such as tapping and clapping.

How do we know when and what young children are capable of doing? Observing children and studying child development research provide many clues for determining appropriate movement play experiences. Ultimately, it is the individual child who provides the answer to our question. Our planning is influenced by the studies of such people as Erik Erikson who told us:

The child's play begins with and centers on his own body. . . . It begins before we notice it as play and consists at first in the exploration by repetition of sensual perceptions, of kinesthetic sensations, of vocalizations, etc.[1]

Erikson also said:

. . . a child "can walk" much before the end of the third year; but to us he is not really on his feet . . . until the ego has incorporated walking and running into the sphere of mastery when gravity is felt to be within, when the child can forget that he is doing the walking and instead can find out what he can do with it.[2]

These two insights provide us with practical information about what the nature of our initial music and movement play with very young children might be (centering on the body) and a possible time line for specific actions, such as accurately stepping to music (four to five years of age). More important, we are reminded that a child's actions are not just body movement, but also an *awareness* of the movement. A growing inside awareness of the movement and its relationship to music is what we are about.

Early Movement Play

Intuitively, parents and other adoring adults play movement games with infants and toddlers that involve body touch and tactile modeling. We touch noses and toes, tickle tummies, and help hands clap together as we rhythmically chant or sing. We rock babies and rhythmically tap them as we sing lullabies or other gentle melodies. We gleefully bounce toddlers on our knee as we chant a nonsense verse. Music and movement are an instinctive, integral part of an adult-child interaction.

BODY TOUCH AND BOUNCING GAMES

The following examples describe how infants respond to music with body touch and bouncing games.

◆   The father sings and rocks while gently tapping the baby's bottom or gently touching her eyes or ears:

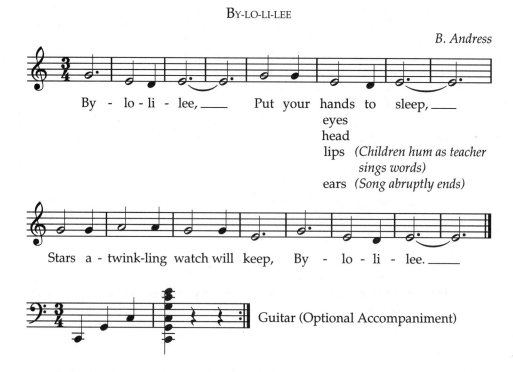

B. Andress, *Music Experiences in Early Childhood*, 1980. Holt, Rinehart and Winston. Used by permission.

◆ The grandpa crosses his leg and gives Jenny a ride on his foot while chanting:

> *Gid*-dy up *hor*-sy, *Gid*-dy up, *whee!*
> *Go* to the *mar*-ket for *Jen*-ny and *me!*

◆ The adult touches parts of the infant's body while chanting or singing:

HERE'S A LITTLE BUG

Terry Andress

Here's a lit-tle bug, crawl-ing up your leg, Craw-ling up your leg. Craw-ling up your leg.

Here's a lit-tle bug, craw-ling up your leg, He's gon-na get your (nose, toe, tummy . . .)

IMITATIVE PLAY

Young children learn through imitative play. They watch, copy what they see, and practice until the ideas become their own. We model many ideas for moving in space both tactilely (touching) and visually (seeing). Tactile modeling is an important technique for introducing young children to how a movement feels. Later, they become more able to imitate ideas that are only visually expressed. The object of imitative play is not to create nonthinking imitators but to provide children with a basic repertoire of movement ideas from which they can draw, embellish, and refine for their own expressive needs.

TACTILE MODELING

These examples demonstrate methods of tactile modeling.

◆ The adult claps the infant's hands together and directs other gestures to accompany the chant:

> Pattycake, pattycake, baker's man
> Bake me a cake as fast as you can.
> Pinch it and poke it and put it in the pan!

◆ The adult extends her index fingers for the toddler to grip, and together they sway from side to side or make a falling-down motion as the adult sings or chants these familiar nursery rhymes. The child is in control and can release her grip to move independently at any time.

> Rock a bye baby in the tree top *(Sway)*
> When the wind blows the cradle will rock
> When the bow breaks the cradle will fall
> Down will come baby, cradle and all. *(Fall down)*

See saw, Margery Daw, *(Sway)*
Jack shall have a new Master;
Jack will be paid but a penny a day
Because he won't work any faster.

◆   The adult and toddler play a "time to move, a time to stop" game. The adult holds the child's hand as they both randomly walk about, stop, look all around, or point a finger at imaginary objects. The "Walking Song" from *Acadian Songs and Dances* by Virgil Thomson is an excellent piece for this activity. Its musical form is A, A, B, A, C, A. The movement is: All walk about during the A section and make up pretend play during B and C.

VISUAL MODELING

Two- and three-year-olds at first tend to be merely watchful during guided movement play, but after much repetition of the play, they become excited, anticipating the predictable actions. The adult presents the story or music and guides the play. Children imitate what they see. Some examples follow.

Playful Hands

This is a favorite hand-play game because it contains much repetition (A, B, A form) and gives the child the chance to feel powerful when he shouts a resounding "No!"

Once upon a time my hands liked to play together.
Sometimes they played very softly, *(Rub hands together)*
And sometimes they clapped very loud *(Clap loudly together)*
Sometimes they shook and shook and shook! *(Shake hands)*
Sometimes they play over the mountains and over the hills. *(Roll hands over one another in forward direction)*
And backwards over the mountains and backwards over the hills. *(Roll hands over one another in backward direction)*
But a big, old bear who lived on the mountain said "No! You can't play on my mountain."
The hands were frightened and ran away to hide. *(Quickly hide hands behind back)*
But the hands really wanted to play together so they would sneak up on the bear and say. *(Slowly and rhythmically bring hands almost together while singing the song)*

COME ON BEAR

Come on bear,   Let us play now, Come on bear,   Let us play now,

But the bear said, "No!"
                (Yes!)

The teacher says to the children, "I guess we will have to say 'please' to the big old Bear." The children say, "Please." The sneaking-up motion, song, and loud "No!" are repeated several times. Each time, more "Pretty, pretty pleases" are added. Finally, the teacher sings, ". . . and the bear said, 'Yes!'" The game is completed with:

> So the hands played very soft
> And sometimes they clapped very loud
> Sometimes they just shook and shook and shook.
> But the most fun was playing over the mountain and over the hill,
> And backwards over the mountain and backwards over the hill.
> And even the big, old bear made his paws play in the same
> way . . . though sometimes he got all mixed up and couldn't do it
> very well! (*Close fists and make wild funny gestures*)

The Waltzing Cat

The teacher prepares dancing cat stick puppets by cutting cat heads from paper or wood. She places a scarf over a 12-inch stick or drinking straw and inserts the stick into the paper or wood head. The teacher distributes one dancing cat to each child and plays a recording of "The Waltzing Cat" by Leroy Anderson. She invites the children to follow what her kitty does: "Sometimes my kitty meows, or dances high in the sky, or sometimes jumps in a very funny way." The piece ends (coda) with a dog barking and chasing the kitty who quickly runs away.

Movement ideas are as follows: Introduction—cat puppet on floor getting ready to dance; A section—smooth, swaying, high and low interrupted with many "meows"; B section hopping/jerky motions; Coda—hide the cat behind back as dog barks. The musical form is: Introduction—A, A, B, A (repeat)—coda.

CREATIVE MOVEMENT

Children should have many opportunities to freely make up dances to music. Know that two- and three-year-olds are just gaining control over body movement and thus do not have a wide variety of dance movements, such as graceful body shapes and sustained or unfolding gestures, for these require muscle control and balance. These children will make jabbing, jerking, and bobbing motions, with feet rarely leaving the security of the floor. Their arms are used more for balance than gesturing. Their spins and turns are joyfully but awkwardly performed. They can ably swish a scarf about, but they would rather wrap themselves in it than use it for a dancing prop. Freely moving to music is still wondrous play for these children, especially if a parent or other loved one is also participating in the play.

This is not a time for a child to pretend, for example, to be a galloping pony because the child may not yet have the necessary imagery capabilities. Concrete, relevant props or focus on body parts are more appropriate. Useful props might include a dolly for rocking, a ribbon wand to swish, a pair of jingle bells, one for each hand, or a jingling tambourine decorated with ribbon streamers.

Young children like to be in full control of the props they use so that they can be discarded at will. Ribbons that are tied to hands or flowing headgear are usually not tolerated for very long. A prop can also become a distraction. There are many occasions when the only requirements for moving should be the child, space, time, and music.

Two-Year-Olds and Young Three-Year-Olds Move to Music

The following examples describe appropriate movement activities for children in this age range.

Hand Dance

The teacher can initiate movement by inviting the children to make their hands dance. A variety of tambourine sounds may accompany the movements, such as tapping, shaking, and rubbing the head of the instrument. The teacher may suggest movements such as "Shaky, shaky hands . . . clappy, clappy hands . . . rubby, rubby hands, high in the sky hands, turning around hands . . . "

The Music Stops, We Stop

The teacher selects any piece of music on an audiocassette (or plays the piano) and asks an aide to manipulate the stop and start buttons on the recorder. The children are invited to walk when they hear the music and freeze when they do not. The style of the music selected will dictate the manner in which the children move. The abrupt stops during the music make this activity a bit less musical but still create an awareness that we move when we hear the music and stop when the music stops. The person controlling the recorder should attempt to stop the music in appropriate places such as at the ends of phrases or sections.

Put Your Little Foot

The teacher prepares for play by placing masking tape Xs on the floor, one for each child. The teacher sings new words to this familiar American dance tune while the adults and children walk randomly around the area. On the word "here," the children put one foot on the nearest X; on the word "found," they point to the X. The adult may wish to take the hand of a child who is a bit bewildered about how to play the game. The teacher may wish to pause briefly at the end of each phrase to allow all children time to find a spot.

PUT YOUR LITTLE FOOT
American Folk Dance Tune

Words by B. Andress

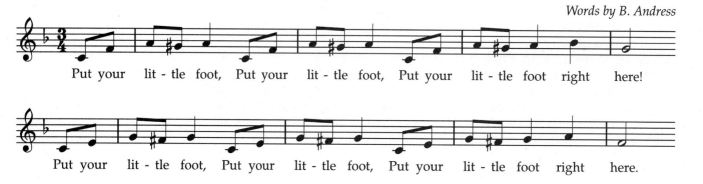

Put your lit - tle foot, Put your lit - tle foot, Put your lit - tle foot right here!

Put your lit - tle foot, Put your lit - tle foot, Put your lit - tle foot right here.

Turn a - round and a - round, Clap your hands make a sound.

Turn a - round and a - round. Show the spot you have found.

Four- and Five-Year-Olds Move to Music

Four- and five-year-old children grow markedly in their ability to move in response to music. Their gestures are more varied and controlled, and their accuracy in responding to musical ideas such as rhythm, repetition and contrast, volume, articulation, and tempo is increasing. Although these children continue to lack many psychomotor skills, they are becoming more able to follow instructions for simple song games and traditional dances, as well as create and organize their own movement pieces. These children are able to pretend, taking great delight in moving like horses and butterflies or sensing the motion of seaweed buffeted by ocean currents. Suggesting images and using other verbal cues are viable tools for initiating movement experiences. The teacher continues to model, describe, and make suggestions as a means of helping children internalize what is happening in their movements and in the music.

TOOLS FOR MOVEMENT

Children need help in acquiring tools for movement. The teacher must model or guide them in discovering how specific movements can be combined with different directions, levels, and energy. The following examples represent an exploration of these ideas through isolated instrument sounds, musical compositions, and word imagery.

Open and Close

In this game, the teacher uses ringing sounds (e.g., finger cymbals, gongs, metallophone) to elicit open and close movements. The teacher may say, "Slowly open your fingers, hands, elbows—all of you—as long as you hear the ringing sound." The children open and close at different levels and in different directions. The teacher may combine some of these ideas and instrumental sounds to create an extended open-and-close dance. For example, "Close all up tight to begin." Small to larger body parts can be opened as small to larger instruments are used: first, finger cymbals, then 7-inch cymbal, and then a gong.

Jabs, Thrusts, Slashes

The teacher can help children experience jabbing, thrusting, and slashing motions by accompanying their movements with short, loud, accented taps on the drum. They begin by using only their arms, jabbing and slashing in different directions.

Then they move their bodies disjunctly in space, adding more power to the thrusts. They end with a sudden burst of energy. "Freeze" is the final gesture.

Zip! Zap! Zing! Zoe!
That's the way my arms go!
(Repeat)
Zip! Zap! Zing! Zoe!
That's the way all of me goes!
(Repeat)
Zip! Zap! Zing! Zoe! **Pow!**

Floating

Floating is a sustained weightless action involving muscle control and balance. The child sits in a chair and ties a pretend string from her right hand to her right knee. Her hand is held about six inches directly over the knee. Slowly, her hand pulls the imaginary string, lifting the leg up as she inhales and down as she exhales. Then she tries the motion with her left hand and leg. The teacher asks the child to stand and repeat the activity by lifting her legs in slow walking motions. The teacher can plan a weightless space walk on the moon and accompany the walk with a metallophone, gong, finger cymbals, or piano strings (by pressing the sustain pedal on the piano while strumming).

Gliding

Gliding is a light, smooth, flowing motion that may be accompanied by soft gong sounds. The teacher allows each sound to fully ring out before he initiates the next one. The children make their fingers into a soft paint brush to slowly paint a new rainbow in the sky each time the gong is softly sounded. The teacher may also suggest that the children turn in new directions and change levels.

Flicking

Flicking is a light, sudden action. The teacher prepares a special hand drum to accompany the suggested movements by placing a few small round pellets (BBs) in an inverted hand drum. The teacher says, "Put your hands in the water and stir the water round and round." (The teacher gently tips the hand drum to make the BB pellets roll around.) Then he says, "Take your hands out and flick the water off." (He taps the bottom of the inverted drum to make short, bouncing sounds.)

Bending and Stretching

The children can explore reaching, stretching, and bending gestures. The teacher reads the following poem, taking time to describe "dew" or a "willow tree." She invites children to move as she again recites the poem. She may substitute more meaningful words if necessary (e.g., hurl, throw). Pause to allow time for the expressive movements to take place as children present their ideas.

GOODNIGHT
B. Andress

Gather in the stars,
Catch the morning dew.
Hurl them through the skies
To make the world look new.

Roll up a white cloud
Fluff it for a pillow.
Put it in the nest
On the branch of the willow . . .
. . . Goodnight little birdie!

Pushing-Pulling

Children can internalize the contrasting energies exerted when they push and pull many different objects.

PUSH ME, PULL ME
B. Andress

push a dinosaur
push a star
pull a mountain
pull a car.
push a doorbell
pull a tooth
push me, pull me
through the roof!

The children can try out some of the acquired movement ideas to create dances in response to music. The teacher can model and suggest some of the ideas, but mostly she should provide opportunities for the children to make their own choices about how they will move to the music.

"Aquarium" from The Carnival of the Animals by Saint-Saëns

This music can be used as the teacher tells the children that they are at the bottom of the sea. They may choose to be seaweed, a fish (big or small), a mermaid, or the ocean currents. The teacher explains that the ocean current is like the wind in the sky, only it is under the sea. Try out the different movements; for example "How would seaweed move?" (planted in sand, arms only gliding, body swaying); "What kind of fish/mermaid will you be?" "Will you be in a school of fish or swimming alone?" "How will the ocean currents change the way the fish or sea-weed move?" (A long, sheer piece of fabric can be draped over the face of the "current.") The teacher invites the children first to listen to the music and then plays it again as the children assume their chosen role and create their "under-the-sea" dance. The teacher should remember to describe or draw attention to interesting movements expressed by the children when appropriate.

"The Royal March of the Lion" from The Carnival of the Animals

This music can be used to encourage children to offer their ideas about how a lion king would move. The teacher discusses and explores the majestic walk of the lion, as king, "How would he hold his head?" (tall and proud); "How do his paws move?" (sustained, flowing movement, but firmly placed); "How will he roar?" (head back, mouth open, perhaps paw raised in an arching, slashing motion). Music possibilities include scurrying-around, get-ready music; trumpet fanfare announcing the lion king; pompous marching music; four lion roars; more march with short roars interspersed; more march; a big-roar finish.

"The Chinese Dance" from the Nutcracker Suite by Tchaikovsky

This music alternates between two distinct musical ideas: the "questioning" phrase—smooth legato (trilling flute)—and the "answering" phrase—staccato (plucked strings). The teacher provides each child with a paper fan and suggests a response to the music: first phrase—stand still while fanning face; second phrase—hide face behind fan and take many small steps while moving to a new position. These two ideas alternate throughout the music.

Prelude in A Major by Chopin

Invite children to move to the music. The teacher observes if the children move freely to this music and whether they seem to sense the equal phrases and reflect this by coming to a short pause at the end of each phrase. She notes the quality of their movement. Is it flowing? Jagged? There does not have to be a right or wrong way to move to the music. There may, however, be stronger ways to express what is heard.

"Stars and Stripes Forever" by Sousa

The teacher asks the children to move to the music. All will probably step or march in some fashion. The teacher enters the game only to suggest that the children step in different directions when he says, "Ready, Change." The words are a signal to go in a new direction of their choice—backwards, to the right or left, turn around, etc. The children are cautioned to move carefully around their friends to avoid bumping. Note: The tempo of recorded march music is often too fast and may create confusion for young children. If this occurs, the teacher should play slower steady beats on a hand drum to present this same activity.

Creative Movement for Older Four- to Eight-Year-Olds

Brief story ideas should be used with four-year-olds because they may not yet have the necessary recall and story sequence skills to interpret a lengthy tale. Five-year-olds and older are more able to perform lengthy movement stories.

The Magic Carpet

A group of 12 children are seated on the floor for music time. A song and a rhythm game have already been performed as a transition to the next activity, which is the song "Bluebird, Bluebird through My Window." An introduction about flying things is in progress. Eager participants offer ideas about things that can fly such as birds, bees, and butterflies. Ralph, who recently saw the movie Aladdin, *interrupts, "Yeah, and magic carpets can fly, too." This instigates excited chatter from all the children. The teacher abandons plans for the bluebird song and immediately switches the activity to a creative movement experience. She says, "Ralph is right. Magic carpets can fly. Let's make our own magic carpet."*

The teacher pretends to draw the outline of a big carpet on the floor. "What color would you like the carpet to be? Who wants to ride on this magic red carpet? Jump on! I hear magical sounds from this carpet." The teacher hastily grabs a page from her notes and begins to rub the paper ends together, making swishing sounds. She begins to hum, inviting the children to help make the sounds. "Better hang on 'cause we are really going to fly high and far away." She leads the group in flying around the room, weaving among tables and making high and low voice inflection sounds that correspond with the up-and-down movements of the flight. The carpet stops to visit various palaces along the way, and the people get off to dance. The teacher announces, "This is a dancing palace. The people like to point their toes." The teacher improvises a pointing-toe song as the children dance. "I see dancers, they point their toes, point, point, point . . . . Time to go. Get back on the magic carpet." The next palace has slowly turning-around dancers. The game ends with the carpet flying back to where it began.

Seizing the teachable moment is a skill that every early childhood teacher must cultivate. Abandoning a well-thought-out lesson plan to fling oneself spontaneously into an improvisatory setting takes courage, because the activity may not go well. If the magic carpet sequence had been planned, the teacher could have been prepared with mystical instrumental sounds such as the metallophone and tambourines. Improvising, her only resources were scraps of paper and her voice, yet the activity played well and involved the children in a more creative venture than just singing about a bluebird.

The Fire Truck

All the fire fighters are asleep. "Ding! Ding! Ding!" The fire alarm rings. Hurry! Put on boots, coat, and hat; run and jump on the fire truck. Here we go, driving very fast to put out the fire. We're here! Jump off the truck; unroll the hose; squirt the water. (High, low, round and round) Fire's out. Roll the hose back up. Get back on the truck and drive slowly back to the fire station; perhaps even go back to sleep.

This movement is effective if it is accompanied by xylophones or a piano; for example, a lullaby for sleeping, loud, high ringing bells (triangle) to wake up, and glissandos for squirting water.

A Storm

The teacher asks the children to be a streak of lightning crashing out of a dark storm cloud. He counts, 1, 2, 3, 4, freeze (reminding them that "freeze" means to stand very still, holding the last position they were in). The children make slashing lightning streaks with their arms on each count. When the children are in freeze position, the teacher asks, "Can you still feel how powerful that lightning was as it slashed through the sky?" The teacher describes the children's shapes: "I see Michael's lightning. It is still very strong and pointing up/down in the sky."
An extended sound and movement story can be as follows:

Dark clouds move mysteriously through the sky (drum roll). *All dancers pretend to be a big, menacing cloud.* Streaks of lightning crash: 1, 2, 3, 4, freeze.

Cymbals: • • • • • (Hold position for four or more counts)

All dancers become the powerful lightning. The storm alternates between these two ideas, and may end with falling rain (rapid xylophone sounds).
All dancers wiggle their fingers or create a movement idea of rapidly falling rain.

Structured Movement Play

Children need a great deal of practice play in order to fully master rhythmic responses to music. Sensing and responding to the underlying beat are practiced with such activities as clapping, tapping, stepping, and rhythmically rolling balls to the music. Children should also have many opportunities to sense contrasting heavy and light beats that are grouped in music to provide a sense of meter; for example, moving in twos: **heavy** light, **heavy** light (marching, stepping), or threes: **heavy** light light, **heavy** light light (waltzing, swaying). Sensing the underlying beat, rhythm patterns, and phrases enables children to successfully perform traditional song games and dances that have rules and a structure.

Rhythmic play with rules begins rather loosely with such song games as "Ring around the Rosie," where all are expected to fall down on the final phrase in the music, or the "Hokey-Pokey," which has many directions and special times for shaking and turning. Teacher must be patient with young children as they strive to perfect their timing and rhythmic accuracy because they are still developing these skills.

Rules become truly demanding when children dance to songs such as the "Old Brass Wagon." Children are expected to walk with a steady beat, circle left to right, and swing a partner, all with rhythmic accuracy. The literature is full of folk and contemporary dance music that has such detailed, how-to directions.

OLD BRASS WAGON
Midwestern Play-Party Game

2. Swing, oh, swing, Old Brass Wagon, (*3 times*)
   You're the one, my darling.

3. Skipping all around, Old Brass Wagon, (*3 times*)
   You're the one, my darling.

The use of choreography for a classical piece of music also represents a highly structured "thing" to be remembered and repeated. Depending on the complexity involved, these activities are usually more appropriate for the school-age, rather than preschool, children.

MORE CHALLENGING MUSIC-MOVEMENT ACTIVITIES

Bingo

The children sing the words, clapping their hands to the long and short rhythmic pattern of B-i-n-g-o. This traditional game continues by eliminating letters, leaving in their place the silent beats or rhythmic idea. After several repetitions, the word *Bingo* is no longer spelled, and only the internalized sense of the rhythm pattern exists. Seven- and eight-year-old children usually perform this song game with ease.

BINGO
American Folk Song

A Choreographed Dance

Propose a strategy for second grade children. Small groups of children are to create a dance piece with instrumental accompaniment using the following criteria:

◆ The dance must be a minimum of 30 seconds long.
◆ It must be accompanied by small percussion instruments.
◆ It involves two ideas, one of which is repeated (A, B, A).
◆ They are to perform the dance for their classmates.

Old Opidiah

This game is an example of a circle dance for older children. Precise rhythmic responses are expected, thus it is definitely a game with rules. The formation is a circle facing inward. The movement calls for the children to move to the right: left foot takes one side step, right foot steps together (measure 1); both feet jump (on the word "jumped") into the circle and immediately back out again (measure 2). The same direction and foot movement pattern are repeated throughout the song.

OLD OPIDIAH
Traditional Game Chant

Musical Setting by B. Andress

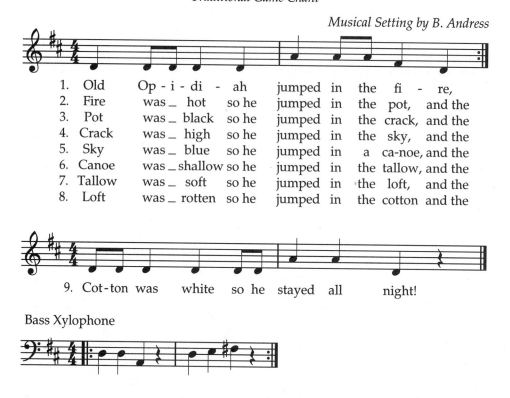

1. Old Op-i-di-ah jumped in the fi-re,
2. Fire was _ hot so he jumped in the pot, and the
3. Pot was _ black so he jumped in the crack, and the
4. Crack was _ high so he jumped in the sky, and the
5. Sky was _ blue so he jumped in a ca-noe, and the
6. Canoe was _ shallow so he jumped in the tallow, and the
7. Tallow was _ soft so he jumped in the loft, and the
8. Loft was _ rotten so he jumped in the cotton and the

9. Cot-ton was white so he stayed all night!

Bass Xylophone

More about Movement Models

EMILE JAQUES-DALCROZE: EURHYTHMICS

Eurhythmics, the study of rhythm, was developed by Emile Jaques-Dalcroze in the late 1800s and early 1900s in Switzerland. The focus of the approach is on hearing and feeling music before dealing with music symbols. Eurhythmics is used

to direct the child's natural capacity for rhythmic expression and to identify it with the rhythms of music . . . . When a child learns to identify his movement patterns with sound patterns, music becomes a language easily understood in terms of his own motor imagery. [3]

Sensing and doing, which involve both instinct and the body, are developed over a period of time before any verbalization or intellectual learning of music is expected. The learner uses a variety of steps, leaps, stops, and gestures while hearing music. Quick reaction exercises are used to challenge the child to move, think, and feel music. Ideally, movements are accompanied by a pianist, who can freely improvise in response to the child's movements or can use his or her own musical improvisations or composed music to prompt an action.

This natural movement approach gives learners the opportunity to move expressively, attend to the music, develop concentration, become aware of specific musical elements, experience rhythmic control and coordination, and respond to traditional musical symbols. The approach stresses not only the "doing" of rhythms, but also the honing of aural acuity and response to visual rhythmic representation. Typically, children explore ideas about dynamics (volume), duration, tempo, metrical patterns, speech and rhythm patterns, phrase and form, and pitch and melody.

Initially, the children are encouraged to use their bodies; for example, "Be a wilting flower or a red crayon in the hot sun." Later, they might move to sound and silence or fast and slow. Crescendo and decrescendo might be explored by having the children kneel in a circle, with all holding onto one hula hoop. As the music volume gradually increases, the hoop is slowly raised; as the volume decreases, the hoop is lowered.[4] One of the most successful ways for children to experience a natural beat feeling in music is to play bounce—catch or roll-the-ball games.

After prompting much sensing and doing play, the teacher may introduce note cards to "picture the music." These note cards may contain rhythmic notation or other musical symbols such as dynamic markings (forte-piano). On seeing the cards, the children's movements reflect the indicated rhythm or musical control symbol.

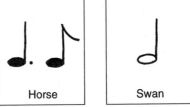

Quick response practice typically entails activities where the child walks a steady beat (¼ meter) while simultaneously clapping two sounds to each beat. The teacher says, "One-two-ready, change." The child, without interrupting the movement flow, switches her body movements, now clapping the steady beat, and walking two steps to the beat.

Virginia Hoge Mead spoke about how eurhythmics experiences differ from other approaches to teaching music:

I believe it is the total absorption of mind, body, and emotions in the experience of actualizing the musical sound. You imagine your body as the instrument and you sense the excitement of being the interpreter, the performer, and the listener all at the same time. You imagine that you and the music are one. [5]

The philosophy and activities of Dalcroze's eurhythmics are in keeping with a child-centered approach. Guiding children through sensing and doing experiences before teaching symbols agrees with a developmentally and musically appropriate approach.

ELAYNE METZ: THE MUSICALITY OF THE CHILD'S MOVEMENT RESPONSES

Educators are always searching for more effective ways to interact with young children. How we elicit their movement responses has long been questioned. When we model a movement, are we being intrusive, denying the child the power of original creativity? If we leave the child to her own resources, how does she enrich and extend her own imaginative movement ideas?

Elayne Metz studied the musicality of young children's movement responses, that is, how their responses reflect the nature and content of the music being heard.[6] Her conclusions provide us with important insights about how to more effectively interact with children during movement experiences. Metz questioned (1) what factors are involved in two-, three-, and four-year-olds' free choice participation in movement activities, (2) what the relationship is between peer and teacher in eliciting movement responses to music, and (3) what these observations tell us about setting the movement learning environment in the preschool.

Three categories were identified for the investigation:

◆ *Conditions*—Information about behavioral dispositions based on participation patterns of children

◆ *Interactions*—The teacher's and children's overt behavior as demonstrated through *modeling, describing,* and *suggesting*

◆ *Outcomes*—The nature of movement responses in the context of the environment, including properties of music- and nonmusic-related movement responses

In part, Metz concluded the following. First, children have a disposition to specific types of participation in movement activities, but time—a delayed response factor—may be a factor in increasing participation. Second, the increase in music-related movement responses corresponds to the degree of interrelatedness among the properties of describing (teacher describes what child is doing), suggesting (teacher suggests possible actions), and modeling (teacher demonstrates what to do). Third, preschool children's responses to music are modified by changes in developmental growth. Modeling changes from pure imitation to invitational or interactional responses as children mature. Fourth, of the types of interactions between teacher and children, describing and suggesting are more successful than modeling alone in eliciting children's music-related movement responses.

Metz's conclusions have implications for how we interact with children within and beyond the scope of movement education. Modeling, suggesting, and describing become effective teaching techniques as we guide children through all areas of the curriculum.

PHYLLIS WEIKART: BEAT COMPETENCY

Phyllis Weikart's movement theories are currently being explored in the classroom.[7] With her approach, Weikart expresses concerns that children must first develop "beat competency" before they can effectively understand rhythm and perform rhythmically. Initial activities should focus more on responding to the beat than on the performance of rhythm patterns. Language is a key factor in enabling accurate movement responses. Children are encouraged to use a four-step movement process: (1) Explain what they will do without moving. ["Knee, knee" (say the Beat).] (2) Tap the knee while chanting the name of the body part (say and do). (3) Tap the knee while whispering the name of the body part (whisper and do). (4) Think "knee" while tapping the body part (think and do). Weikart's approach presents many opportunities for children to respond to the beat with folk dance and music in other styles.

SUMMARY

Children should move to music for the sheer joy of expressing themselves. Their movement to music involves creative as well as structured responses. Children at every stage of development should have many opportunities to improvise or choreograph movements that help express what they hear in the music. There is no right or wrong way to move, but certain ways may be more appropriate than others.

Structured dance responses are dictated either by traditional folk/composed music or the choreographed efforts of others. Such movements and music can be performed the same way in different times and places. Because of their structured form, they can be handed down through the generations. Folk dance, ballet, and other planned movement to music are examples of structured responses. Structured movement in response to music also refers to classroom activities that demand musical accuracy, such as performing a steady beat, rhythm patterns, or describing repetition and contrast.

Movement is an overt descriptive tool that provides insight about how the child is sensing and understanding music. It is important that a quality early childhood music program helps children acquire a repertoire of movement gestures and provides many opportunities for testing their ideas through expressive and structured movement play.

THINGS TO DO

1. Develop an appropriate strategy that involves children in creating their own movement study such as becoming a carousel or an ice cube in the sun. Describe the target age group. What music or sound stimuli will you use? How do you predict children will respond?

2. Plan a movement and music activity where children are held accountable for one or more of the following: (1) rhythmic accuracy, (2) repetition of patterns, (3) repeatable gestures, or (4) describing other specific ideas heard in the music. Such an activity might involve folk dance, response to the musical form of a given selection, or a rhythmic chant and dance.

RESOURCES

Andress, B. "Research to Practice: Preschool Children and Their Movement Responses to Music." *Young Children* (November 1991): 22–27.

Dalcroze Society of America
613 Putnam Drive
Eau Claire, WI 54701

The High Scope Press
600 N. River Street
Ypsilanti, MI 48198

NOTES

[1]Erik H. Erikson, *Childhood and Society*, rev. ed. (New York: W. W. Norton & Company, 1964), 220.

[2]Ibid., 85.

[3]Elsa Findlay, *Rhythm and Movement: Applications of Dalcroze Eurhythmics* (Evanston, IL: Summy-Birchard Company, 1971), 3.

[4]Ibid., 14.

[5]Virginia Hoge Mead, *Dalcroze Eurhythmics in Today's Music Classroom* (New York: Schott Music Corporation, 1994), 5.

[6]Elayne Metz, "Movement as a Musical Response among Preschool Children," *Journal of Research in Music Education* 37 (Spring 1989): 48–60.

[7]Phyllis Weikart, *Round the Circle* (Ypsilanti, MI: The High Scope Press, 1987).

9

Music Play Centers

Much research has been done about the impact of play in the lives of young children. Most theorists have a definition of what play is but, though they all agree it is important, there is little mutual consensus about what the definition is. The problems in defining play are reflected in the following statements:

Schiller: The aimless expenditure of exuberant energy.

Froebel: The natural unfolding of the germinal seeds of childhood. Instinctive practice, without serious intent, of activities that will later be essential to life.

Dewey: Activities not consciously performed for the sake of any result beyond themselves.

Gulick: What we do because we want to do it.

Stern: Play is voluntary, self-sufficient activity.

Patrick: Those human activities which are free and spontaneous and which are pursued for their sake alone.[1]

More helpful information abut the nature of play is available to us. Piaget made a distinction between play as mastery and play as assimilation. In contrast to its use in adaptive thought (see Chapter 1), in play there is a predominance of assimilation rather than accommodation.

. . . the child goes from one scheme to another, no longer to try them out successively, but to master them without any effort at adaptation . . . . The activity is no longer an effort to learn, it is only a happy display of known actions.[2]

Berk reported that Vygotsky accorded fantasy play a prominent place in his theory, granting it the status of a "leading factor" in development,[3] as the following frequently quoted remarks reveal:

Play creates a zone of proximal development in the child. In play, the child always behaves beyond his average age, above his daily behavior; in play, it is as though he were a head taller than himself. As in the focus of a magnifying glass, play contains all developmental tendencies in a condensed form and is itself a major source of development.[4]

We no longer need to be convinced of the importance of play. Instead, we are now at the stage of how to most effectively accommodate a music play program in a classroom setting. If we want to work effectively with young children, we must (1) continue to enrich and create opportunities for one-on-one or small-group play and (2) change our perspective of how we view the classroom learning environment, especially in school-age classrooms where the teacher-child ratio is greater. The environment must provide for a continuing use of learning centers that contain representational and symbolic toys that allow children to develop imaginatively and cognitively in accordance with their developmental level. We accept this learning approach for preschool and kindergarten children without hesitation, but class sizes and curricular constraints discourage the prevalence of learning center environments for first- and second-grade children. Thus, ready or not, this age group sadly falls into a "whole-group" delivery system.

Teachers of school-age children need to renew their efforts to accommodate the learning center approach. Space, schedule, teacher time, and energy appear to be the greatest hindrances to implementing such a program. Special scheduling for center activity may alleviate some of the problems; for example, one day a week or once a month might become "center days." A room specially set up for this kind of activity could hold about ten area or music table plays for the children's exploration. For example, in the music classroom, preset, portable cubicle displays may be quickly rolled in and out to accommodate the music teacher's regular classes (see the section on storage and retrieval). For example, the first grade class at 9 o'clock explores centers that are later covered with a sheet or otherwise visually "put away" for the incoming sixth grade class at the 10 o'clock hour. The centers reappear for the second graders at 11 o'clock (see storage and retrieval).

Ideally, music play centers are created within the context of the overall classroom environment whether they are in a preschool, a primary grade level, or a music classroom. Certain areas may be dedicated as permanent music spaces, while others may be ever-changing music exploratory play environments. Children can choose to participate in the centers for as long as they are interested, returning frequently or not at all.

Music play environments can be compiled or constructed from found objects or from traditional classroom and orchestral instruments. The objective is to provide an enticing play area that triggers curiosity and motivates children to become involved in making and responding to music either independently or within a small group. Such areas must inherently have musical validity through which the child can enhance musical skills, understanding, and appreciation. The adult must plan settings that enable the child to:

- interact with developmentally appropriate hands-on musical objects and sounds.
- interact with meaning-centered musical ideas.
- acquire a song repertoire.
- interact with specific genres of classical literature (e.g., opera, programmatic, and absolute music).
- move expressively to a variety of recorded music.
- explore musical sounds.
- identify, differentiate, and categorize sounds.
- explore sight and sounds of musical instruments.
- develop musical skills on various instruments.
- respond to visual representations of sounds and songs.
- integrate music with other curricular ideas.
- discover music as a means of communication.

Programs for independent music exploration should include areas for (1) indoor and outdoor play, (2) table play, (3) designated small area plays on the floor, and (4) permanent centers such as music book corners, ensemble centers, music storage shelves, and areas for listening and expressive movement.

The models described next offer suggestions for creating music play settings within the classroom. Some play areas involve relatively inexpensive, consumable items while others require more involved funding, workmanship, and long-term storage. Teachers may need to acquire materials gradually for several of these settings and provide for efficient storage and retrieval.

Models and Materials for Music Play Settings

TABLE PLAY SETTINGS

Table play settings usually consist of small objects, instruments, and musical game boards with pieces that can be manipulated. These items are placed on a child-size table. Children know that the objects must remain on the table for use by other children, rather than be carried off to another play area.

Marching Soldiers

The teacher places an audiocassette recording of the "March of the Toys" from *Babes in Toyland* by Victor Herbert in the play area. She creates four different pictures of houses representing towns and laminates and tapes these pictures in different areas near the edge of a round table. Small toy wooden soldiers are used as game pieces.

For the musical play, the children are challenged to recognize the sound of a specific instrument (trumpet), which signals a slight change in music and play. The children first hear the introductory fanfare and then march their wooden soldier to and around the first town. When they hear a trumpet fanfare, they go to the next town and march around until they hear another fanfare. This procedure

continues until the children march their toy soldiers through all of the towns. The play ends with the children marching their soldiers, gradually becoming softer down the road and under the table until they are hidden from view. What other toys could be marched to this music?

Although the play is designed to follow the changing sections in the music as signaled by the trumpet fanfares, children may elect to invent their own "march-around-the-towns" game. This is quite acceptable; movement in any direction while tapping the steady beat is a valuable music play activity for very young children.

The musical form for this activity is: Introduction (fanfare)—A, B; Trumpet fanfare—A; Trumpet fanfare—C; Trumpet fanfare—A, C, C; Trumpet fanfare—A (becoming softer).

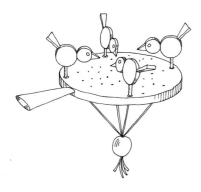

Pecking Chickens

This play uses "Ballet of the Unhatched Chicks" from *Pictures at an Exhibition* by Mussorgsky. The teacher records the music on an audiocassette tape and places it in the area along with a chicken-pecking toy. (This toy can be found at craft fairs and toy shops.) When the toy is moved in a circular motion, the weight of the suspended ball causes the chickens to peck the board with clattering sounds.

For musical play, the children use these sounds to accompany the music. They may make random pecking sounds throughout the music or, if they are developmentally ready, they may play, pause, and sway during various sections of the music. The form of the music is as follows:

A	PAUSE	A REPEATS	PAUSE	B	A REPEATS
Circular motion to make birds peck	Hold ball to stop	Birds peck	Stop	Hold ball and make birds sway	Birds peck

Paw Paw Patch

The teacher introduces the song to the children during group time and then prepares a music play mat on which the children may tap the beat and play at picking up "paw paws" as they again sing. The teacher prepares the table play by enlarging and laminating the play mat and placing it on a table for the children's use. Disks such as checkers or other cardboard or plastic pieces are placed in the Paw Paw Patch area of the play mat.

PAW PAW PATCH
Traditional

Where, oh where is pre - ty lit - tle Su - zy?

Where, oh where is pre - ty lit - tle Su - zy?

Where, oh where is pre - ty lit - tle Su - zy?

Way down yon - der in the Paw Paw Patch.

For the musical play, the adult first models and then invites one child at a time to play the game by singing the verse of the song. The child's index finger is placed at the starting place on the mat (Begin). The player rhythmically taps his

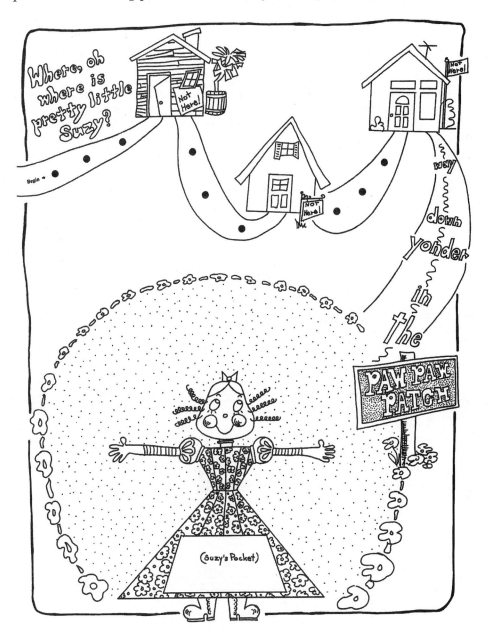

E. Achilles, "Paw Paw Patch," *You, Your Children and Music*, Vol. I, Issue 7. Arizona Early Childhood Music Collaborative Project. Used by permission. Permission to reproduce this play mat for personal use is granted to users of this textbook.

index finger, moving along the path to look for Suzy. The tapping involves a sequence of touching the three dots and a house to the underlying beat of the music. On the last phrase of the verse, the player's finger slides downward on the path (Way down yonder in the Paw Paw patch).

> Where, oh where is pretty little Suzy?
> *(Spoken)* She's not in this house!
> *(Sing three times)*
> Way down yonder in the Paw Paw Patch.

The player rhythmically picks up the "paw paws" and places them in Suzy's pocket while singing the refrain:

> Pickin' up paw paws, put 'em in your pocket . . .
> Way down yonder in the Paw Paw Patch.

Little Boy Blue

"Little Boy Blue" may be sung (depending on the child's ability to sing the wide skips in the melody) or chanted. The teacher should make sure the children know the song or chant before he places the play mat on a table for independent use. The teacher enlarges the play mat and picture pieces and cuts out four shapes (flower, house, tree, and haystack) and the sleeping Little Boy Blue. The pictures are matched with their shapes on the play mat. Little Boy Blue is hidden under one of the shapes.

In the musical play, the adult demonstrates how the game is played by singing the song, stopping to point to and discuss the pictures on the page. The teacher sings:

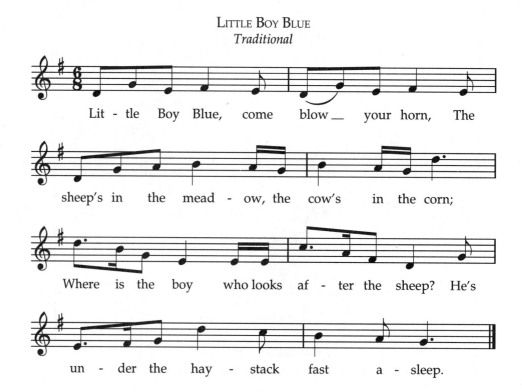

LITTLE BOY BLUE
Traditional

Lit - tle Boy Blue, come blow __ your horn, The
sheep's in the mead - ow, the cow's in the corn;
Where is the boy who looks af - ter the sheep? He's
un - der the hay - stack fast a - sleep.

Little Boy Blue, come blow your horn,
The sheep's in the meadow . . .

He then says, "Just look at all those sheep. No one is taking care of them. They are getting into all kinds of trouble—playing in the mud, eating the flowers, playing games where they can fall down, playing with the water hose, and nibbling at the little girl's dress." He sings the next phrase:

. . . the cow's in the corn.

LITTLE BOY BLUE
Song Play by Barbara Andress

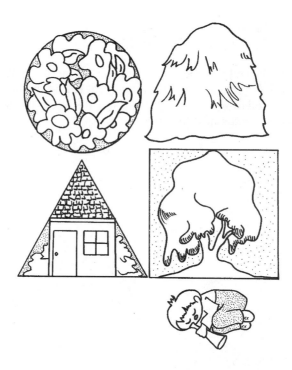

B. Andress, "Little Boy Blue," *You, Your Children and Music,* Vol. II, Issue 3. Arizona Early Childhood Music Collaborative Project. Used by permission. Permission to reproduce for personal use is granted to users of this textbook.

Teacher says, "I see the cows in the corn. How many cows are eating the corn?"

Where is the boy who looks after the sheep?

Teacher sings, "Is he under the flowers? Tree? House? Haystack?" The children lift each shape until they find the hidden Little Boy Blue. The game is completed with "He's under the haystack/house/tree/flowers fast asleep."

The children independently play the game many times, hiding Little Boy Blue under the different shapes for a friend to find.

SPECIAL DESIGNATED PLAY AREAS

Areas can be designated quickly as music play centers in the following ways:

◆   By marking the floor area with masking tape

◆   By placing a hula hoop(s) on the floor as circle markers

◆   By placing a small, colorful area rug or portable carpet squares on the floor

◆   By turning the piano so that one end faces the wall and the other end projects into the room to create a cubicle/corner

◆   By separating two four-drawer file cabinets to create a small play space in between

◆   By adapting cardboard boxes for crawl-in centers

Small instruments or objects to be manipulated may be placed within these areas for exploratory play. Most children respect the rule that instruments, mallets, and other game pieces must remain within the specified areas.

LARGER PLAY AREAS

Larger play areas are settings in which children enter a designated space and become a part of a pretend, exploratory, or construction event. There is usually some "staging" involved in these play areas.

Musicians at Work

The teacher prepares a setting in which children can play out the various roles of a musician: composer, conductor, and performer. He designates a place(s) in the room for the musician's studio (composer) and rehearsal hall (conductor and performers). He stocks each area with equipment/instruments that the musicians need.

The composer needs:

◆ Large and/or small sheets of lined staff paper (staff paper can be purchased in chart-size pages)

◆ Large music notation stamps (stamps can be purchased or the shapes cut out in relief on the sides of large gum erasers available from art supply stores)

◆ Ink pad

The children enjoy randomly stamping notes, rests, and other traditional symbols on their pretend music pages. They will not understand the meaning of the symbols, but they will become aware of the "look" of written music. The conductor and performers may wish to pretend to play the music written by the composer.

The conductor needs:

◆ A conductor's baton (purchase a short baton at a music store; blunt the tip if it is too pointed)

◆ A wire music stand (assembling a wire music stand can be a great construction project)

◆ Several sheets of printed music

◆ Recorded music and cassette tape player (child conducts as recorded music is heard)

◆ A few small percussion instruments for the conductor's musicians to play

◆ A few chairs arranged in a half circle for performers

The conductor raps her baton on the stand to gain the attention of the imaginary or real performers, starts the music, waves the stick up and down during the music, stops the music, turns and bows to the audience, and invites the performers to stand and take a bow.

The performers need:

◆ Instruments in small boxes or cases (used small violin cases to hold their percussion instrument would be fun for the performer to carry around)

◆ A small wire music stand (tabletop cardboard stands are also available from music dealers)

◆ Several sheets of printed music

The performers get ready to play by taking out their instruments and music and setting up their stand. They watch the conductor as she tells them when to start and stop playing.

Echo Play

Sometimes teachers can find plush toys such as teddy bears or birds that echo what a child says or sings. Usually, the child must push a heart emblem or button while singing a short phrase to the toy, and the electronic device in the toy echoes what is sung. The toy becomes a play partner in pitch matching or echo games.

TEDDY BEAR PLAY. The teacher places a toy such as an echoing teddy bear in the topically planned "Teddy Bear" song play area. The child can sing brief patterns from the song for the bear to repeat.

MORE BEAR PLAY. The adult builds a mountain with two large stacked pillows. The child sings the song and moves the bear up and down the mountain as follows:

THE BEAR WENT OVER THE MOUNTAIN
Traditional Folk Song
(Beginning pitch: G)

The bear went over the mountain *(Sing three times)*
To see what he could see.

For the interlude, the child moves the bear stepwise up the mountain while singing:

```
                                F—up
                          E—up
                    D—up
              C—up
```

The other side of the mountain *(Sing three times)*
Was all that he could see!

For a special ending, the child moves the bear stepwise down the mountain while singing:

```
        G—down
              F—down
                    E—down
                          D—down
                                C—down
```

Three Billy Goats Gruff

The teacher purchases three different sizes of slit-log drums at a craft show or from a music vendor. Although each drum has several indefinite pitches, each has a relatively low, medium, or high sound depending on its size. The teacher adds legs and a head to the drums to create billy goat characters. She constructs a bridge or uses the center's balance board and places the goat slit-log drums, bridge, and a large cymbal with beater in a play center. The children may play out the story of the Three Billy Goats Gruff using the instruments to express the ideas.

For example, the goats one by one trip trap over the bridge (sounds on the slit-log drum); the troll who is hiding under the bridge jumps up and says, "You can't cross my bridge!" (clang the cymbals). The story continues until it is played out.

Very young children often do not use the play area to tell a story; they are quite content to tap on or ride the goats and walk over the bridge. This can become an improvised song play time with the adult singing, "I see Julio riding on the goat" or "Here goes Bobby over the bridge."

Train Play

The teacher constructs a wooden locomotive that contains various small percussion instruments. He begins with an open-sided cube in which a small cowbell is hung and mounts it on a platform that holds a sandblock on each side and extends out to hold a small wooden drum that becomes the engine boiler. The smokestack is made by inserting a clave tone block in the drum. The V-shaped cow catcher is covered with a serrated ratchet board that makes clacking sounds. Removable mallets are placed on each side of the drum. Immobile or movable wheels are added to complete the locomotive. The child explores the many sounds found on the locomotive and uses the instruments expressively while singing songs such as "Little Red Caboose" or "Ride a Train."

RIDE A TRAIN
Spiritual

Words by B. Andress

Ride a train lit-tle chil-dren, Ride a train, lit-tle chil-dren Ride a train, lit-tle chil-dren, There's room for man-y on board.

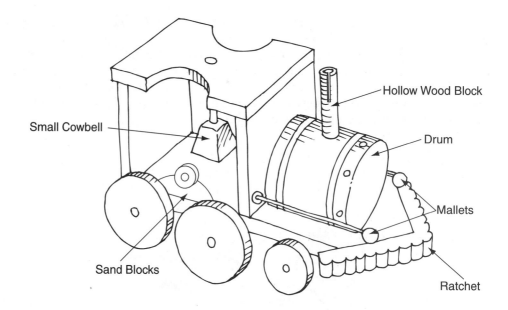

Block play is a most valuable manipulation activity for young children. The teacher can extend the train play by constructing musical wooden blocks to be used as railroad coaches in the long train. Various sounds can be added such as rattles, jingle bells, or pitched bells for open-sided gondola coaches. The children arrange the blocks behind the locomotive, producing a variety of timbral sounds as a part of their construction play.

A Dancing Place

Children love to see themselves move. One corner of the room may be used as a permanent dancing place. Safe, Plexiglas mirror material can be purchased in 4-by-8-foot sheets. (The vendor will cut the pieces to any desired size.) The teacher affixes two 4-by-6-foot mirrors to the corner walls or onto a plywood hinged screen. This size will amply reflect the children's stretching, reaching, and whirling motions. The teacher places a cassette tape recorder and tape loop in the area and entices the children to the area by frequently changing the props and music. Typical dancing place materials would be dancing dolls.

DANCING DOLL PARTNER. One or more child-size rag dolls are made for dancing partners (patterns are available at fabric stores). The teacher dresses the dolls with children's clothing or clothes that topically reflect the music to be used. The dolls' legs are weighted with sneakers so that they can be manipulated to jump or tap both feet. The dolls can be used for the following activities.

◆ *Country Dancing*—The teacher dresses the dolls in overalls, blue jeans, neckerchiefs, or granny skirts. The children dance the dolls to country or square-dance music such as "Hoedown" from *Appalachian Spring* by Copeland. Loud, boisterous dancing will occur.

◆ *Ballroom Dancing*—The dolls are dressed in formal attire with jewels and flowing fabric and dance to a Strauss waltz.

◆ *Arabian Dance*—The teacher prepares a tape loop of "The Arabian Dance" from the *Nutcracker Suite* by Tchaikovsky. The dolls wear fancy clothes, veils, and flowing head scarves. Several colorful scarves and a tambourine may be placed in the area as additional props.

LIGHTS AND MOVEMENT. Movement play is special when all the children are involved either as performers or as the audience. The teacher darkens the room, plays the music, and combines movement with objects such as flashlights, black-lights, disco mirror balls, color wheels, and colored gels on overhead projectors.

RIBBON STREAMER HOOPS. Long, narrow ribbons are tied to a hoop. One player holds the hoop vertically in front of a fan at a safe distance. The children dance through, around, and about the streamers. Before the play, the teacher should experiment to see how long the ribbons should be so they don't get tangled in the fan.

SPOON STRAW STREAMERS. Plastic spoon straws are straws with a small spoon at one end and are available from restaurant supplies vendors. The teacher punches a hole in the spoon section and then ties the ribbons through to create a colorful dancing wand. The plastic straw provides a safe staff for the wand that bends easily if a dancer is accidentally jabbed.

RING STREAMERS. Long, narrow ribbons are tied to plastic rings. The children wear the rings, one on each middle finger as they move to music (Achilles, MENC Sample Fair 1990).

Peter and His Friends

The teacher can introduce a "Peter and His Friends" play during group time and invite the children to replay the story independently. The story characters are Peter, which can be a soft pillow with facial features, and specially designed playful animal instruments such as a guiro duck, a finger cymbal bird, and a tom-tom cat.

The music and story of *Peter and the Wolf* by Prokofiev can be adapted to meet the children's developmental level. The teacher records various musical themes from the work, alternating Peter's theme with the music of each new friend. In one version, Peter walks to his theme and one by one meets and greets newfound friends: a bird, a cat, and a duck. Peter walks around, looking up and down and all around to find each friend. "He looked up, He looked down. He looked all around. And a little 'birdie' is what he found." The animal instruments are played

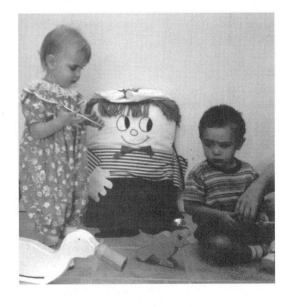

Duck Guiro
Courtesy of
Peripole-
Bergerault,
Inc.

when the children hear their musical themes. In this version, the wolf is not introduced and the duck does not get swallowed. More mature children can be introduced to the entire musical story.

There are many books on the market that beautifully illustrate the story of *Peter and the Wolf*. The teacher may want to place a book in the area as a part of the children's play options.

Music Book Corner

The teacher prepares a space for the music book corner with soft pillows and a shelf or other container for a rotating collection of music-related books. Many commercially prepared books are available that delightfully illustrate traditional children's songs. These books are fun to sing rather just read. Teachers may also find many books that can be adapted to music play. For example, a book that shows pictures of a carousel on subsequent pages as it goes faster and faster, then slower and slower, effectively illustrates ideas about tempo (accelerando-ritardando).

These books may be introduced musically during group time and then placed in the music corner for the children's independent playtime. If the initial presentation involves an accompanying tape or manipulation figures, the teacher might set up a small table in the area for playing with the featured book of the week.

The following suggestions are typical of useful materials for a music book corner. Because books go out of print, specific references should be used as models rather than as permanent resources. The following list of singable books is but an introduction to the many books that illustrate familiar children's songs.

Adams, Pam. *There Were Ten in the Bed*. England: Child's Play, Ltd., 1979.

————. *I Know an Old Lady Who Swallowed a Fly*. England: Child's Play, Ltd., 1973.

Emberly, Edward. *London Bridge Is Falling Down*. Boston: Brown, 1967.

Jeffers, Susan. *Silent Night*. New York: E. P. Dutton, 1984.

————. *All the Pretty Horses*. New York: Scholastic, 1974.

Jones, Carol. *This Old Man*. Boston: Houghton Mifflin, 1990.

Keats, Ezra Jack. *The Little Drummer Boy*. New York: Collier Books, 1968.

Kovalski, Maryann. *The Wheels on the Bus*. New York: Little Brown & Co., 1987.

Langstaff, John. *Oh, A-Hunting We Will Go*. New York: Atheneum, 1974.

Lawson, Carol. *Teddy Bear, Teddy Bear*. New York: Dial Books, 1991.

Peek, Merle. *Mary Wore Her Red Dress*. New York: Clarion Books, Ticknor & Fields, 1985.

Rae, Mary Maki. *The Farmer in the Dell*. New York: Viking Kestrel, 1988.

Westcott, Nadine. *Skip to My Lou*. Boston: Little, Brown, 1989.

————. *Down by the Bay*. New York: Crown, 1978.

————. *Peanut Butter and Jelly*. New York: Dutton Books, 1987.

Following are some specific suggestions for music book corner activities.

Aylesworth, Jim. *Old Black Fly*. New York: Henry Holt & Company, 1991. This book can be sung to a rhythmic variation of the spiritual "Joshua Fit the Battle of Jericho."

Baum, Susan. *Today Is Monday*. New York: Harper Collins, 1992. This book has illustrations of a familiar, traditional, cumulative song. It provides an excellent visual reminder as it unfolds into a long strip as each new verse (day of the week) is introduced.

Hurd, Thacher. *Mama Don't Allow*. New York: Harper & Row, 1984. This is the adventurous tale of some swamp musicians who aren't very musical but find themselves performing at the Alligator's Ball, where they narrowly escape being on the menu. The song "Mamma Don't 'Low No Gitar Pickin' Round Here" runs throughout the story (words and music are printed in the book). The teacher creates a table play including the characters from the story and a lot of alligators. He invites the children to dramatize the story by using the characters and singing the song. The children may want to create their own "Lullaby of Swampland." To play out this story, they need two dowel figures for mom and dad; swamp musicians—saxophonist, drummer, guitarist, and trumpet player—dowel figures with instrument stickers; and purchased or made alligators.

Jorgensen, G., and P. Mullins. *Crocodile Beat*. New York: Scholastic, 1995. The poetic words in this book are typical of many books that can be read to a recorded rhythm pattern. The teacher makes a lengthy cassette tape of a drum rhythm from a synthesizer (sometimes called businessman's bounce, jazz, or rock) and reads the book to the taped accompaniment.

Leman, Martin. *Ten Cats*. New York: Holt, Rinehart and Winston, 1981. The words of this counting book can be sung as a scale song. The children sing approximately one pitch per counted cat. Upon reaching nine cats, the children sing rapidly down the scale and then back up to complete the count of ten cats and the scale.

Wood, Audrey. *The Napping House*. New York: Harcourt Brace Jovanovich, 1984. The teacher redubs music to accompany the reading of this cumulative story. She begins with a lullaby or some other sleepy-time music, which accompanies the first part of the story when all the creatures are sleeping. She invites the children to snore each time the story refers to "grandma sleeping." The music changes in the tape to coincide with the rude awakening of all the creatures. The wake-up music should be something startling and raucous, such as a loud percussion ensemble. Suggested music: "Sweet Dreams" from Children's Album, Op. 39, by Tchaikovsky, and "Percussion Melee" by Ganz.

Williams, Sue. *I Went Walking.* New York: Harcourt Brace Jovanovich, 1990. All the words of this book can be sung as a three-tone chant. The teacher introduces the book during group time. Later, when children are playing in the music book corner, one child can sing both parts or two children can play out the questions and answers.

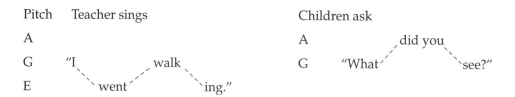

Pitch	Teacher sings		Children ask	
A			A	did you
G	"I walk		G	"What see?"
E	went ing."			

Deming, A. G., and Willington, M. "Who's That Tapping at the Window?" New York: Puffin Unicorn Books, 1994. The song is taught during group time, and then the teacher sets up a table play area in the music book corner. She does the following:

◆ Draws a house on an upright presentation poster/chart

◆ Cuts out a window and door

◆ Places stick creature puppets in front of the house whose names rhyme and are color coded, following illustrations in book (e.g., cat and rat-gray; wren and hen-yellow; dog and frog-green)

◆ Prepares one puppet face that will fit into the door and window

◆ Makes available a wood block and mallet and an xylophone

◆ Places the book in the play area

One child makes a knocking sound on the wood block. The children show the puppet face at the door or window and sing, "Who's That Tapping at the Window?" Another child finds the rhyming puppet names such as the cat and the rat and answers as per the story. Another child knocks, and another face appears at the door or window singing the question. Another two rhyming puppets answer, and so on. The story has a surprise ending that is dramatized by a child playing raindrop sounds on the xylophone.

WHO'S THAT TAPPING AT THE WINDOW?
American Folk Song

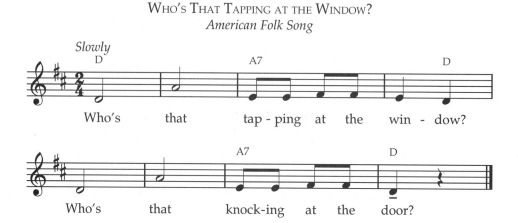

Music Theaters

Many games can be played in these large or small performing arts centers. Some examples are described next.

MICROPHONE PLAY. Children can be motivated to sing by placing a pretend microphone and one of the center's low, wide, building boxes in the music theater. The teacher explains that the box is a stage and the microphone is for singing. Children have seen performers use microphones, so they need little nudging to play out roles on their pretend TV, studio, or stage. They often interview friends, create their own songs, or sing composed ones.

FINGER-PUPPET MUSICAL THEATER. For this play, the teacher prepares a small cardboard or lightweight wooden box with a curtain as shown below. A

child places finger-puppet characters on his right hand and inserts it in the theater from the bottom; his left hand holds the box by its extended front handle. The child can present song stories and puppet movements to selected listening pieces. When playing independently with the theater, the child may wish to sit in front of the dancing place mirrors for a better view of the action.

Finger-puppet Music Play. The teacher records the song "One Elephant Went out to Play" on a tape loop and places the recorder in the theater area. Crocheted elephant finger puppets can be donated by a person who crochets or purchased from a craft fair or toy store. Three or four puppets are needed to dramatize this song. One elephant finger puppet pops up and dances in the theater space, then two, and so forth, as each verse of the song is sung.

Glove Finger Puppets. There are many glove finger puppets on the market that depict the characters in children's stories and music. A collection of these gloves can be acquired to provide many hours of musical play in the miniature theater.

Shadow Puppet Theater. A table-size shadow screen theater is created with books in the classroom and a devised cloth screen. Using two large spiral-bound chart books for the wings of the stage, the teacher constructs the shadow screen by attaching a rectangular piece of white fabric (the size of one chart book cover) to a horizontal wood stick on the top and a 1-inch round wooden dowel on the bottom. She drills a hole in each end of the top stick and slips one mallet through each top hole down into the spiral binding to secure the shadow screen to the chart books. A bright light or color wheel is placed beyond the screen to complete the stage.

Cutouts of shadow puppets may be prepared from cardboard or masonite and placed on long sticks. The children will want to experiment with where the characters should be placed in relation to the screen to produce the best shadows (probably very close to the screen). Characters for songs may be created and used such as Little Miss Muffet and the slowly descending spider.

A Listening Post

Two-inch PVC pipe and couplings are used to construct a sound-controlled listening post. The children speak into or place their ear on the upright sections of the assembled listening post. They discover that even the softest whisper or song is amplified as it travels through the pipe network. One child may sing softly into an upright end, sending a song to a friend who is listening at the other end. Materials needed include: six 6-inch lengths of pipe; one 12-inch length of pipe; three right-angle couplings; four elbow couplings; and one T-shaped coupling. The post is assembled as illustrated below.

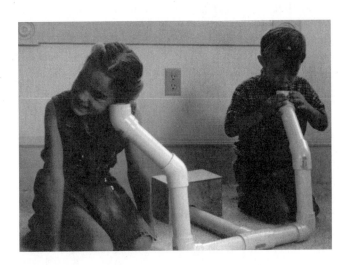

Idea shared by
Susan Kujawski,
Litchfield, AZ.
Used by permission.

Next, the teacher adds a right-angle coupling with the open end facing up to the end of the 12-inch pipe. A small constructed box is placed over the end. A small cassette recorder may be placed inside the box with the music softly playing. The lid is secured on the box so that the recorded music is muted and doesn't disturb other play in the classroom. The children must place their ears to the open ends of the listening post to hear the rich, full sounds of the amplified music. Additional pipe and couplings can be used to construct a more extensive listening network.

Stairstep Play

Large classroom blocks are used to create steps with three or four risers. Portable steps may also be used. The teacher places resonator bells on the steps that reflect the pitches needed for the activity. Two children play the game; one is the stepper, the other is the bell player. The stepper tells the bell player which bell to tap by jumping up or down or skipping over a step. Random stepping/playing may ensue, or children may step out a melody. "Hot Cross Buns" is a good choice for this game (pitches C, D, E).

Storage and Easy Retrieval of Preset Centers

Teachers can easily become overwhelmed with concerns about storing and retrieving the many diverse materials needed for an early childhood hands-on music program. Not only is it a large task to develop activities, compile materials, and implement the learning environments, it is a large task to store these items for repeated use. The logistics of resetting the various environments with posters, instructional visuals, and small instruments for use during a one- to two-week time span in the classroom can become a problem. The following suggestions may help teachers get organized.

Cardboard backdrops for specific music play areas can be created from commercially prepared project display boards (available at office supplies; approximately 25 inches by 36 inches when closed). Descriptive information/pictures, typical of a bulletin board, can be affixed to the display board. (When purchasing books, the teacher may want to buy two copies—one for reading and the other to be used as a picture source for the display board.) The finished display is protected by a clear, plastic laminate paper. The display board may be subject to tipping, so it should be placed against a wall or some other sturdy backing. The display board folds out to define the play space and can then be folded flat for storage. Small items that complement the play are placed in plastic bags or boxes.

A portable three-divider screen can be constructed to create multiple play cubicles. After determining the suitable height and width for the available space, the teacher creates three sturdy shadow box-type bulletin board screens. They are hinged together in book fashion with long piano hinges so that they can open out into three play spaces. Locking wheels on the base of each bulletin board offer mobility. When the screen is in place, a wood spacer or lock-open hardware can be placed on the top edge between each screen for stability.

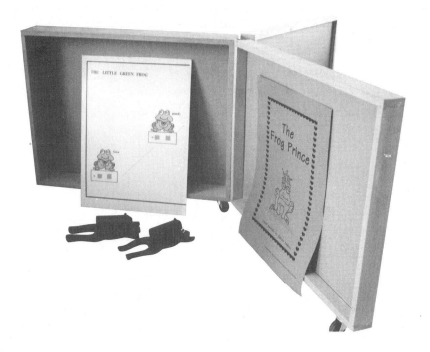

Depending on the planned usage, the backboards of each section may be masonite, pegboard, corkboard, whiteboard, or even acrylic mirror. The teacher prepares different topical materials for each cubicle and leaves them there for as long as they are needed. The center can be rolled into a corner when it is not in use.

Typical cubicle play set-ups might be as follows:

◆ *Section 1, Teddy Bear Play*—Children manipulate toys to dramatize verse 1 of the song. Teddy bear pictures are placed iconically up and down, depicting part of the melody. Also included are one stuffed bear, one small shoe, and one doll-size bed with a blanket for putting bear to sleep.

◆ *Section 2, Starlight Star Bright*—Stars and two triangles are hung on the pegboard surface. Several desk bells are placed on the floor of the cubicle for gentle tapping. Children sing the song and tap the ringing sounds for accompaniment.

◆ *Section 3, Nursery Rhyme Posters*—Soft nursery rhyme pillows fill the area. Children play with the pillows while singing the rhyme depicted. (Fabric stores sell material that has song pages printed on them. The prints often depict nursery rhymes or characters. Rather than making this fabric into a book, the teacher can sew and stuff it to make song pillows.)

SUMMARY

Music learning environments take time to prepare and implement in the classroom. The settings presented in this chapter range from small table play areas to larger designated spaces. The advantages of providing children with exploratory hands-on settings that allow them to make decisions and experience quality musical sounds more than justifies the disadvantage of having to prepare and maintain such settings. Teachers rarely begin with multiple centers; rather, they gather and develop materials over a period of several years. An effective way to begin is to pool your efforts with those of several teachers. Each teacher may be responsible for developing one or two centers, and then completed ideas and centers are shared with other group members.

If teachers get too swept up in obtaining materials for centers, they may lose sight of the educational goal. When planning any activity for children, we must maintain a constant concern for the validity of the learning experience. We cannot afford to waste children's time on the meaningless and trivial.

THINGS TO DO

1. Select four of the music play centers discussed in this chapter and identify one musical understanding inherent in each of the activities. If necessary, refer to Chapter 4 for the appropriate basic music concepts.

2. Select a music understanding you want to communicate such as a melodic idea: music moves by steps and skips, or a rhythmic idea: music moves with a steady underlying beat. Plan a center that you feel would help children develop an awareness of the musical understanding you select.

NOTES

[1]A. V. Sapora and E. D. Mitchell, *The Theory of Play and Recreation*, cited by Joe L. Frost in *Toward an Integrated Theory of Play* in *The Young Child and Music: Contemporary Principles in Child Development and Music Education*, ed. Jacquelyn Boswell (Reston, VA: Music Educators National Conference, 1985), 7.

[2]Jean Piaget, *Play Dreams and Imitation in Childhood* (New York: W. W. Norton & Company, 1962), 92–93.

[3]Laura E. Berk, "Vygotsky's Theory: The Importance of Make-Believe Play," *Young Children* (November 1994): 31.

[4]L. S. Vygotsky, "The Role of Play in Development," in *Mind in Society,* eds. M. Cole, V. John Steiner, S. Scribner, and E. Souberman (Cambridge, MA: Harvard University Press, 1978), 101.

10

Music for Young Children with Special Needs

The materials and techniques described so far in the book are also appropriate for teaching children with special needs. A high-quality learning environment is as important for these children as it is for other children. Because each child's developmental level must be considered, teachers or care providers must strive to understand individual differences and adapt their programs, materials, and instructional techniques to effectively promote learning. Adults must enforce the idea that children with special needs have the right to be enrolled in attractive, developmentally appropriate programs that are staffed by concerned, attentive, and able teachers.

Historically, children with special needs have been assigned to segregated, self-contained special education classrooms or mainstreamed within other classes. Now, many children are in inclusive classrooms.

Self-contained special education classrooms typically are in special schools that are solely for children with disabilities, or they are separate, designated classrooms within a regular school. In the past, people often assumed that all disabled children were mentally retarded—a serious disservice to many physically disabled children with normal intelligence. Children who were mentally challenged were (and often still are) identified as trainable or educable based on IQ testing. Regardless of their disability, all special education children were often lumped together in age-defined classrooms. Self-contained classrooms are still used in school systems, but educators have taken a more enlightened approach to placing these children.

Mainstreaming evolved in the 1970s when the Education for all Handicapped Children Act was passed. Mainstreaming involves placing the child in the "least restrictive environment." The child divides his or her time between special education classes, with specially scheduled resource teachers, and regular classes. Individual Education Programs (IEP) are designed to help children function in the least restrictive environment. In this program, the special education teacher advises the classroom teacher about how to work with the students, so basically it is two programs with two teachers. Mainstreaming is still practiced in some schools.

Inclusion of the special needs population into regular classes was implemented in the early 1980s. The concept of the inclusive classroom is that all doors are open between self-contained and regular classrooms, and both students and teachers work together. In this type of program, special education teachers take on the role of personal support teachers, moving from student to student. The whole class is part of the inclusive process. IEPs are also designed for children in this program.

There is no doubt that children with special needs require special understanding about their unique learning styles and capacities. Some schools and systems provide information about students with special needs, but too often care providers or teachers are expected to include these children within the classroom without benefit of background information about the challenges the children face. Classroom teachers then become responsible for seeking information about the child's needs and appropriate courses of remediation. The imperative for these caregivers, then, is to seek advice from and collaborate with those experts who are responsible for the progress of these challenged learners.

Identifying Children with Special Needs

In order to meet the needs of children with special needs, teachers must be knowledgeable about their developmental impairments and factors involved. Welsbacher used the following categories to describe children at risk:[1]

◆ *Established Risk*—Children with professionally accepted conditions including physical impairment, mental retardation, sensory deficits, neurological dysfunctions, and early childhood handicapped (ECH).
◆ *Biologically at Risk*—Children in whom no clear abnormality is detected immediately. The possible risks are from pregnancy complications, injury, toxic substance, prematurity, and low birth weight (LBW), among others.
◆ *Environmentally at Risk*—Children who are biologically and genetically intact and normal at birth but threatened by their environment: quality of maternal and medical care; opportunity or lack of social, educational, and sensory stimulation.

Welsbacher felt that early intervention with appropriate music experiences can and does enhance the language, cognitive, and motor skills of special-needs children.

Special Needs in the Classroom

Children with special needs function best in a structured environment that involves predictable routines and effective teacher modeling, suggesting, and describing. Interactions should be one-on-one as well as in full groups. Many special-needs children are unable to independently "discover," so they need to be taught how to do it. Describing the child's actions and what he is sensing is an effective technique for teaching how to discover.

Group music sessions for challenged children are planned in much the same way as they are for other children (see Chapter 4, p. 64). The teacher begins and ends with music or an activity that is familiar. The teacher's pace of introducing new materials differs from that used with typical primary-level children; however, the technique is not markedly different from that used for all preschool children: The teacher introduces a single, new idea with no attempt to elaborate on or expand it to the next level of interaction, usage, or understanding within the same session. Whether the music activity is done individually or within a small group, it needs to be reintroduced and expanded in small increments. For example, in order to demonstrate the understanding that musical cues are sometimes used to indicate that the music is coming to an end (ritard—a gradual slowing down), the adult may use the following sequence:

◆ *Session 1*—The teacher sets the structure for a "stop the music game." The child is first given time to explore the sound of a resonator bell. A mallet is used to tap many sounds.

◆ *Session 2*—The child repeatedly plays the sound of the resonator bell (pitch G) while the teacher plays a whole piece such as "Hot Cross Buns" on the recorder (beginning song pitch E). After completing the song, the teacher says, "All done!" while making a dramatic gesture of holding the recorder in the sky. The child is encouraged to imitate by holding the mallet in the sky. The same game is repeated many times.

◆ *Session 3*—The duet is repeated, but this time the teacher plays an exaggerated ritard (gradually slower) on the final phrase(s) as a warning that the song is about done. The teacher and child again hold the mallets and recorder in the sky while saying, "All done!"

Adapting the Environment for the Special Learner

Children with special needs must cope with a vast array of developmental impairments. They often have a complex combination of two or more impairments: for instance, a child may be autistic and also orthopedically challenged. It is not our purpose to present a comprehensive listing or definition of the many developmental problems that these children face; the intent is to offer a few examples that demonstrate how musical interaction can contribute to their remediation and personal growth. Enabling children with special needs to participate in musical activities often is as simple as adapting equipment, instruments, and the environment.

THE ORTHOPEDICALLY CHALLENGED CHILD

Following are a few suggestions for helping teachers adapt the environment for orthopedically challenged children.

Children with limited coordination are often unable to grasp a pick. A rubber door stop may be used instead for strumming string instruments such as an autoharp, guitar, or cello.

Children tend to pick up mallets by grasping the head (ball end) because it appears to be a handle to the stick. This, of course, makes the mallet unusable for tapping sounds on instruments. Mallets with a head on both ends of the stick may be purchased or made to solve this problem. The two-headed mallet also prevents the children from sticking the nonhead end in their eyes.

The size of striking surfaces is important for this special population. Bars on glockenspiels or small xylophones are often very small and narrow, which makes them difficult to strike. Larger barred instruments, such as an alto metallophone, a bass xylophone, or, ideally, the large single-pitched bass bars, should be used instead.

Xylophone-type instruments or bass bars should be placed in a position to accommodate the child's ability to hit the right bar or hit it at all. The teacher can help the child practice his swing. A long scarf or streamer on the end of a stick may help the child improve an even swing. The streamer prop enables the child to grasp the stick in the same way he holds a mallet. When the swinging action is more evenly performed, the adult may partner with the child and manipulate the instrument to intercept the child's mallet.

CHILDREN WITH VISUAL IMPAIRMENT

Children who are visually impaired fare very well in the music play environment. They can usually follow verbal instruction and learn songs and instrumental accompaniments through listening. Their sharp tactile senses allow them to easily touch and play instruments.

Few changes in lesson presentation are required to accommodate learners who are visually impaired. Certainly, the teacher must be more aware of the need to describe all ensuing actions so that the child fully comprehends instructions and expectations. Experience has shown that, without even being asked, classmates readily assist children who are impaired in participating in activities by directing hand movements, partnering, or otherwise guiding gestures during a movement or other music activity.

The teacher does need to make minor changes in approach, equipment, and play settings to enable the visually impaired child to participate more fully. Following are a few suggestions.

Spatial differences when playing melodies are more easily sensed by some children through touch on a keyboard rather than playing mallet instruments such as bells or xylophones. Other children, however, do well with mallet instruments, especially step bells. Braille letter names should be placed on all keys and mallet instruments to identify each pitch.

The teacher and peer aides can provide an increased sense of security when assisting the child who is trying to find objects. Rather than grasping the child's hand and moving it to the desired object, the hand-under-hand guidance method should be used. The teacher places her hand under the child's hand and then guides the movement to pick up a mallet or find an instrument.

A sense of spatial distance is easier to feel if a touch trail is used to reach objects. The child slides her hands across a surface rather than moving them through the air.

If a movement activity is overly complex, the teacher can provide the child with a dancing puppet, small percussion instrument, or other prop to manipulate while sitting in place.

Rather than grasp the child's hand when he participates in an expressive movement activity, the teacher can provide for more independent, self-controlled motion. A support for the child is placed in an open space; support can be a short bar on the wall, the back of a very sturdy chair, or a shoulder to which the child may cling. Bending, reaching, and minimal foot motion are then possible without the intrusion of another person's guidance.

School-age children may role play "Being the Music Conductor." The child is verbally instructed to move her hand in a down-up direction when she hears music in ¾ meter. She is then given a specially shaped wire coat hanger guide for response to music in ¾ meter. The child holds the hanger with her left hand, places her right finger inside the hanger, and follows the prepared triangular shape: beginning at the top, sliding down, to the right side, then back up. The child may also use an empty picture frame in like manner to sense music that moves in fours.

Child's
Right

CHILDREN WITH AUDITORY IMPAIRMENT

Children who are auditorily impaired experience varying degrees of deafness. These children can and do participate in making music. The teacher can expect many sounds to be cacophonous as the children explore ways to use their voices. The children strive to sing songs, and they also explore improvised vocal play such as sounds of sirens and animals as a part of the musical activities. Percussion or string instruments that produce vibrations provide useful sensory input. The children are often fitted with sound-enhancing devices that are prescribed for their specific auditory problem. The teacher is usually advised about how to use these devices and otherwise communicate with the child.

Children with auditory impairments often go to school earlier than hearing children. In their beginning classes, they usually use signing and speech reading, or both. Most teachers in the classroom now simultaneously use signing and speech reading. A majority of public school programs for hearing impaired children use a whole-language approach that includes one of the exact sign systems such as Signing Exact English (SEE). However, American Sign Language (Amslan) is still widely used in many parts of the country. In addition to signing and speech reading, it is important that the teacher use other visual clues and props when presenting material to the children (e.g., pictures, puppets, expressive facial and body gestures).

Suggestions for Musical Interaction

The teacher should continuously consult with the auditory specialist about use and adaptation of music equipment and teaching techniques to meet the individual child's needs. The following ideas may be appropriate and useful for some children with hearing impairments.

- ◆ The teacher should use visual aids that communicate the topic or ideas within songs; puppets and story or pointing boards are most useful.

- ◆ When singing "Old MacDonald," rather than sign all the words of the song, the teacher can sign and lip-say only the name of each animal. (All children will want to participate in the fun of this action.) A child may also be invited to determine which animal all children will sing about by pointing to a prepared farm animal picture board.

The teacher can encourage a child to practice animal sounds by placing the child's hand on her throat to feel the vibrations produced by "oink," "moo," or "neigh" sounds. The child then places his hand on his own throat to imitate what was felt. This activity can be expanded to include key words from other songs.

The emphasis is on distinguishing tactilely the differences between the *production* of different sounds, and the *hearing* of them (combining tactile sensations with residual hearing, the level of hearing that is usually present to some degree in all but profoundly deaf children).

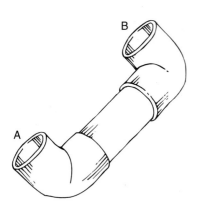

- ◆ The teacher may use instruments with large resonating chambers (such as autoharps and resonator bells) for the child's personal exploration and expression, as well as for accompanying songs and other musical activities. The sound vibrations become almost tactile in these instruments and can help the child make a connection between feeling and hearing.
- ◆ The teacher can use a large plastic tube or PVC pipe song phone to amplify sound. The teacher sings into one end (A) as the child holds the other end to her ear (B). The child immediately echoes by singing into (A) while continuing to hold (B) to her own ear.
- ◆ The open end of a small tub drum or bongo drum may be held over the child's ear while the teacher or the child gently taps on the drum head.
- ◆ The teacher can help the child sense sound vibrations by strumming an autoharp while holding the back of the instrument to the child's ear.

CHILDREN WITH LANGUAGE DELAY

Many at-risk children experience gaps in the normal acquisition of speech. Speech involves verbally expressing oneself and receiving information. Children must be able to function both in an expressive mode (speaking), including the articulation of speech sounds, and a receptive mode (listening). The unintelligible child who has difficulty forming the beginning and ending sounds of words may have expressive problems (inability to actually form and articulate the sounds) or may have receptive problems (inability to hear or perceive the differences in the sounds and thus to copy them properly). Nearly all problems for children with language delays are either expressive delays or receptive delays. With minimal additional planning, music time affords a variety of opportunities for children to more freely deal with language, thus improving their communication skills.

The teacher plays a musical game during group time. He is sensitive to the needs of two children within the group who are language delayed. The play is centered around the song "Teddy, Bear, Teddy Bear." (p. 97) The teacher gives each child a small, plush teddy bear. During the song, the children make the bear turn around and touch the ground as indicated in the lyrics. The teacher improvises an interlude in which language skills may be enhanced. He sings a two-tone chant (G, E):

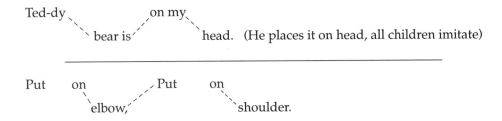

Ted-dy   bear is   on my   head.   (He places it on head, all children imitate)

Put   on   elbow,   Put   on   shoulder.

After several demonstrations in which body parts are identified by the teacher, individual children are invited to be the leader, deciding where to put the teddy bear. Michael, the unintelligible child (articulation delayed), sings, "U-ah-an [put on hand]." The teacher looks pleased with his response and replies, using one important word enunciated clearly, "Oh! **Hand**!" The teacher sings clearly to the other children:

Put   on   **hand**!

Marie is receptive; she hears the words but doesn't have the capacity to answer. She is expressively delayed. The teacher is prepared for this interaction with a small fixed-bar xylophone. Realizing that identifying many body parts is beyond Marie, the teacher modifies the game. He first sings and gestures up or down with the bear several times to model the game change for Marie. The song chants are repeated with an xylophone replacing the bear. The instrument is held high or low to represent up or down sounds as the song words indicate:

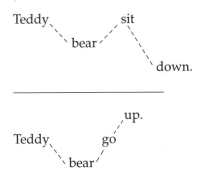

Teddy   bear   sit   down.

Teddy   bear   go   up.

Marie may answer with the words "down" or "up."

The inclusion of this interlude with the singing of the traditional song provides a brief opportunity for the teacher to focus on specific needs of a few special children within the group setting.

The Receptive Delayed Child

Many normally functioning young children have difficulty remembering where they have been or what an event entailed. However, children who persistently avoid a label or specific response may be receptive delayed (inability to auditorily comprehend). These children are usually very talkative but do not necessarily understand what they are saying. Asking multiple questions, rephrased in different ways, may help the child comprehend the question and answer it. Following is an example of a musical game that can be used with a receptive delayed child.

The teacher prepares a table play with several blocks arranged to form houses in a town. The teacher places a figure carrying an envelope in the town. She explains, "This is the man who brings the mail." The mailman knocks on all the doors to bring mail to the people who live in the houses. When he knocks, the people sing, "Who's that knocking at my window? Who's that knocking at my door?" (song on p. 178).

Teacher sings: "Who is knocking at the door?"

Receptive Delayed Child (RDC): "Him."

Teacher: "Who?"

RDC: "That guy!"

Teacher: "What is he called?"

RDC: (After additional probing) "Mailman."

Teacher: "What does he bring to the house?"

RDC: "That. Those things."

After hearing several altered questions, the child answers, "letters" or "mail."

The Articulation Delayed Child

Many articulation delayed children don't know what to do with their tongues, so using repeated words and sounds in song plays reinforces needed word practice. These children need oral stimulation such as tongue wiggling, clicking, and smacking. Songs with repetitive words or sounds become very useful in remediating this child's speech problem.

The song "Old Joe Clark" or its word parody "Clap Your Hands" (p. 96) not only use repetition in the first three words, but also use only one syllable, "la," throughout the entire chorus. Singing "la-la-la-la" is an excellent tongue-wiggling practice for these children.

The Language Delayed Child

Many songs and other music activities contain a great deal of repeated word play that provides excellent oral stimulation for language delayed children. A one-word toddler song such as "Kitty" (p. 93) is effective in articulation play because it repeats a single word (sounds stressed: k, t).

A parody song may be used to introduce new words to a familiar melody such as "Skip to My Lou." The child is involved in oral play such as smacking, clicking, tongue wiggling, and pursing his mouth to form special sounds.

> Kiss a little Miss (smack, smack, smack) . . .
> Kiss a little Mis-sy Mo, Mo!
>
> Click a little tongue (click, click, click) . . .
> Click a little tick-tack tongue. Tongue!
>
> Sing a little song (la, la la) . . .
> Sing a little la-la-la song. Song!
>
> Little baby sleeping (sh, sh, sh) . . .
> Little baby sleeping, sh. Sh!

The voice must be supported by proper air flow to produce words, thus musical games that involve such activities provide oral stimulation. For example, with the song "Jeremiah Blow the Fire" (p. 134), children hold their index finger upright as a pretend candle. They sing or produce "puffs" or "pps" sounds to blow the candle out, feeling the air on their fingertip candle.

Another "puffing" play is to make a sailboat by holding one hand palm up and suspending a soft tissue over the palm with the opposite hand. The teacher tells the children this is a boat and that it needs wind blowing on its sail to make it go. If the wind does not blow the sail, the boat cannot move. The teacher holds the sail to each child's mouth and invites him or her to help the boat go by blowing on the sail.

> Here's a little sailboat
> Sailing out to sea
> Along came a big wind
> And blew it home to me.

(Child blows on the tissue as the teacher moves the boat accordingly)

Another useful game is one that provides practice in producing a sustained air flow. First, the teacher demonstrates by blowing up a balloon and slowly letting the air escape. He then invites the children to become the balloon full of air and then to let the air out while making a continuous "sh-h-h-h-h" sound. He repeats the deflating balloon demonstration simultaneously as the children perform this sound. Next, he sets the balloon aside and invites the children to take a breath and hum/float a sound as the balloon's air is escaping: "See who can make their balloon very slowly go flat." He asks the children to take a breath and let it out while softly counting one, two, three, four. . . . They are to stop counting and be very quiet when they run out of air. "How far were you able to count?" Children may become quite competitive and strive to achieve the largest number on one breath.

Many specific speech problems can be addressed with musical play; we have discussed only a few here. The purpose of these examples has been to show that, with very little effort, musical play can be inoffensively extended to provide practice play for children with language problems while also promoting musical growth. Caregivers are reminded that speech is one of the most complex functions that the body performs—it requires coordinated motor skills, cognition, respiratory movement, and other physical activities. A means to better language skill is singing.

SUMMARY

The slow progress of children with special needs is often accompanied by frustration because of their inability to communicate easily or otherwise function. This intense frustration level often leads to apathy, misbehavior, or other antisocial responses. The more informed the teacher is about a child's specific problem, the greater is his or her understanding about what triggers these undesirable actions. At their best, these children are anxious to please and tend to be uncommonly patient, polite, and caring.

The child-centered music play approach described for typical young children can also be used to interact with special-needs children; that is, it is based on a child's developmental level and then introduces skills and understandings in small increments. Hands-on music play items are used to provide necessary concrete experiences from which understandings can evolve. Children with special needs require more time to interact with materials and ideas and may never achieve the mastery level of typical children. Our role is to help these children reach their greatest potential.

It is most gratifying to see the growth and social-emotional interaction of typical children who have had the opportunity to experience friendship with a child with special needs. The sharing and caring for one another is rewarding for everyone in the class. An inclusive approach in early childhood programs is most effective for promoting understanding about people who must live differently. Understanding that people with special needs are able to share and contribute is an important lifelong lesson for all to learn.

THINGS TO DO

1. Observe a public, private, or church school classroom in which a child(ren) with special needs has been placed. Become familiar with how the child functions and responds generally, not just musically.

    a. Briefly describe the nature of the child's impairment and the learning environment.

    b. Are music activities a part of this environment? If so, describe.

    c. How does the teacher accommodate this child's learning style?

    d. Do you feel the teacher effectively balances tending to the child with special needs and tending to other children in the classroom?

    e. How do classmates react to the inclusion of this child in their activities?

    f. Would you have interacted differently if you were the teacher?

    g. What clues has this observation provided for your "dos and don'ts" in planning a music session for children with special needs?

2. Choose one song that you feel would be useful for a language delayed child. Explain why you think the song would be effective.

NOTE

[1]Betty Welsbacher, "Meeting Needs: Music Education Experiences of Prekindergarten Children at Risk," in *Readings in Early Childhood Music Education*, eds. Barbara Andress and Linda Walker (Reston, VA: Music Educators National Conference, 1992), 92–98.

11

Multicultural Music in Early Childhood

A rich array of music representing many diverse cultures is available to teachers of young children. Some of the music represents the traditions of children within the teacher's own classroom, but more important, the music represents the diverse traditions of people with whom children will interact throughout their lives. A sensitivity to a culturally diverse world and understanding and interacting in an unbiased manner with all people are important lessons for young children.

Music of diverse cultures has been included in school curriculums for many years. Earlier, the chosen music, though not deliberately meant to offend, lacked authenticity and was often stereotypical. The 1920s and 1930s texts contained such stereotypical materials as "Hi-ya-ya-ya" Indian music; images of lackadaisical Mexicans dozing under oversized sombreros while strumming guitars; lyrics like "Old darkies, how my heart grows weary"; and contrived pentatonic music accompanied by such lyrics as "Wing Foo, China boy, upside down." Today, we are appalled that educators could ever have been so insensitive to cultural differences, so careless with the authenticity of ethnic music, and so unaware that they were actually reinforcing racial bias in our young people. Music educators were not alone in this misdeed; it was the accepted approach in general education and society as a whole.

Music educators now better understand and value the importance of music of other cultures and how effectively this literature can be introduced to children. The research of ethnomusicologists (a person who studies music of all peoples) has brought forth wonderful examples of authentic multicultural music that children can use for dancing, singing, playing ethnic instruments, or just listening. Typically, teachers presented this literature through topical units that featured various countries, for example, the music of Japan, Christmas around the World, or meeting instruments of the world. We are now aware that although the music is more authentic and appropriate, presenting it in unit form represents a "tourist approach." These short-term visits do little to help children understand the uniqueness of the people. Teachers are now challenged to include music of diverse populations as an integrated part of weekly activities, as well as for special study in in-depth units.

Our efforts now should focus on sharing the beauty and excitement found in music of diverse populations; understanding how and why their music is organized and performed; and promoting and developing children's understanding, tolerance, respect, and sensitivity toward people who are different from themselves.

Although it is important for children to understand differences among people, it is equally important that they understand the ways in which we are similar. Unity is as important as diversity. Striving to bring together people of diverse cultures to form and enrich the whole community is a noble goal.

The goal of multicultural education is:

First, to teach children to respect others' culture and values as well as their own; second, to help all children learn to function successfully in a multicultural, multiracial society; third, to develop a positive self-concept in those children who are most affected by racism—children of color; fourth, to help all children experience both their differences as culturally diverse people and their similarities as human beings in positive ways; and, fifth, to encourage children to experience people of diverse cultures working together as unique parts of a whole community. [1]

Multicultural Music in Today's Early Childhood Classroom

The music of various cultures should be used not only for topical units or certain holidays and events, it should permeate weekly activities throughout the year. Music experiences can become a significant part of antibias lessons. Children may play with manipulatives and visual representations of children of all colors, compare traditional Anglo songs performed in several languages, interact with authentic songs and instrumental performances from various cultures, and become aware of composers, conductors, and performers of various ethnic groups who have contributed significantly to the music we all enjoy. Music of many cultures may be used to teach about form, expressive controls, rhythm, and melody. In short, these ethnic selections can be used to teach musical understandings as well as traditional children's tunes have done.

Developmental and musical appropriateness of the literature and activities should remain a constant concern when introducing young children to multicultural music. The songs should be singable, the listening examples meaningful, and goals for playing the instruments achievable. Selecting appropriate multicultural literature for very young children is not always an easy task. One challenge is that the song's language may be different from the child's first language. Another challenge is that unique melodic and rhythmic patterns are not always as predictable to the listener whose ears are attuned to hearing only music from the Western culture.

The songs described in the next sections are representative of selections that have relatively simple language, melodic, and rhythmic challenges. They should be performed easily by young children. These examples are a potpourri of songs from diverse cultures that can be used daily, weekly, or for yearly events. We have made no attempt to represent all cultures. It is assumed that master teachers will seek out materials, performances, and community expertise from various ethnic groups to extend their rich musical resources.

Body Touch Games

Favorite songs during group music time often involve body touch games. Typical of these songs is "Clap Your Hands" (p. 96). Follow the singing of these familiar songs with this Hispanic game "Pon Pon Pon."

PON PON PON
Child's Pointing Game
Mexico, D.P.

Shared in the oral tradition by Maria Trinidad

Pon, pon, pon.   Pon, pon-i-pon.   Pon __ el-de-di-to   en la ma-ni-ta
Put, put, put.   Put, put-ty, put.   Put your lit-tle fin-ger   on your __ hand. __

2. . . . en la ca-ri-ta. (face)
3. . . . en la na-ri-ci-ta. (nose)
4. . . . en la o-re-ji-ta. (ear)
5. . . . en los o-ji-tos. (eyes)

"Pon Pon Pon," *Hispanic Music for Arizona Children,* B. Andress, ed., Arizona Early Childhood Music Collaborative Project, 1993. Used by permission.

The musical play is for the children to sing and rhythmically tap their right index finger in their left palm while singing "Pon, pon pon. Pon pon-i-pon. Pon el dedito en la. . . ." On the final word, the children point to other body parts named in the song: carita, naricita, orejita, and ojitos. The teacher encourages the children to sing the words in both Spanish and English. Spanish-speaking children are invited to teach classmates the Spanish words for new body parts that can be added to the song play.

For extended play, the game may be played with a partner. Each partner taps his own palm, but points to the other child's face, nose, ear, or eyes.

Infant Games

"Pon Pon Pon" can also be played by a parent and infant. The parent gently guides the baby's finger to tap on the palm and then points to the designated body parts.

The "Baby Walking Song" is sung by Apache mothers to encourage their babies to walk. The mother or another helper holds the baby's hands as she takes

BABY WALKING SONG
Traditional White River Mountain Apache

Shared by Bonnie Lewis

Gah   bi-zhaa-zhé _____   ch'in a' chi'i zhoosh.
Oh,   lit-tle rab-bit, __   walks to moth-er.

Shíí   ch'éh   Osb beeh.   Woł   Woł
Look!   Look!   For milk.   Slurp!   Slurp!

"Baby Walking Song," *Apache Music for Arizona Children,* B. Andress, ed., Arizona Early Childhood Music Collaborative Project, 1994. Used by permission.

Rough pronunciation guide: Gah, bi-shaw-shay; Chin a chi-zhoosh (repeat); Shee shay oshb beeh. Whooz. Whooz.

her first steps. For this activity, a large rag doll and a small drum with a beater are needed. The teacher invites the children to help the baby learn to walk. As the children stand in a circle, one child holds the doll, helping it to walk, as the other children sing the song both in Apache and English. A soft, steady drum beat may be played by the teacher to accompany the singing. The drum is played during the interludes (time between verses). The doll is walked, then handed to the next child in the circle. The song is repeated until all children have walked the baby.

Lullabies

The literature is replete with lullabies from many cultures. Children may sing lullabies from other cultures when they pretend to rock babies or use dolls, or the adult may sing them during rest time. The classroom should be stocked with dolls of color whether or not the class includes children of color.

Duerme Pronto (Go to Sleep)
Spanish Folk Song

Duer - me pron - to, ni - ño mí - o, duer - me pron - to sin llo - rar,
Go to sleep, my lit - tle ba - by, Go to sleep and do not cry.

que es tás en los bra - zos de tu ma - dre que te va a can - tar.
Moth - er's arms will hold you gen - tly While she sings a lul - la - by.

"Duerme Pronto," *Holt Music—Grade K*, 1988. Holt, Rinehart and Winston. Used by permission.

For extended play this song may be used when children are beginning to play simple melodies on Orff-type xylophones. The pitches F, G, A, C are repeated upward three times and then played back down, A, G, F.

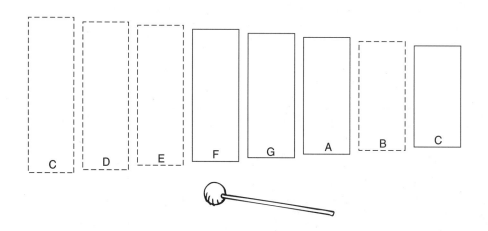

NINNI, BABA (HUSH, MY BABY)
Folk Song from India

Nin - ni, Ba - ba,   Nin - ni, __   ma - khan ro - ti   chi - ni
Hush, my ba - by: Come, Sleep,   bring-ing qui - et   slum-ber,

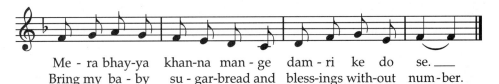

Me - ra bhay-ya   khan-na man - ge   dam - ri   ke   do   se. __
Bring my ba - by   su - gar-bread and   bless-ings with-out   num-ber.

"Ninni, Baba," ©1960 *East West Songs,* World Around Songs, Inc., 20 Colberts Creek Road, Burnsville, NC 28714. Used by permission.

Animals and Birds

Young children are fascinated by jungle animals. The teacher may include authentic African music as a part of the lesson when presenting music such as "The Royal March of the Lion" from *The Carnival of the Animals* by Saint-Saëns (lesson suggestion on p. 153) or a song from the Disney movie *The Lion King.* Singing an authentic African song about a lion and hippopotamus can be exciting, especially when the limited words are easily pronounced and repeated often as in the Zulu song "Ingonyama." In this song, people argue about whether their brave leader should be compared to the lion or to an even greater creature, the hippopotamus.

INGONYAMA
Zulu

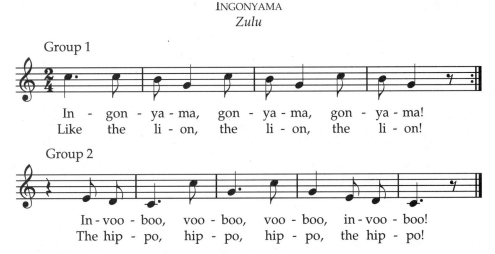

Group 1

In - gon - ya - ma,   gon - ya - ma,   gon - ya - ma!
Like   the   li - on,   the   li - on,   the   li - on!

Group 2

In - voo - boo,   voo - boo,   voo - boo,   in - voo - boo!
The hip - po,   hip - po,   hip - po,   the hip - po!

"Ingonyama," *African Songs,* World Around Songs, Inc., 20 Colberts Creek Road, Burnsville, NC 28714. Used by permission.

In "Chichi Papa," a group of birds is being taught to sing by a leader bird. If necessary, the performance of this song can be simplified by asking the children to sing only on the words "chichi papa." The remaining phrases are sung by the adult.

Chichi Papa
Japan-Hawaii

Chi - chi pa - pa, chi - pa - pa,
su - su - me - no gak - ko - no sen - se - wa,
mu - chi - o fu - ri, fu - ri chi - pa - pa,
chi - chi pa - pa, chi - pa - pa.

"Chichi Papa," *Fun and Folk Songs,* World Around Songs, Inc., 20 Colberts Creek Road, Burnsville, NC 28714. Used by permission.

On the Farm

A variety of songs about farm animals are an important part of the early childhood song repertoire. In addition to traditional farm songs such as "The Farmer in the Dell" or "Old MacDonald," farm songs of other cultures should be performed.

Los Pollitos
Guayaquil, Ecuador

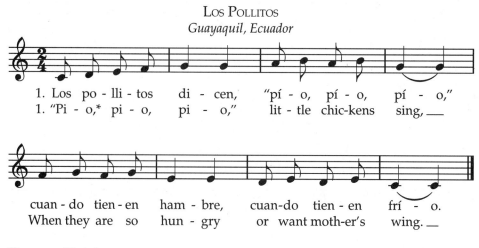

1. Los po - lli - tos di - cen, "pí - o, pí - o, pí - o,"
1. "Pi - o,* pi - o, pi - o," lit - tle chic - kens sing, __

cuan - do tien - en ham - bre, cuan - do tien - en frí - o.
When they are so hun - gry or want moth - er's wing. __

*Pronounced Peé-oh.

Children enjoy singing these Apache words to an already familiar song.

HASTĮĮN MACDONALD BI KÍ YAA
Apache

Has - tįįn Mac Don - ald   bi   kí   yaa.   Hey   nay   nay   ya   ho.

Di   kí   yaa   yee má - ga - shi   na - kai.   Hey   nay   nay   ya   ho.
(cow)

Moo   moo   hiłts'ag.   Moo   moo   hiłts'ag.   Ku   moo,   lu   moo   Dahot' é - hé   moo   moo.

Has - tįįn   Mac   Don - ald   bi   kí   yaa.   Hey   nay   nay   ya   ho.

2. Di kí yaa yee gúchi (pig) nakai
    Hey nay nay ya ho.
    Oik, oink, hiłts'ag
    Oik, oink, hiłts'ag
    Ku oink, lu oink
    Dahot' éhé oink, oink!
    Hastįįn Mac Donald bi kí yaa.
    Hey nay nay ya ho.

3. Di kí yaa yee gídí (cat) nakai
    Hey nay nay ya ho.
    Meow, meow hiłts'ag
    Meow, meow hiłts'ag
    Ku meow, lu meow
    Dahot' éhé meow, meow!
    Hastįįn Mac Donald bi kí yaa.
    Hey nay nay ya ho.

4. Gúshé (dog)

5. Nal'eeł (duck)

"Hastiin MacDonald Bi Ki Yaa," *Apache Music for Arizona Children,* B. Andress, ed., Arizona Early Childhood Music Collaborative Project, 1994. Used by permission.

Weather

The song "It's Raining, It's Pouring" (p. 135) is performed easily by children because the melody is simple and accompaniments can be played on xylophones or wood blocks. In place of the traditional English version, this Mexican version may be sung.

Children may wish to add rain sounds as an introduction, during the interludes, or as a special ending (coda) to the music. The teacher prepares the xylophone by marking the pitches to be used with masking tape: C, D, E, G, A, c'. Children may play random pitter-patter sounds or make up a little tune.

QUÉ LLUEVA!
Children's Song
Mexico, D. P.

¡Qué llue - va! ¡Qué llue - va! la chi qui ta di - cien - do los
It's rain - ing, It's rain - ing; Th-e little girl is say - ing; The

pa - ja - ri - tos can - tan, las nu - bes se le - ran - tan,
lit - tle birds are sing - ing, All the clouds are leav - ing,

¡Qué sí! ¡Qué no! ¡Qué cai - ga el cha - pu - rr-ón!
Oh, yes! Oh, no! Oh, let the rain fall down!

¡Qué sí! ¡Qué no! ¡Qué cai - ga el cha - pu - rr-ón!
Oh, yes! Oh, no! Oh, let the rain fall down!

Literal Translation:
It's raining! It's raining!
The little girl is saying
The little birds are singing,
All the clouds are leaving.
Oh, yes! Oh, no!
Oh, let the downpour fall.

"Que Llueva!" *Hispanic Music for Arizona Children*, B. Andress, ed., Arizona Early Childhood Music Collaborative Project, 1993. Used by permission.

Dramatic Play

Versions of stories such as *Snow White* or *Sleeping Beauty* are in the literature of several cultures. Children can play the roles of various characters as all sing the song. The following song examples have many verses, which might seem overwhelming for young learners, but the songs are doable because the words within each verse are repeated many times. The teacher introduces each new verse, then the children echo one of the words in the verse.

Teacher: Once there was a princess,

Children: a princess, a princess . . .

THE SLEEPING PRINCESS
Swedish Folk Ballad

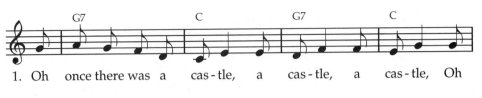

1. Oh once there was a cas-tle, a cas-tle, a cas-tle, Oh

once there was a cas-tle, long a - go.

2. The guards were at the portals . . . long long ago.
3. The King and Queen they lived there . . .
4. They had a little daughter . . .
5. She was a royal Princess . . .
6. The Princess had a party . . .
7. The Princess was a spinning . . .
8. She prick'd her little finger . . .
9. The castle was enchanted . . .
10. One hundred years they slept there . . .
11. The bushes grew so slowly . . .
12. And thorns grew thick around them . . .
13. A handsome Prince came riding . . .
14. The Prince cut down the bushes . . .
15. He wandered in the castle and found the pretty Princess . . .
16. He woke the pretty Princess . . .
17. He asked her then to wed him . . .
18. They had a royal wedding . . .

An Ecuadorian version of this dramatic play is follows.

ROSITA
Guayaquil, Ecuador

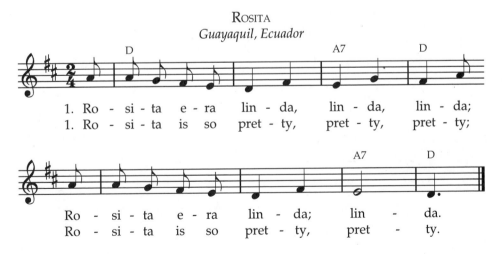

1. Ro - si - ta e - ra lin - da, lin - da, lin - da;
1. Ro - si - ta is so pret - ty, pret - ty, pret - ty;

Ro - si - ta e - ra lin - da; lin - da.
Ro - si - ta is so pret - ty, pret - ty.

2. Rosita tiene cuidado, cuidado, cuidado . . .
   Rosita is in danger, danger, danger . . .

3. Ya viene hada fea, fea, fea . . .
   Now comes the witch* so wicked, wicked, wicked . . .

4. Cien años dormir debeis, debeis, debeis . . .
   A century sleeps the fair maid, fair maid, fair maid . . .

5. Todos duermen con Rosita, Rosita, Rosita . . .
   They slumber with Rosita, Rosita, Rosita . . .

6. Se crece el seto, seto, seto . . .
   Then see how high the hedge grows, hedge grows, hedge grows . . .

7. Ya viene joven príncipe, príncipe, príncipe . . .
   Here comes the prince so handsome, handsome, handsome . . .

8. Rosita será mi reina, reina, reina . . .
   My queen will be Rosita, Rosita, Rosita . . .

9. Bailemos todos felices, felices, felices . . .
   Now we are dancing gaily, gaily, gaily . . .

*Substitute reina (queen) if use of the word *witch* is inappropriate.

Pride, Freedom, and Peace

The teacher plays a recording of or sings "America the Beautiful" and discusses the idea that people of different colors, shapes, and sizes from around the world came to live in America. The teacher adds that the people have different ways of living and celebrating life, and that we are very proud of our country because it is made up of these many different people.

The illustrated book *People* by Peter Spier is an excellent resource for introducing "America the Beautiful" because it depicts the many physical ways that people are different.

Another way to help children better understand the meaning of the words is to create visuals to accompany the song. The teacher can use sketches, tearsheets from magazines, posters, or photos, and display each picture as the descriptive phrase is sung.

AMERICA THE BEAUTIFUL

Words by K. Bates
Music by S. Ward

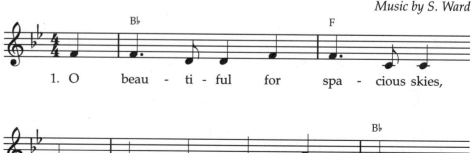

For pur - ple moun - tain maj - es - ties

A - bove the fruit - ed plain!

A - mer - i - ca, A - mer - i - ca,

God shed his grace on thee,

And crown thy good with broth - er - hood

From sea to shin - ing sea.

The book *America the Beautiful* by K. Bates and N. Waldman beautifully illustrates the lyrics of the song by depicting many wondrous sights from sea to sea, including our finest national parks.

People of all cultures sing songs about national pride and how they value freedom. All wish for peace.

ZUM GALI GALI
Israeli

Introduction

Zum ga - li ga - li ga - li, Zum ga - li ga - li,

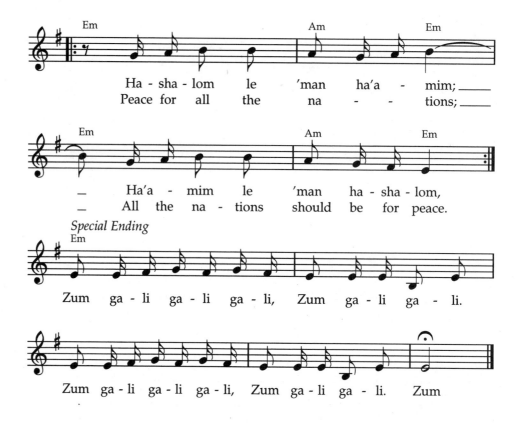

Ha - sha - lom   le   'man   ha'a - mim; _____
Peace   for   all   the   na - - tions; _____

_ Ha'a - mim   le   'man   ha - sha - lom,
_ All   the   na - tions   should   be   for   peace.

Special Ending

Zum   ga - li   ga - li   ga - li,   Zum   ga - li   ga - li.

Zum   ga - li   ga - li   ga - li,   Zum   ga - li   ga - li.   Zum

Singing a song in another language gives a child who speaks that language a sense of self-esteem. It is fun for him or her to be the one who truly understands the words and their pronunciation and to recognize a familiar family song. Songs in other languages do not, however, provide an understanding of the people. Multicultural music experiences need to go beyond singing different-language songs to why and how these songs are important to the people who sing them.

Exploring Instruments of Other Cultures

Diverse cultures use instruments that range from simple to exotic. Within the United States, many unique folk and traditional instruments are of great interest to young children—for example, the southern Appalachian dulcimer; the rhythmic Jumping Jack; Native American drums, rattles, shell and bell leg adornments; flutes; Hawaiian ukuleles; and small Polynesian percussion instruments. Ethnic instruments include Mexican guitarones, guitars, maracas, bongos, congos, claves; African slit log drums, cabasas, M'biras; and Oriental gongs and finger cymbals.

Young children can explore the shapes and sounds of various instruments and, in many instances, use them to accompany songs. Children will be interested to know that a musical instrument in some cultures is more than just a sound source, it can also be a revered symbol. Such an instrument is the Native American drum. The drum is a thing of nature, made of a hollowed-out tree stump and an animal skin. The teacher may want to explain to the children that the Pow

Wow drum is not just a musical instrument. The drum is to be treated with respect. The beat of the drum closely resembles a human heartbeat, and it is referred to as "the heartbeat of mother earth."[2]

Playing an ethnic instrument may be difficult for young children, just as playing traditional classroom or orchestral instruments can be. They should be encouraged to touch, pluck, strike, and explore the sounds of authentic instruments, which may be acquired from music and/or import stores. When obtaining ethnic instruments is not possible, other more accessible instruments may be adapted to replicate their sounds. For example, some Native American drums can be easily prepared for classroom use. The Apache water drum was originally made from an animal skin tightly affixed to a clay jug. Today, the clay pot is replaced by a metal pot.

Making and Playing an Apache Water Drum

Materials needed include the following:

◆ *Resonating Chamber*—deep metal pot approximately 8 by 12 inches (obtain from restaurant supply store)
◆ *Drum Head*—leather chamois skin (from auto supply store)
◆ *Tension*—two 1-inch innertube or large, thick rubber bands

To assemble the drum:

1. Soak the chamois skin in water. Wring the sides to remove excess water.
2. Pour the water approximately ¼ inch deep into the bottom of the drum.
3. Tightly stretch the wet chamois skin over the open end of the drum and secure it in position with the innertube rubber bands (wrap each rubber band twice).
4. Continue to stretch the skin by tugging and adjusting the rubber bands.

The drum head should be played when it is damp. The child grips the drum with one hand by the excess folds of the chamois skin. With the opposite hand, she holds a bent twig beater (a small-headed mallet may be substituted for the twig beater).

The drum is used to accompany singing and dancing. A constant steady-beat pattern is used. The singer's words often indicate a change in the dance, but the beat of the drum remains constant.

Playing a Stringed Instrument

The Japanese koto is a large, expensive, multistringed instrument that is placed on the floor. The performer sits on the floor, pressing the strings with one hand while strumming or plucking with the other. Replicate the idea of playing this instrument. Place pictures of kotos in the environment. The size and sound of the instrument can be discussed and a recorded example played if available.

The four strings on a dulcimer or ukulele can be tuned to two pitches: A (doubled) and B (doubled). The instrument is placed on the floor in front of the seated performer. An ostinati (repeated pattern) is played on the strings by a child to accompany the teacher as she sings "Sakura." Other children may listen or use paper fans to improvise their own traditional Japanese-style dance as the music is performed.

SAKURA (CHERRY TREES)
Japanese Folk Song

English by K. F. R.

(Repeat throughout the song)

A   A   B   A   A   B

Using Music to Promote Understanding and Respect

Much has been written about integrating antibias programs within the curriculum for young children. The authors stress that very young children are already beginning to form lifelong attitudes about stereotyping gender, race, age, or physical impairment. Children at the preschool and early elementary levels are not too young to deal with these concerns. Even the most subtle actions of adult models or objects in the learning environment can influence young children's positive or negative evaluations. Including antibias materials within the program does not just happen; teachers must make a conscious effort to structure the environment to include activities and materials that address antibias concerns.

SUGGESTIONS FOR ANTIBIAS ACTIVITIES

Following are some suggestions for incorporating antibias activities into a curriculum. The teacher should use abundant visual aids depicting diverse images of children and families: disabled, gender, family groupings, people of color. The NAEYC publication, *Anti-Bias Curriculum, Tools for Empowering Young Children* by

L. D. Sparks, contains many suggestions for initiating discussions about feelings and concerns children may have regarding diverse cultures.[3] Sparks' suggestion for using "persona" dolls is excellent because the dolls place focus on a culture or concern rather than on an individual child within the classroom. Personna dolls such as "Maria" can introduce a Hispanic song; a physically disabled "mother in a wheelchair" can sing a lullaby; or the "African-American family" may be used to play out "The Farmer in the Dell."

Hand and finger puppets depicting diverse populations are available from most teaching supply vendors. These puppets may be used to guide songs such as "If You're Happy and You Know It." Puppets depicting, for example, African-American or Asian children are used to clap hands, cry, sleep, or otherwise depict mood changes as indicated in the song lyrics. It is important that characters representing all races be used rather than just white characters.

The teacher should depict the lives and music of diverse cultures as an integral part of today's society rather than merely historically. Native American children do not necessarily dress in traditional regalia and dance at Pow Wows. These children also wear blue jeans, tennis shoes, T-shirts, and enjoy rap music.

Materials should be sought that not only allow correlation between literature and music, but also deal with diverse populations. For example, the book *Silent Lotus* by J. Lee evolves around a young girl named Lotus who lives in a Far Eastern country. Lotus is auditorily impaired, and when she is rejected by other children, she finds great joy in dancing. She ultimately becomes one of the finest dancers in the king's court.

After hearing this story, the children can create their own version of a Balinese court dance by placing their hands in a lotus bloom position and using other gestures illustrated in the book. The dance may be accompanied by recorded music such as "Mesem" from *Music for the Balinese Shadow Play*. This gamelan music has many pitched gong sounds that ring on and on. Slow, gentle, flowing movements are used as the children change arm positions and sway gently side to side. This lesson provides many opportunities for learning about another culture and for becoming aware of the challenges confronting a child who is auditorily impaired.

Ben's Trumpet by Rachel Isadora is a children's book about a young, black inner-city boy who wants nothing more than to play a trumpet. His dream is realized when a jazz musician comes to his rescue. This is a good opportunity to introduce the ideas of how members of the jazz combo come together to introduce a melodic idea, and then each instrumentalist improvises on that melody to complete the set. At this time, pictures of successful African-American jazz musicians such as Louis Armstrong (Satchmo), Fats Waller, and Bessie Smith can be displayed. These pictures become more meaningful when brief examples of each musician's music are heard.

Music doesn't always have to be presented in a formal lesson. The teacher can set the tone for a mid-morning group time reading of *Ben's Trumpet* by playing one of Satchmo's recordings as the children arrive at school in the morning.

The Enormous Watermelon by B. Parkes and J. Smith is a delightful book about Old Mother Hubbard who seeks the help of other nursery rhyme characters to harvest an enormous watermelon. The story is great fun and provides an opportunity to sing nursery rhyme tunes. There is a similar African-American folk tale called *The Enormous Yam*. The tale is about an African-American farmer who raises an enormous yam so large that he cannot harvest it alone. Characters come along one by one, and they all work together to pull the yam out of the ground. As each new character tries to help, the song phrase is sung.

The story ends with all the helpers eating an enormous yam pie. The retelling of this story is a good opportunity to cast the helpful characters as multiracial, with the moral being that all people can work together to successfully complete a task.

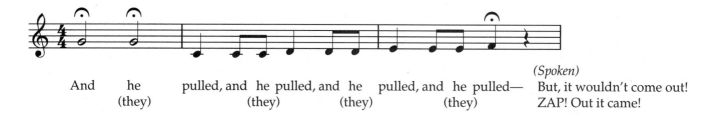

And   he   pulled, and he pulled, and he   pulled, and he pulled—   *(Spoken)*
(they)   (they)   (they)   (they)   But, it wouldn't come out!
                                                                                          ZAP! Out it came!

The teacher who is serious about mounting an effective antibias or multicultural curriculum can gather many hands-on materials and directed teaching objects. One effective way to organize these materials is to create "culture kits." These kits are boxes with labels that indicate the contents, such as "Hispanic," "African-American," or a special topic. The boxes contain the teacher's collection of materials for a given culture. For example, a Hispanic kit may contain pictures of traditional and contemporary Hispanic people; regalia (clothing for dress up or dancing such as serapes, hats, fans, lace scarves); maracas; small bongos; guiros; claves; music recordings (mariachi music, folk dance, the story of *Pedro El Y Lobo*); small folk art examples (pottery, carvings, tin work, silver); small flag of Mexico; song collections; children's books; pictures of food; and crepe paper fiesta flowers and decorations.

SUMMARY

Music is a powerful tool in shaping attitudes and expressing innermost feelings. Music has always been used by all cultures to pass down traditions and express pride in race and nation. Sharing music of many cultures provides insights about the history and emotions of those people. Young children are capable of understanding, performing, and appreciating music of diverse cultures when it is selected and presented in a developmentally acceptable manner. Young children have not yet learned to reject strange-sounding instruments or melodies; their curiosity still allows for an openness and unbiased exploration of music and the people who create it.

The use of music in an antibiased program to help students understand differences in people is an approach that should be cultivated in today's classrooms. Teachers should find many ways to include not only traditional and contemporary music of various cultures, but also classroom activities that incorporate multiracial perspectives. It is important to include visual representations that depict people of many races, both genders, all ages, and with various impairments in music-making tasks. Teachers must consciously plan experiences that reflect a system that values how individuals are different and yet, in many ways, the same.

Music is an important tool to help children become more sensitive and to develop caring attitudes. Creating an awareness that the music of diverse populations is beautiful, exciting, and full of wonderment is a worthy goal for an early childhood program.

THINGS TO DO

1. Select two songs that reflect diverse cultures that you think young children can sing, play on an instrument, or move expressively to. Describe how you would present the songs to the children, and discuss their expected response.

2. Make a brief list of successful contemporary musical performers, conductors, or composers of color who are good role models for young children. Explain why their music or performance is effective.

3. Research children's literature to find one children's book that can be used both for its music or movement content and its sensitivity to antibias concerns. One example is a singable, illustrated version of "Mary Had a Little Lamb" by B. McMillan that depicts Mary as an African-American child and the teacher as a male rather than a female.

4. Compile one culture kit that you think will provide effective resources to help the children in your classroom understand a particular group of people.

REFERENCE

Native American Music—Canyon Records, 834 N. Seventh Ave., Phoenix, AZ 85016.

NOTES

[1]F. E. Kendall, *Diversity in the Classroom: A Multicultural Approach to the Education of Young Children* (New York: Teachers College, Columbia University, 1983), 3.

[2]*Native Mosaic: Drum, Flute, Song* (Phoenix, AZ: The Heard Museum; and The Phoenix Symphony).

[3]Louise Derman-Sparks et al., *Anti-Bias Curriculum: Tools for Empowering Young Children* (Washington, DC: National Association for the Education of Young Children, 1989).

12

Integrating Music throughout the Curriculum

Understanding, valuing, and enjoying music are the major goals of musical experiences for young children. We are foremost concerned that experiencing music for music's sake be a worthy curricular goal. However, as an integrative force throughout various curriculum areas, music plays a significant role for all learning. Such integration signifies that music does not stand alone; it is part of people's total experience.

We have already referred to music that permeates young children's daily experiences as permeable learning (Chapter 4, p. 58). Permeable learning and integrated learning are similar, but different enough to warrant their separate labels. A permeable learning experience is more spontaneous in nature and often occurs with somewhat less deliberate planning, whereas integrated learning often requires deliberate action, distinct resources, and communication among various members of the teaching staff. There is no doubt, however, that both the permeable and integrated approaches are closely aligned conceptually and as systems for delivering learning experiences to children.

An integrative or permeable learning approach provides an additional source in the system for communicating how music (1) is used as a means to creatively express innermost thoughts, (2) flows throughout daily lives of people in various times and places, and (3) is a significant tool for better understanding extra-musical ideas.

Creative Expression of Innermost Thoughts

The class is reading about threatened environments. During class time, the children create a poem about the importance of the trees in the rain forest. The poem is taken to the music class, where a musical setting is created to help express the words.

The children snap their fingers, slap their thighs, and stamp their feet to create ever-increasing raindrops that abruptly end in a deadly silence when the trees are all cut down and the rain no longer comes. The children create a pictorial score of their rain music.

The poem and musical score are taken to the art class, where pictures are drawn to further express the children's concerns. All materials are then returned to the homeroom, where the teacher binds the works into a big book for future reference and enjoyment of the children.

Music in Time and Place

Mary Pautz, a member of the curriculum planning team for the Milwaukee Symphony Orchestra's Arts in Community Education (ACE), described the following "time and place" activity through an integrated curricular approach.

Picture in your mind a classroom transformed into the continent of Africa—a desert, a rain forest, and a savanna. Animals created in art class peer out of their natural habitats. We can feel the sand under our feet, the rain forest trees towering over our heads, and the tall savanna grass rustling as we pass. Welcome to Africa! Share the children's experiences of choosing and using Swahili names (in place of their own); printing Adinkra cloth vests; weaving kente cloth mats; creating pasta necklaces; painting masks on our windows; taking safaris to the zoo, the public museum, and the art museum; sharing exceptional African and African-American children's literature; welcoming guests into their classroom to teach them about Kwanza, Ethiopia, and African-American traditions; composing an African poem in Spanish, complete with instrumentation; experiencing Kwanza, a seven-day African-American celebration of life; listening to music by Duke Ellington and William Grant Still; and participating in an unforgettable experience with an African drummer/storyteller.

Music as a Tool for Understanding Extra-Musical Ideas

A musical experience may initiate an idea for another study focus or enrich learnings already introduced as a part of another curricular activity.

The children are playing in the "store area" with its shelves of pretend merchandise such as small cereal boxes, milk cartons, and canned goods. The checkout counter with its cash register and play money are in place, and a shopper is gathering items in a small shopping cart. Much dialogue is exchanged about how much each item costs. Group music time immediately follows the free play experience. The teacher introduces a silly song that focuses on money.

MAMA GAVE ME A NICKEL
Traditional

Ma - ma gave me a nick-el, to buy a pick-le. I
did-n't buy a pick-le, I bought some chew-in' gum!

Chorus:
Mm-mm-mm-mm-mm-chewin' gum, mm-mm-mm chewin' gum.
Mm-mm-mm-mm-mm-chewin' gum, mm-mm-mm chewin' gum.

2. Mama gave me a dime to buy a lime.
   I didn't buy a lime. I bought some chewin' gum.

3. Mama gave me a dollar to buy a collar.
   I didn't buy a collar. I bought some chewin' gum.

The children make exaggerated chewing motions as they sing the chorus of the song. The words "bubble gum" are substituted for "chewin' gum" on the third verse. A special ending (coda) is planned, where the children pretend to blow a large bubble that explodes when a loud thump on the drum is heard.

All laugh at their silly song, then the teacher presents a problem-solving game by showing the children two nickels and one dime. She chants:

Two nickels make a dime
Two nickels make a dime
Shopping time, sing a rhyme
Two nickels make a dime.

"If I spend a nickel to buy one piece of chewin' gum, how many pieces of chewin' gum can I buy with a dime?" "If I spend a nickel to buy one brontosaurus, how many . . .?" "If I spend a nickel to buy one strawberry, how many . . .?"

In subsequent sessions, the teacher uses the same song with other coin values: "Mama gave me a penny to buy a 'Jenny'" (pointing to a child). "Mama gave me a quarter to buy a pointer" (show pointer finger).

These examples of an integrated approach demonstrate that the learning experience may be guided by one teacher or through the collaborative efforts of several area specialists. Whomever has the responsibility for teaching, he or she must remember that an effective integrated curriculum goes beyond the use of, for example, the "Mexican Hat Dance" to study Mexico or singing a toothbrush song for a dental health unit. Effective integration occurs when children are involved in a process that combines skills and understandings that are acquired in various areas of study.

Integrated Curriculum Activities

An integrated curriculum includes art, dance, drama, health, language arts, math, music, physical education, reading, science, and social studies. The combined content is developmentally appropriate, ensuring that children continue to effectively develop their social, personal, perceptual, and thinking skills.

The following examples of activities integrate one or more curricular areas to form meaningful experiences for young children. The suggested activities may be taught by one person or divided among several members of the teaching staff.

INTEGRATED CURRICULUM FOCUS: ART, MUSIC, MOVEMENT, LANGUAGE ARTS, AND SOCIAL STUDIES

Theme: Community Helpers and Big Machines Build Our Towns

Young children have a fascination with backhoes, road graders, cement trucks, and other heavy machinery. Children often insist that parents pull off the road to watch diggers in action.

The teacher can prepare to focus on how machines help us build roads, bridges, and buildings by making available resource books, videos, and posters about heavy-equipment vehicles. Following are some useful children's books on this theme:

Korman, J. *Tonka Working Hard with the Mighty Loader.* Pawtucket, RI: Scholastic, 1993.

Hughes, F. *Tonka Working Hard with the Mighty Mixer.* Pawtucket, RI: Scholastic, 1993.

McNaught, H. *The Truck Book.* New York: Random House, 1978.

Scarry, R. *Cars and Trucks and Things That Go.* New York: Golden Press, 1974.

A videotape that shows heavy-construction equipment moving boulders and grading roads is *Road to Construction Ahead* (Focus Video Production, 1991). This tape's narration, sights, and sounds of the machines hold the children's avid attention.

The teacher may discuss the big machines' actions and invite the children to draw pictures of objects the big machines help build. Posters of earth movers, graders, front loaders, and cranes can be displayed. Children can place the pictures they have just drawn on a bulletin board near their favorite construction vehicle.

A recording of ponderous music such as "The Steel Foundry" from *Symphony of Machines* by A. Mossolov can be played. The teacher initially invites each child to move to the music like a big machine. When the children are ready for cooperative play, they may be asked to move with a partner or within a larger group to make one big machine—the up and down parts of the loader, the wheels, or the pusher/puller. Children may wish to work in contrary motion with one pushing and the other pulling. A very large machine may be created by the class as, one by one, each child adds a part to the whole.

Another activity is to have the children make big books about diggers, movers, and haulers. For one book, the teacher asks the children to say words that express how the heavy equipment moves: up and down, back and forth, round and round. The teacher writes the ideas on several pages, placing the words so that they depict suggested motions (e.g., round and round may be written in a spiral).

For another type of book, the children are asked to think up words that express the sounds the equipment makes, such as "thud," "thump," "squeak," "crunch," and "beep." Thump and thud words may be thick and heavy while squeak and beep words may be small and squiggly.

Additional big books might describe the look of the machines. If desired, the teacher can add pictures, bind the books, and place them in the classroom resource library.

INTEGRATED CURRICULUM FOCUS: MUSIC, EXPRESSIVE MOVEMENT, AND THE VISUAL ARTS

Theme: Fantasy

For this theme, the teacher displays a print of the painting *Green Violinist* by Chagall and discusses the uniqueness of the violinist, dog, and men who appear to float above the rooftops. The teacher explains that this could not really happen, and that the artist was sharing his ideas of fantasy. Together, the teacher and children make a list of ideas for fantasy pictures from which the children will choose one to create. Examples include toothbrushes growing on trees, a chair with wings, houses floating on clouds, boats walking down the street, a box with feet, or flowers growing out of the sun.

While displaying the children's completed pictures, the teacher suggests the idea that fantasy pictures often have a dream-like quality and invites the children to play with dream-like ideas. For example, they might walk and gesture as if they are in a dream or fantasy land (slow motion or faster than normal); create music to accompany the walk [sustained ringing sounds (with soft gongs or rubbing cymbals) or dissonant pitched resonator bells or metallophones (Fs and F♯s and Bs and B♭ played at the same time]; or perform this dream-like fantasy for others.

INTEGRATED CURRICULUM FOCUS: MUSIC, MOVEMENT, ART, SCIENCE, AND LANGUAGE ARTS

Theme: Imaginary and Real Creatures

While the children listen to a composition such as *Banshee* by Henry Cowell, they are to think of an imaginary creature. The teacher prompts them with questions such as "How does it move?" "How big is it?" "What does it eat?"

The class is divided into three groups. Each child receives a large piece of newsprint paper and colored pens. Each group draws parts of the creature (Group 1 draws the head, Group 2 draws the body, and Group 3 draws the legs). Then the children select the head of one, the body of another, and legs of a third and assemble an imaginary creature. Each assembled creature can be modified or unified by group decision. Then creatures are mounted on a large piece of paper. Throughout this activity, the children periodically listen to the recording. The new creatures are discussed, and each child is asked to write or otherwise contribute one or two sentences about the creature. The teacher reads the sentences as the creature pictures are displayed.

Now the children explore vocal sounds and movements for the imaginary creatures, such as sustained or choppy "oh's, ah's, ee's" or "zing, bing, ting's". The children create these sounds at will, so the music will have many dissonant sounds. The teacher can accompany the vocal sounds with continuous rubbing of sand blocks. A sound and movement composition can be created to accompany the pictures and descriptive sentences.

The teacher can also explore reference books for pictures of real creatures that are unique in appearance such as bugs, beetles, starfish, or jellyfish.

Idea from an Arizona Comprehensive/Integrated Arts Strategy.

INTEGRATED CURRICULUM FOCUS: MUSIC, ART, AND GEOMETRIC SHAPES

Theme: A Classroom Art Exhibit in the Style of Mondrian

Piet Mondrian painted pictures with simple geometric shapes divided by bold black lines. To play out the theme, the teacher obtains a poster-size print of a Mondrian painting such as *Composition*. He reproduces this painting by cutting out construction paper geometric shapes (squares and rectangles) in the same sizes and colors that appear in the original art. He then makes a puzzle board with strips of black tape that replicate the dividing lines in the painting and uses the geometric shapes as puzzle pieces.

The teacher places the Mondrian poster, puzzle board, and geometric shapes in a play area and invites the children to complete the puzzle so that it matches the

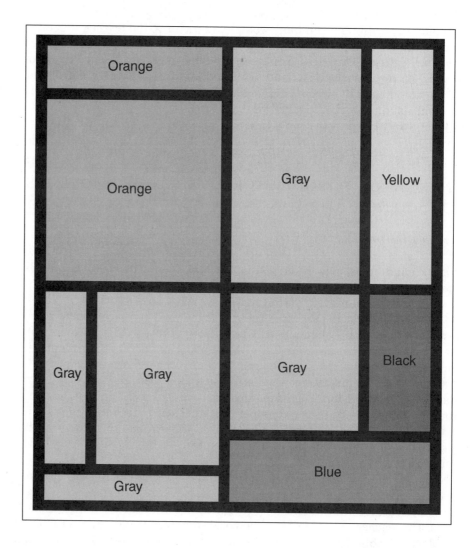

original painting. They discuss how the artist used only squares and rectangles to make his painting. The children then make their own picture using squares and rectangles. Precut construction paper shapes (squares and rectangles) in different colors, narrow black dividing strips, scissors, and glue are needed for this activity. Shallow-edged lids from medium-sized boxes can be used as a base for the collage. The children glue the shapes inside the flat portion of the lid, then add the dividing strips. The completed picture also has a box edge that can function as a ready-made frame.

The children and the teacher create a "classroom art gallery" of the children's pictures and examples of Mondrian's work. The exhibit could be called "In the Style of Mondrian." Other classes, parents, and friends can be invited to attend the gallery opening. The teacher helps the children choose appropriate background music to be played as visitors view the works of art. They discuss what kind of music should be played at an art exhibit: "Would we hear a symphony orchestra?" "A marching band? (probably too many musicians to fit into an art gallery or museum)" "A rock band? (probably too loud for people to discuss the pictures)" Discussion might lead the children to decide that the background music should be performed by an instrumental soloist or a small group (harpist, pianist, or string quartet). If possible, the teacher may invite a musician to perform or obtain recordings of the group/soloist that the children have selected.

INTEGRATED CURRICULUM FOCUS: ART AND MUSIC

Theme: Matching and Classifying

Young children often explore ideas of same and different by manipulating matching cards that depict line drawings of animals or shapes. This experience can be enhanced by having children interact with the works of master artists. Pairs of art postcards of high topical interest to children can be obtained from city art museums or framing shops. The teacher then prepares topical kits with a series of paired cards for matching.

For matching pictures of children, the following works could be used:

◆ *Katia Reading*, Balthus

◆ *Boy with Striped Shirt*, Alex Katz

◆ *In the Meadow*, Pierre-Auguste Renoir

◆ *The Calmady Children*, Sir Thomas Lawrence

◆ *Young Breton with a Goose*, Paul Gauguin

◆ *Eve of St. John*, Peter Hurd

◆ *The Migration of the Negro. No. 58*, Jacob Lawrence

◆ *Young Girls*, Mary Casatt

For matching animals in art, the following works might be used:

◆ *The Hunt of the Unicorn*, detail from the seventh tapestry in the series *The Hunt of the Unicorn*

◆ *Black Buck Miniature*, probably by Mansur, from the album of Shah Jahan

◆ *Hippopotamus*, Egyptian Dynasty 12

◆ *Statue of a Cat*, Egyptian, Ptolemaic Period

◆ *White Bull*, Franz Marc

◆ *The Tiger*, Franz Marc

For finding and naming musical instruments, the following could be used:

◆ *Drummer*, detail from *The Three Pagan Heroes*, French tapestry

◆ *The Music Lesson*, John George Brown

◆ *Seated Harp Player*, Marble Cycladic, third millennium B.C.

◆ *Horn Blower*, African, Court of Benin

◆ *A Hunter with a Spear Sounds His Horn*, detail from *The Unicorn Tries to Escape*, the third tapestry of the series *The Hunt of the Unicorn*

◆ *Sailor's Holiday*, Robert Brackman

◆ *The Fifer*, Edouard Manet

A highly recommended book with supportive materials that extends this activity and other uses of art postcards is *Mommy, It's a Renoir!* by Aline D. Wolf.

INTEGRATED CURRICULUM FOCUS: SCIENCE AND MUSIC

Theme: Dancing Rice

Sounds and vibrations in music provide a natural link to a science curriculum. To guide children in exploring ideas about sound and motion, the teacher discusses sound waves and vibration, and then covers an open can with a balloon, stretching it tightly across the top. Rice is placed on top of the balloon cover and the can is set on top of the speaker of a tape recorder. The teacher plays a recorded musical selection such as a lively march. The children will be excited to see the rice move and dance with the sound vibrations.

Activity prepared by Mary Pautz for the Milwaukee ACE project. Used by permission.

INTEGRATED CURRICULUM FOCUS: READING, MUSIC, AND MOVEMENT

Theme: Web for Reading Rainbow Experiences

Reading Rainbow programs can be obtained from the Instructional Television Department at local public television stations. Each program integrates music and children's literature in a unique way. The featured books listed below are only a small part of each program.

Brett, J. *Berlioz the Bear.* New York: Putnam's Sons, 1991.

Hurd, T. *Mama Don't Allow.* New York: Harper & Row, 1984.

Martin, B., and J. Archambault. *Barn Dance.* New York: Henry Holt and Company, 1986.

Mathers, P. *Sophie and Lou.* New York: Harper Collins, 1991.

Seeger, P., and M. Hays. *Abiyoyo.* Pawtucket, RI: Scholastic, 1986.

Walter, M. *Ty's One-Man Band.* New York: Four Winds Press, 1980.

Winter, J. *Follow the Drinking Gourd.* New York: Knopf, 1988.

The following web (interconnected learning scheme) was created for the Reading Rainbow television program "Sophie and Lou." The segments of the program are indicated in rectangles; strategies for classroom activities to enrich the theme of the program are in circles and ovals. Resources for suggested musical enrichment activities are *Wee Sing Fun & Folk* and *Wee Sing Sing-Along* songbooks; Bernstein's "Mambo" from *Dances of West Side Story;* and *Classics for Kids,* RCA CD.

A junk gamelan (based on the Indonesian instrument) may be prepared by gathering items such as pots, pans, broiler racks, and hubcaps. These junk items are then used to create metallic gong and ringing sounds typical of an Indonesian gamelan.

Shared by Mary Pautz and Jill Anderson, Milwaukee, WI. Used by permission.

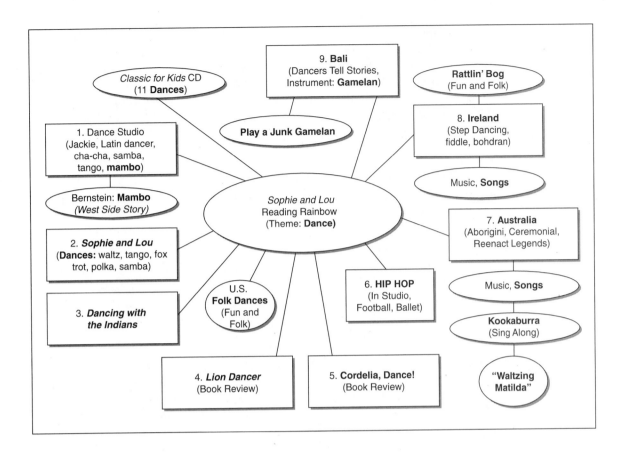

INTEGRATED CURRICULUM FOCUS: READING, ART, MUSIC, MOVEMENT, AND SOCIAL STUDIES

Theme: Special People in Our Lives

The teacher can acquaint children with the significant contributions that Josephine Baker made to America and the world by reading a story about her childhood days in turn-of-the-century St. Louis. Musical examples and the book *Ragtime Tumpie* by A. Schroderer can be obtained for this activity.

Joplin, Scott. "The Ragtime Dance" from *Piano Rags*. New York: Nonesuch Records H-71248.

Smith, Bessie. "St. Louis Blues." CBS Columbia Records G-30818.

"Sonny Boy" from *The Fabulous Josephine Baker*. RCA Victor 09026-61668-2.

Ragtime Tumpie relates the story of a young African-American girl who, though poor, was a very happy child. She scavenged around the city for leftover fruits and vegetables, and even picked up fallen coal around the railroad tracks to help her family. Her greatest joy was dancing to the ragtime and blues music she heard as she passed by the cafes and honky-tonks. She loved the syncopated rhythms and the sounds of the banjos, saxophones, harmonicas, fiddles, and drums. She ultimately won a contest, keeping alive her dream of becoming a great entertainer. And a great entertainer she did become, for her name was Josephine Baker.

Josephine Baker became a great star of her time, appearing on Broadway and in Paris. She helped the French Resistance fight for freedom during World War II and received medals for bravery. The teacher can prepare to tell Baker's story by marking appropriate places on the pages where ragtime music, the blues, or a rhythmic response might be inserted to enhance the storytelling. Suggestions include the following.

◆ Softly play "The Ragtime Dance" as the story is read.
◆ Invite children to tap their toes with the music after the words, "The catchy rhythm jumped to her toes and her foot began tapping . . ."
◆ Add the sounds of drum sticks (pencils on tabletops) for " . . . Eddie beat the sticks on the cracked cement."
◆ Change the recorded music to an excerpt from "The St. Louis Blues" when Tumpie dreams of this lazy, slow, sad music.
◆ Return to the sounds of ragtime when Tumpie dances; invite the children to dance with Tumpie.
◆ Upon completion of the story, discuss that "Tumpie/Josephine" was a real person and that this was the way she sounded when she sang. Play all or an excerpt from "Sonny Boy."

The teacher may ask the children to draw pictures of Josephine as a little girl, as an adult entertainer, and as a brave freedom fighter. A microphone and audio-cassette player can be used to record the children's statements about what they liked best about this special child or women. Their recorded statements can be replayed while viewing the artwork.

SUMMARY

An integrated/permeable learning approach may be guided by one teacher who wisely brings together skills and understandings from other disciplines within the curriculum. However, such a teacher is not readily available for all integrated programs. An integrated approach may also be a collaborative effort among several teachers who share their expertise. A collaborative approach does not mean that music teachers become reading or science teachers, or that classroom teachers are necessarily responsible for music. It does mean that each discipline retains its integrity as teachers communicate, plan together, and are flexible, enthusiastic, curious, and willing to share their expertise and time.

Regardless of the staffing approach used, children should have the opportunity to learn from the various perspectives that an integrated curriculum provides. Through an integrated/permeable learning approach, one learning is introduced, enriched, and builds upon another. Such an approach provides yet one more exciting way to deliver quality educational experiences.

THINGS TO DO

1. Select a book from children's literature that provides multiple learning experiences. Create an interconnected learning web that graphically demonstrates the many ways the book might be explored through an integrated curriculum approach. Assume that your ideas will be implemented by a group of collaborating teachers. Discuss how the responsibility for learning segments will be routed and accomplished.

2. Design an integrated/permeable learning experience for typical four-year-old children. How will this design differ from your plans for seven-year-old children?

13
Collaborative Music Programs

Developing quality music programs for young children is a time-consuming and continuing endeavor. Even if teachers have the makings of a good program, the problem of delivering it to all young children in private and public schools can seem insurmountable. Music teachers have the necessary musical skills, but they usually are not assigned to work with children below the kindergarten level. On the other hand, childcare providers have the daily responsibility of children, but often lack the necessary musical skills to implement a program. Herein lies the greatest frustration in providing this young population with quality musical experiences.

The reality is that only a few music educators are fortunate enough to work personally with children in preschools or childcare centers, and many care providers and classroom teachers need much support to present an appropriate program. The challenge is to empower care providers and classroom teachers to take on the responsibility.

As discussed earlier, music educators present many in-service sessions for early childhood educators. Music educators initiate local, regional, and national workshop sessions at meetings of the National Association for the Education of Young Children (NAEYC) and Music Educators National Conference (MENC). MENC members assist in developing curriculum guidelines and resources for use in private and public preschool settings. Community colleges and universities regularly offer workshops and coursework in this special area, in which care providers may or may not have the opportunity to enroll. Some universities offer community outreach sessions, where parents and/or their children may enroll in excellent early childhood music programs. MENC publishes descriptions of several of these promising practices.[1]

As motivating as these professionally sponsored activities may be, they have a short-term effect. What is needed is a continuous source of expertise for care providers and teachers who interact daily with young children. It appears that if we are to adequately share expertise using our present delivery system, we must form strong collaborations between music educators and other educators in the early childhood network.

REACHING OUT

Collaboration requires that we reach out to establish communication with colleagues in various related fields of knowledge-based specialization. Knowledge-based specialists may be found within the perimeters of one's own profession, such as music, or within the field of early childhood education. Either the early childhood specialist or the music specialist must take the responsibility for initiating a dialogue.

Ways to reach out may include the following:

◆ Organize a task force within your own profession whose major goal is to establish a network with those in other areas of knowledge-based expertise.

◆ Contact a university, four-year college, or community college knowledge-based specialist in the early childhood or music department. Make an appointment or meet for lunch to discuss mutual concerns for children, coming events, current resources, or perhaps a collaborative activity. Express interest in learning about one another's concerns for program development and in-service activities. Faculty members are often key people in leadership roles in their profession and are an integral part of a greater network. They are usually generous with their time, resources, and advice.

◆ Attend various network sessions of knowledge-based specialists. Often, local music educators and early childhood educators schedule monthly breakfast or luncheon meetings during which information and ideas are shared. Plan to attend not only the meeting of your own professional group, but those of colleagues in related fields. Share dates of your upcoming workshops and conferences with the new group; be sure they know they are welcome to attend.

◆ Encourage your profession to invite colleagues in related fields to in-service sessions. Waive registration fees for these guests. If and when the number of attendees becomes financially prohibitive, the host organization may have the happy problem of establishing an affiliate membership strand, where fees are greatly reduced, but still enough to help cover expenses of the event.

◆ Individual childcare centers should establish contact with knowledge-based specialists in the public schools within their geographic area. Many in-service activities may be mutually planned or attended by representatives at both sites and with no additional cost to the planners. The center and the public school might each appoint a liaison whose role is to provide information about concerns or activities that can be shared.

Collaborative Projects

Several collaborative efforts have been explored, implemented, and refined. These projects may serve as useful starting points for interested educators. The following descriptions include suggestions for establishing networks among professionals, in-kind service contributors, and grantors, all of whom share the goal of providing quality musical experiences for young children. These network and activity suggestions range from simple to complex.

A MODEL FOR A STATEWIDE COLLABORATIVE PROJECT

The Arizona Early Childhood Music Collaborative Project was developed and implemented to represent an involved, comprehensive approach to collaborating with many related groups in music and early childhood education. Many facets and details for implementing the model are presented, although only selected projects within the whole may be useful or replicable in other settings. The use of operas, newsletters, and workshop networking may be useful ideas for educators who are investigating collaborative approaches. Resources developed for the Arizona project are not currently available unless they are listed as available from a publisher. The printed materials referred to in this section are intended as models to describe the nature and breadth of materials that one might generate to assist teachers in the classroom.

The planners of the five-year Arizona project (1991–1996) sought to buy in to an existing network through which music in-service sessions and materials could be disseminated to care providers and early childhood teachers throughout the state. The child development programs at several community colleges were amenable to the idea of collaboration and served as the major link between the trainees, care providers in the field, and music educators. On-site advisors who supervise the yearly coursework of more than 1,000 candidates for the Child Development Associate (CDA) certification were identified as the initial and most important group for in-service because they have the responsibility for assessing the quality of trainees' work.

PROJECT DESCRIPTION

The Arizona project established and maintained a network of music educators and other professionals who were primarily responsible for the care and education of young children. These educators designed and implemented ongoing music services that reflected developmentally and musically appropriate experiences for three- to eight-year-old children. The program was phased in over a period of several years. The initial stages set about enhancing the quality of the then-current music and movement studies as required in the Child Development Associates (CDA) certification program administered at the community college level. Later, the project extended its offerings to include additional in-service for early childhood care providers and teachers currently in the field. Upon successful completion of the various phases of the program, the Arizona Music Educators Association (AMEA) awarded each participant an Early Childhood Music Certificate of Recognition, indicating the participant's higher level of achievement in guiding quality musical experiences for young children. The standards used for the certificate reflected those prepared by the Music Educators National Conference.[2]

FUNDING

Sponsorship for the Arizona project, including funding and in-kind services, was received from The Governor's Office for Children; Department of Education; The Arizona Music Educators Association; The Arizona Arts and Creativity in Early Childhood; Commission on the Arts; the Alliance for the Arts; and Central Arizona Community College Child Development Associate Program (CDA). Special projects were funded by grantors such as American Express. Funding changed from year to year, with grantsmanship being a major responsibility of the project's task force.

MISSION STATEMENT

The goal of the *Early Childhood Music Collaborative Project* is to affirm early childhood as a joyful time for interacting within a rich musical environment which stimulates curiosity and a disposition for a lifelong inclusion of music as a personal expressive force.

The *Early Childhood Music Collaborative Project* provides a forum for early childhood and music educators as they work together in developing quality educational experiences for children ages three to eight years of age.

Permeating all interactions is the philosophical commitment to child-centered learning; the value and role of music throughout the early childhood years; and the integral role of parents, community members, care providers, and music educators in providing quality education experiences for young children.

SPECIFIC GOALS

The project will:

- Use music as a catalyst to establish a network between the existing multiple organizations that serve the needs of young children.
- Create an awareness and encourage all areas of the music education profession to extend their traditional role to include the needs of preschool children.
- Identify music and early childhood educators who wish to serve as mentors, clinicians, and/or authors of developmentally appropriate written and recorded materials such as hands-on music kits, newsletters, and song collections.
- Create an awareness in early childhood educators as to the importance of quality early childhood music education and provide materials for so doing.
- Enhance the quality of the Child Development Associate (CDA) syllabus to reflect early childhood music standards and descriptions as established by the Music Educators National Conference.
- Empower CDA advisors to effectively guide and supervise their trainees.
- Provide a series of local and regional in-service sessions for CDA advisors, and public and private school care providers/teachers.
- Commission operas to be written especially for the preschool audience and cause them to be performed throughout the state.
- Provide scholarships to teachers of young children who wish to extend their skills in presenting musical experiences.

SUPPORTIVE ACTIVITIES OF THE PROJECT

Workshops

Eight regional workshops were presented yearly for teachers in childcare centers and public schools. These sessions were free to the participants. Honorariums and travel expenses for clinicians were funded solely by the project or as a shared expense between the project and other collaborating entities such as public or private preschools and community colleges. The co-sponsors at times provided housing, publicity, duplication of printed materials, refreshments, and part of clinicians' expenses. A local music clinician was identified in each region, who was then funded by the project to present a brief follow-up session. The objective was to help local music and early childhood educators become aware of their respective expertises.

Twenty-four, one-hour, on-site workshops were presented in designated childcare centers upon request from the centers' care providers. These sessions were tailored, for example, for specific care centers with small staffs or for larger, combined groups that requested a session during their in-service program.

Acknowledging that public school music education has been focused on the school-age child, the project held yearly regional workshop training sessions for a limited number of music educators who were interested in acquiring a better understanding of early childhood music. This cadre of educators became clinicians for the project.

Scholarships

Scholarships ($50 for tuition) were awarded each year to approximately 50 teachers/care providers for enrollment in a one-credit community college early childhood music course. Options for fulfilling this requirement included an on-site program or scheduled Saturday or evening classes. The scholarship project was administered by early childhood generalists on the task force.

Publications

Publications were prepared for preschool and primary school teachers and care providers. These materials were authored by music educators and printed by the Arizona Department of Education (ADE), with minimal distribution to public schools and more comprehensive distribution to preschools.

NEWSLETTERS. "You, Your Children and Music" was a newsletter issued approximately six to eight times a year. It incorporated child-ready, hands-on materials (play mats) as well as "how-to-do" and "why-we-do" ideas for teachers. (See "Little Boy Blue," p. 168, and "Paw Paw Patch," p. 166). The idea behind the newsletters was that preschool teachers often have a minimal budget for appropriate music materials, yet children need manipulative play items as a part of their music learning. The newsletters helped to partially fulfill this need.

PARENT SUPPORT MATERIALS. "Music Play Time in the Home" was a series of newsletter masters that were produced as a resource for various groups that provide educational leadership to parents of young children. The newsletters shared developmentally and musically appropriate activities that could be presented easily by parents at home. The materials presented a hands-on approach using traditional children's songs and improvised song play as a means of involving children in making music alone and with other family members. The intent was that families would find joy in making music together and extend the play to include music from their own cultures and family traditions. A master set of ten newsletters was made available each year to teachers/care providers, who then duplicated and distributed each issue to the parents of their children.

Music Play Time in the Home
An Arizona Early Childhood Music Collaborative Project Parent Newsletter

Music Play in the Kitchen

Performing music as food is being prepared or eaten can become a great time for busy parents to interact with their children. Singing familiar songs, playfully changing the words, making up new verses becomes great fun for the whole family.

Sing about The Muffin Man

In the traditional song the question is asked "Do you know the muffin man? The child answers, *"Oh, yes I know the muffin man"*. Could the worlds be changed to sing about food that is being prepared or eaten: *Oh, do you know the potato/carrot/cookie man? Do you know the cleaning/ dusing/ sweeping man?*

The Muffin Man

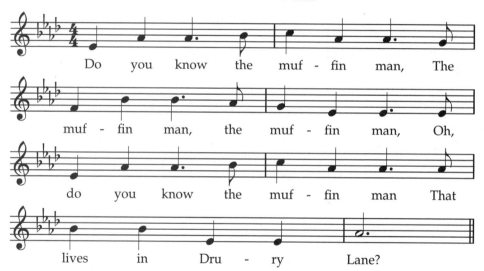

Do you know the muf - fin man, The
muf - fin man, the muf - fin man, Oh,
do you know the muf - fin man That
lives in Dru - ry Lane?

Dramatically play out a song

Perform Little Miss Muffet. Follow the instructions and prepare the puppet and props as indicated on the reverse side of this page. Sing the traditional song manipulating the characters as the story unfolds. Upon repreated play, change words so that Miss Muffet is eating different foods: *Eating her __ (pizza) __ and whey . . .*

Perform a spider song medley

Begin with Little Miss Muffet, add a second verse and another familiar spider song:

 Eency old spider, sat down beside her
 Wanting her curds and whey.
 Miss Muffet said, "Shoo! get out! Go up some water spout!"
 So Eency went on his way: (Sing: "Eeency Weency Spider . . .")

AECMCP Sponsors: The Arizona Department of Education, Arizona Music Educators Association, Central Arizona College Child Development Associate Training Program, Arizona Commission on the Arts, and the Governor's Office for Childen.

Lit - tle Miss Muf - fet   sat   on   a   tuf - fet,

Eat - ing   her   curds   and   whey; _____   A -

long   came   a   spi - der   and   sat   down   be - side   her, And

fright - ened   Miss   Muf - fet   a - way. _____

Materials:

2 - paper cups

1 - 4" stick

1 - matchstick

1 - 10" string

Assembly:

- Cut one cup for a 2" high stool

- Cut one cup as a spider.
  Poke a hole in bottom of cup for string.
  Attach string on inside using match stick.
  Tie opposite end to 4" stick.
  Wind string to make spider go up or down
    to frighten Miss Muffet.

- Cut out Miss Muffet.
  Fold into sitting position.
  Place on stool.

Procedure:

- Sing and use characters to play out the
    drama of the song.

spider's eyes

SPECIAL-FOCUS PUBLICATIONS. Projects were undertaken each year to provide music and recordings for classroom use. Printed song collections with audiocassette tapes were made available at no cost to the project recipients. Typical materials were "Hispanic Music for Arizona Children, Book I and II" (see "Pon Pon Pon," p. 197), "Apache Music for Arizona Children," and a "Traditional Collection of Children's Songs." For each publication, ethnic consultants were involved in an effort to include authentic and appropriate music of the state's unique cultures. For example, a public school district and tribal members collaborated to prepare the Apache music materials (see "Baby Walking Song," p. 197).

Backpack Operas

A collaboration between the state Choral Directors Association and the project was formed to provide developmentally appropriate opera experiences for young children. The intent was to make this genre more appealing to young audiences and to involve high school–age students in the performance. The choral directors viewed this collaboration as an opportunity to extend the perimeters of their educational role, provide an exciting vocal experience for young children, and build a "feeder" system for their programs over the years.

THE OPERA. The opera was commissioned to be written by a member of the Choral Directors Association. The charge was to prepare material that was musically attractive to high school–age performers and developmentally appropriate for young children. The opera was to be performed at sites with limited audience space, and few costumes and props. Rehearsal time and supervision by the high school choral instructor was to be kept to a minimum. An overview of *Old MacDonald Had a Farm*, a typical opera from this project, follows. This story is about a farmer and his upbeat animals who decide to travel to the city. Upon arriving in the city, they discover there isn't much to eat and few places for animals, so they happily return to the country.

THE OPERA CAST

◆ Old MacDonald, also known as "Mac," is a happy-go-lucky farmer who presides over a motley crew of animals, each with its own personality, but united in a desire to leave the farm to explore the delights of the city. Mac loves his farm but also exhibits an interest in seeing the exotic city life.

◆ Betsy is Mac's cheerful wife who is comfortable with her own set of responsibilities. She probably works harder than her husband, because he prefers to spend a lot of time in the village visiting with the people.

◆ The cat is perpetually after the rat, but only half-heartedly.

◆ The rat is paired with the cat, but is not deathly afraid of her.

◆ The pig is "Mr. Cool"—certainly self-proclaimed. He exhibits a continual swagger and general sense of disdain and superiority.

◆ The chicken aspires to the title of "Miss Cool" and is unwilling to let the pig have the "Cool" title without a fight.

◆ The cow/pianist is a pleasant character with a quality of dreaminess to her demeanor. She aspires to be more than a cow—she wants to dance and sing and be like other more active animals. She is ultimately resigned to her milk-giving position in the scheme of things.

Typical of the opera's music is the following excerpt sung by the cow while awkwardly dancing:

It Isn't Easy to Be a Cow (Excerpt)

am a cow who tries, and tries, and tries. _____ It's hard to be some-thing that you're

not. It's hard to play it cool and feel so hot. I've been un - ea - sy yes, ev - er

since I've tried to be a frog, I've tried to be a frog and not a prince. __ 1. I want to

PLANS FOR PERFORMANCE. The opera was performed by high school choral students, who were supplied free of charge the opera scores and educational packets. The education packets were also distributed to directors or teachers of participating preschool centers and public schools in their geographic area by representatives of the high school choir. The participating care provider or teacher had the responsibility of coordinating the activity and preparing the children for the event. To do this, the teacher took the following steps:

◆ Requested and scheduled a performance of *Old MacDonald Had a Farm* with the high school student performing group.

◆ Made sure that the performers were aware of any site limitations and the anticipated size of the audience.

◆ Obtained the backpack opera teaching materials from the director of the high school performers and became familiar with the contents.

◆ Wrote information abut the date, time, site, and performing group on the playbill (enclosed in kit) and exhibited it prominently in the classroom area.

◆ Informed family members about the concept of children's song play activities and the upcoming opera so that they could share the child's excitement regarding the event.

THE TEACHING MATERIALS. Packets were prepared for the preschool or primary-level teacher that included the following items:

1. *Playbill*—A poster to advertise the performance.

2. *Teacher's Guide*—Suggestions for helping children understand that opera is a story that is sung. The teacher could use this guide to help children create their own song stories/operas. For example, the adult initiates the play by sing-songing: "Hello! I'm the old lady who lives in the shoe. I have so many children I can't remember all their names. Help me sing their names." The teacher sings the names using pitches G and E:

"Cin-
dy"

The children echo the names, then each child sings names for the teacher and others to echo. The teacher sings, "We have certainly sung the names of many children." The play continues with the teacher singing,

> There was an old lady who lived in the shoe,
> She had so many children she didn't know what to do!
> What do you think she should do?

The children dialogue-sing various ideas such as "take them to play," "make them clean their room," "bake them a cake." The teacher ends the play by singing,

> She gave them some broth, without any bread,
> And kissed them all soundly and put them to bed!

> *(All make smacking kissing sounds)*

3. *Letter to Parents*—A letter to parents that explained the event and children's use of song story plays. A sample letter follows.

Dear Parents:

   Your child will have an opportunity to see a performance of an opera that has been specially composed for preschool/primary-age audiences. The performance will be a delightful introduction to this type of music, as well as involve your child in creating his or her own made-up song stories (opera). The children's own songs will often be rambling tunes that do not necessarily reflect traditional song rules or form. The fact that these tunes can be so freely sung means that the words and musical storytelling are the major focus of the play.

   Please listen, encourage, and feel free to join your child in opera play that involves singing songs and musical conversations. Know that the two teachable ideas that help move an opera plot along are *action* songs and *feeling* songs. The song play your child engages in will reflect these ideas.

   Many thanks for being so actively interested in your child's musical play.

Sincerely,

4. *Story and Song Themes*—Included were story and song excerpts from the opera *Old MacDonald Had a Farm*.

5. *Puppets and Patterns*—Manipulative materials such as puppets and plastic spoon singers were provided for the children's use in playing out this and other operas such as *Rumpelstiltskin*.

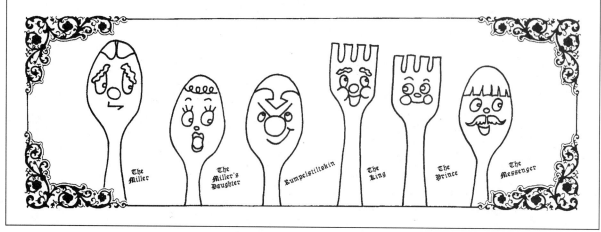

6. *Concert Courtesy*—Suggestions to the teacher for introducing concert courtesies. For example, "Be aware that during the performance, group control is the responsibility of the on-site preschool director/care providers/teachers. The young student performers will be concerned only with the musical production. Expect that children will become excited in response to the fun of the story action.

    "Help your children become aware of appropriate audience courtesy. Children should applaud after each solo is sung (optional); when the cast bows at the end of the opera; as each character individually takes a bow; as the pianist is acknowledged; as the cast again bows; and when the director of the group is acknowledged or thanked."

In planning this opera series, much attention was given to preparing the teacher, children, and performers so that all would have a positive experience. It was gratifying to observe the interaction of the high school performers with the preschool children. The teenagers demonstrated great caring, sharing of their talents, and natural instincts as teachers of young children. They often spontaneously solved their own performance problems:

One high school group performed Old MacDonald *in a small room with the preschool children seated on the floor. The performance went well and, at the end, the characters were to dash offstage. The performers suddenly became aware that there was no offstage area. Without a word, they regrouped, took a bow, and, without adult suggestion, took it upon themselves to go among the young audience, shaking hands and asking questions about favorite characters and songs. The delighted preschoolers touched the pig character's nose and the feathers of the chick character. An adoring fan club was born.*

Examples such as this reinforce the idea that in collaborative activities everybody wins.

Additional Ideas for Collaborating with Other Groups

INSTRUMENTAL PERFORMANCES FOR YOUNG CHILDREN

Small ensemble concerts such as duets, trios, or quartets may be planned for young children. The model calls for high school instrumental performers to form small ensemble groups to perform in preschools. The high school ensembles may be traditional, such as string quartets or brass trios, or two friends who play trumpet and drums who might wish to collaborate on a performance.

The collaborative effort involves the early childhood community, early childhood music educators, and the State Band and Orchestra Directors Association. The procedure is much the same as for the Choral Directors model for opera. Music scores are needed for various ensembles; college and university instrumental or composition majors may be able to compose arrangements of familiar songs from children's literature for the ensembles. The project sponsors have the responsibility of printing the scores, providing guidelines for the high school performers, and preparing concert materials for the teachers.

Guidelines for High School Instrumental Performers

Whenever possible, the participating high school students should assume major responsibility for planning their programs. They need to address the following questions when planning performances: Will the ensemble be large or small? Will we perform a traditional piece or try some unique combinations? Will we perform music prepared in band/orchestra class, specially arranged nursery/traditional children's songs, or a selection from our own solo repertoire?

Model for a Preschool Performance

The following steps would be taken to plan a 25-minute string ensemble performance:

1. Open with a suitable selection from this year's performance repertoire (be sensitive to the length of the selection).

2. Perform an arrangement of "Hickory Dickory Dock."

3. Introduce the instruments with a puppet master of ceremonies. When introduced, each performer explains unique features and sounds of his or her instrument, and then plays the melody of a child's tune such as "Mary Had a Little Lamb" or "Hot Cross Buns."

4. The group performs the round "Frere Jacques" in the key of C, then invites the children to use their own string instrument to play along. (Note: the teachers will have prepared string fiddles for each child by stretching a rubber band around the sides, bottom, and over the opening of a Styrofoam cup. The bottom of the cup is placed on the child's ear; the rubber band is plucked over the opening of the cup. The child hears a rich, pitched string sound while accompanying the string ensemble. The cup can actually be

tuned to the first or fifth step of the scale, C or G, by squeezing the sides in or out and adjusting the band. Children can then play a one-pitched drone with the string ensemble. The number and age of children in the audience determine the practicality of using tuned cups.)

5. End the concert with an excerpted selection from this year's repertoire.

Additional Instrumental Ensembles

Unique performing groups can also be used for programs. For example, a trumpet, flute, and snare drum ensemble can present an Americana program involving bugle calls such as taps; patriotic songs; a crescendo-decrescendo parade idea; or a drum cadence that tells others in the parade when it is time to play.

A violin (Peter), flute (bird), oboe (duck), and clarinet (cat) ensemble can introduce Peter's friends by playing only excerpted themes from *Peter and the Wolf*.

An electronic keyboard and guitar ensemble can perform prepared music as well as explain the many different sounds that can be produced. They may wish to improvise "out-in-space" music by darkening the room and providing children with flashlights. (Performers should be sensitive to audience control during this part of the presentation by playing only briefly if the group becomes overexcited.) The children may be allowed to have a hands-on experience by playing the performers' instruments.

High school performers are encouraged to plan and organize their own programs. Original program ideas, however, should be monitored for appropriateness by the director before they are performed in concert.

Obviously, more planning is required for an instrumental collaborative project. The materials suggested may serve as a springboard for teachers who wish to further pursue such a project.

Parent-Toddler Music in City Parks and Recreation Systems

Collaboration with educators and directors of city government programs is an often overlooked means of implementing and funding early childhood music programs. Staff for Saturday Schools, sponsored by the parks system, can be recommended by music and early childhood professionals. The concept for the program should be mutually planned by those responsible for the sessions. Funding, real and in-kind, may come from the city, registration fees, or matching funds from groups such as the state's art commission, industries, or private donors.

One such model involves 15 duos/trios of parents and toddlers who participate in a six-week program of one-hour weekly sessions. The parents first attend an orientation session at which they are made aware of their role in musically playing with their child during the sessions. Parents are assisted by two teachers as the children interact in a minimum of ten music play areas. Typical areas are (1) "Jack and Jill" using step bells; (2) a dancing place with large mirrors, props, and recorded music; and (3) instrumental ensemble play where guitars and Orff-type xylophones are tuned for successful improvisational play. During each session, children and parents interact in the centers for approximately 40 minutes, then group music play is guided for the remaining 20 minutes. Guided group music play consists of singing, playing instruments, listening to music selections, and moving expressively.

The session ends with parents and children exploring the music library checkout kits. These kits, often packaged in small plastic bags, are available for take-home music play. The library has approximately 40 checkout kits containing in-struments, books, tapes, and related materials. Following are some examples of kits.

Autoharp Kit

A total of five tuned autoharps are available for checkout with information about use and safety of the instrument, a songbook with chords marked, and a variety of picks. Parents are instructed to plan a special sharing time to use the autoharp to ensure positive, safe, supervised play. Tuning forks are deliberately eliminated from the take-home kits because strings often break when unskilled parents attempt to tune the instrument.

Book and Tape Kit

An illustrated traditional children's songbook with specially recorded cassette tape music are combined into one kit. The three-minute tape contains just one song and is recorded by the teacher rather than purchased. (See p. 245 for a list of usable books.) The city library system can collaborate on these kits by securing books from its resources.

Dancing Doll Kit

A scarf doll is prepared by attaching a large, colorful scarf over a small ball on a stick with a rubber band. The doll and an audiocassette tape of dancing music are included in the kit. The music may be a waltz, a tune from a Disney movie, a contemporary rock or jazz selection, or a folk song.

Music Conductor's Kit

Contents of this kit are the book *The Philharmonic Gets Dressed* by K. Kuskin and M. Simone, a cassette tape of favorite children's classical music, and a conductor's baton. Parents read the book, then play the tape as the child pretends to be the conductor of a fine orchestra.

Hispanic Music Kit

This kit holds a small, eight-inch sandpaper guitar, one pair of small maracas, one pair of claves, a cassette tape of Spanish music selections, and a picture of mariachi musicians. The child dances or accompanies the recorded music using the ethnic instruments.

SUMMARY

The number of children in preschools and primary schools is staggering. Delivering music programs to all of these children requires a far-reaching effort by many different professionals and organizations. It is more efficient to enter a new music project into an existing network than it is to establish a new system. Music programs are usually a most welcomed enhancement to the existing venue. A viable option for introducing a program is to collaborate with people involved in established programs such as those offered at the community college level. Combined expertise provides optimal programs, and combined networks hasten the delivery of information to children.

THINGS TO DO

1. We have described at length the roles of both music educators and early childhood educators. As a reader of this book, you probably fit into one of these groups. Seek out a colleague in the related field, music or early childhood, and discuss the music program from each of your perspectives.

   a. Identify a specific early childhood program.

   b. What is the nature of the existing program?

   c. In your opinions, can it be improved? How?

   d. What would each of you be willing to do to improve the program?

   e. Briefly describe a collaboration with a third party (another organization or person) that you would both like to undertake to provide quality music experiences for young children in your care.

   f. Report on this discussion to others in your class, center, or school.

2. Divide into publication teams. Plan and prepare a two- to four-page newsletter that you feel will be valuable to (a) care providers or (b) parents. Share your prototype with other members of the class.

RESOURCES

Music Educators National Conference, 1902 Association Dr., Reston, VA 22091.

Stocker, David. *Old MacDonald Had a Farm*. EC Schirmer Music Company, Inc., a division of ECS Publishing, 138 Ipswich St., Boston, MA 02215.

NOTES

[1]Barbara Andress, ed., *Promising Practices: Programs and Projects* (Reston, VA: Music Educators National Conference, 1989).

[2]See *Opportunity-to-Learn Standards for Music Instruction* and *The School Music Program, A New Vision* (Reston, VA: Music Educators National Conference, 1994).

Appendix

Glossary of Musical Terms

Accelerando (ah-chel-lay-rahn-doh)—Gradually becoming faster.

Accent—Louder or with emphasis. Normally, the accent falls on the first beat of the measure.

Articulation—How sound is initiated and packaged; smooth-connected, jagged-disconnected.

Ballet (bal-lay)—A dance or set of dances performed to a musical accompaniment usually telling a story or picturing an idea entirely with dance and pantomime.

Ballet Suite—Selected numbers from the music of a ballet arranged for orchestral performances.

Beat—Recurring rhythmic pulse underlying music.

Bordun (boor-doon)—First and fifth tone of the scale sounded simultaneously and played repeatedly.

Canon—A strict form of music in which all voices or parts have the same melody, although beginning at different times. A simple form of a canon is a round.

Chant—Words spoken rhythmically.

Chord—The sounding together of several tones, usually three or more.

Chromatic Scale—A scale moving by half steps, containing 12 half steps within the octave (C, C#, d, d#, e, f, f#, g, g#, a, a#, b, c').

Coda—A special or extended ending added for emphasis.

Crescendo (cray-shen-doh)—Gradually becoming louder.

Decrescendo (day-cray-shen-doh)—Gradually becoming softer.

Diatonic Scale—Eight-tone scale such as C, d, e, f, g, a, b, c'.

Dissonance—Tones of chords sounding together that are "jarring" when heard.

Duration—Relative longness or shortness of sound.

Dynamics—The gradations of loudness or softness of tones.

Elements of Music—Pitch, rhythm, harmony, dynamics, timbre, texture, and form.

Fanfare—An introduction played by a flourish of trumpets for ceremonial, hunting, or military purposes.

Form—Overall structural organization of a composition; same and different musical ideas.

Forte (for-teh)—Loud.

Fortissimo (for-tih-see-moh)—Very loud.

Gavotte (ga-vot)—Early dance form.

Genre—A style or category of music such as gospel, rock, or march.

Harmony—Combination of tones sounded simultaneously.

Improvisation—To perform music spontaneously from the imagination rather than from memory or from a written score.

Interlude—A piece of music played as a bridge between sections.

Interval—The distance in pitch between two notes, sounded either together or separately.

Introduction—An opening section of music to prepare listeners for what is to follow.

Key—The "family" of notes found in the scale of the keynote (do), and their relation to this keynote.

Legato (leh-gah-toh)—In a smooth, connected manner.

Major Scale—A succession of eight tones within an octave that move in whole steps except for two half steps between tones 3 and 4 and 7 and 8.

Measure—Music contained between two vertical bars.

Medley—A number of well-known tunes played in succession.

Melody—Organized pitches that move up or down or remain the same to form a tuneful sound.

Melodic Contour—The same, up, or down flow of the melodic phrase.

Meter—A grouping of beats determined by underlying accents.

Meter Signature—A fraction found at the beginning of each piece or therein. The upper number indicates the number of counts in each measure, the lower number indicates the note that lasts for one count.

Notes—Music symbols indicating pitch or rhythmic information (whole, half, quarter notes).

Octave—An interval in which a tone is repeated eight tones higher, such as C–c'.

Opera—A musical drama that is sung with appropriate action, costumes, and scenery, and is accompanied by an orchestra.

Operetta (little opera)—A light opera that may have some spoken dialogue.

Ostinato—A short, persistently repeated melodic or rhythmic pattern.

Overture—A piece of orchestral music introducing a musical work such as an opera.

Patschen (pah-chen)—To slap thighs with one's hands.

Pentatonic Scale—A scale consisting of five tones, resembling the five black keys of the piano, or pitches such as C, D, E, G, A; widely used in folk music.

Phrase—A portion of a melody representing a unit, usually four measures in length; a "musical sentence."

Piano—Soft.

Pitch—Highness or lowness of musical sound.

Prelude—Introductory music played before a musical work, play, or ceremony.

Program Music—Music based on a story, a picture, or some idea other than the music itself.

Range—Highest and lowest notes of a song, voice, or instrument.

Rest—A music symbol indicating silence.

Rhythm—Relatively longer and shorter sounds/silences in various groupings.

Ritard—Gradually slower.

Rondo—A recurring musical refrain that alternates the same idea with contrasting keys (A, B, A, C, A, D, . . .).

Root—The lowest note upon which a chord is built.

Round—A simple canon in which all voices sing or play the same melody but begin at different times.

Staccato—A tone played in a crisp, detached manner.

Staff—Five narrow, spaced horizontal lines on which music is written.

Style—The distinctive manner in which the elements of music are organized, reflecting their use throughout various times and places (e.g., baroque, rock, or gospel).

Syncopation—The placing of an accent on a beat ordinarily not accented.

Tempo—The speed at which music is to be performed.

Theme—A portion of a melody that has melodic or rhythmic importance because of repetition or development.

Timbre (tam-bur)—Quality of tones that distinguish one instrument/voice from another.

Tonality—Tones as they relate to a harmonic center or point of rest.

Tonic Chord—The chord built in thirds above the first degree of the scale; for example, in the key of C major, the tonic chord is c, e, g.

Waltz—A graceful dance that moves in moderate triple meter (¾) with a pulse on first beats.

Whole Tone Scale—A scale consisting of six tones (rather than the usual seven tones), each of which is a whole step apart.

Glossary of Musical Terms is a revised list from *Music Guide for Arizona Elementary Schools*, Arizona Department of Public Instruction, 1964.

Pronouncing the Last Names of Composers

Bach (bahk)
Beethoven (BAY-toe-ven)
Brahms (brahmz)
Chopin (sho-pan)
Debussy (duh-bew-SEE)
Elgar (el-gar)
Grieg (greeg)
Haydn (HIDE-n)
Ibert (ee-BEAR)
Kabalevsky (caw-bah-YEF-skee)
Kodaly (koh-DALL-yee)
Liadov (lee-AH-duf)

Moussorgsky (moo-SORG-skee)
Mozart (moat-zart)
Ravel (rah-VELL)
Rimsky-Korsakov (rim-skee-KOR-sah-kof)
Saint-Saëns (seh-SAW)
Schumann (shoo-man)
Sousa (SOO-sah)
Shostakovich (shah-stuh-KOH-vich)
Stravinsky (strah-VIN-skee)
Prokofiev (proh-KOH-fee-ef)
Tchaikovsky (ch-eye-KOFF-skee)

Resource Materials

PROFESSIONAL ORGANIZATIONS

American Orff-Schulwerk Association (AOSA)
PO Box 391089
Cleveland, OH 44139
  Journal: *The Orff Echo*

Association for Childhood Education International (ACEI)
11141 Georgia Ave.
Suite 200
Wheaton, MD 20902
  Journal: *Childhood Education*

Dalcroze Society
613 Putnam Dr.
Eau Claire, WI 54701
  Journal: *American Dalcroze Journal*

Music Educators National Conference (MENC)
1902 Association Dr.
Reston, VA 22091
  Journal: *Music Educators Journal*

National Association for the Education of Young Children (NAEYC)
1834 Connecticut Ave., NW
Washington, DC 20009
  Journal: *Young Children*

Organization of American Kodaly Educators (OAKE)
1457 S. 23rd St.
Fargo, ND 58103
  Journal: *The Kodaly Envoy*

MUSIC TEXTBOOK SERIES

Macmillan/McGraw-Hill
1221 Avenue of the Americas
New York, NY 10020

Silver Burdett Co.
250 James St.
Morristown, NJ 07632

EARLY CHILDHOOD PUBLICATIONS FROM THE MUSIC EDUCATORS NATIONAL CONFERENCE

Andress, B., ed. *Promising Practices: Prekindergarten Music Education.*

Andress, B., and L. Walker, eds. *Readings in Early Childhood Music Education.*

Feierabend, J. *TIPS: Music Activities in Early Childhood.*

Graham, R. *Music for Special Learners: Mainstreaming, Individualization, and Special Methodologies.*

Overby, L., ed. *Early Childhood Creative Arts.*

Palmer, M., and W. Sims. *Music in Prekindergarten: Planning and Teaching.*

SONGBOOKS

Beall, P., and S. Nipp. *Wee Sing and Play, Wee Sing Silly Songs, Wee Sing and Play,* 1984, 1982, 1981.
Price/Stern/Sloan Publishers, Inc.
410 N. La Cienega Blvd.
Los Angeles, CA 90048

Feierabend, J. *First Steps in Music for Infants and Toddlers,* 1995.
First Steps in Music, Inc.
PO Box 73
Simsbury, CT 06070

Fierabend, J., and G. Kramer. *Music for Little People,* 1986.
Boosey & Hawkes, Inc.
200 Smith St.
Farmingdale, NY 11735

Hall, M. A. *Snug-a-Love Songs* (book and tape) and *Take a Bite of Music, It's Yummy*
Music for Children
96 County St.
Norwalk, CT 06851

Jenkins, J. *The Ella Jenkins Song Book for Children,* 1966.
Oak Publications
33 W. 60th St.
New York, NY 10023

Kenney, M. *Circle round the Zero,* 1983.
Magnamusic-Baton, Inc.

10370 Page Industrial Blvd.
St. Louis, MO 63132

Kleiner, L. *Kids Make MUSIC* (book and video), 1994.
Bogner Entertainment, Inc.
PO Box 641428
Los Angeles, CA 90064

One Thousand Jumbo, the Magic Songbook
Charles Hansen Music & Books, Inc.
1860 Broadway
New York, NY 10023

Raffi. *The Raffi Singable Songbook*
Chappell
14 Birch Ave.
Toronto, Ontario, Canada

Sharon, Lois, and Bram. *Elephant Jam,* 1980.
McGraw-Hill Ryerson Limited
Toronto, Ontario, Canada

Thurman, L., and A. Langness, *Heartsongs,* 1986.
Music Study Services
PO Box 4665
Englewood, CO 80155.

Warren, J. *Piggyback Songs and More Piggyback Songs*
Totline Press
Warren Publishing House
PO Box 2255
Everett, WA 98203

RECORDINGS

Children's Favourites. (Saint-Saëns, *Carnival of the Animals*; Copland, *The Cat and the Mouse*; Rimsky-Korsakov, *The Flight of the Bumblebee*).

Children's Weekend Classics (*Peter and the Wolf, The Sorcerer's Apprentice*).

EMI-Angel. *The King's Singers Present Kids' Stuff.* (*I Know an Old Woman; Frog Went a Courtin'; The Grand Old Duke of York*).

Fiedler's Favorites for Children and More Fiedler's Favorites for Children. (*Nutcracker Suite* selections; *Whistle While You Work; Chim-Chim-Cher-ee; In the Hall of the Mountain King*) Boston Pops Orchestra, RCA Recordings.

Folkways Records. *Early Early Childhood Songs, Call-and-Response Rhythmic Group Singing, Play Your Instrument and Make a Pretty Sound, and You'll Sing a Song and I'll Sing a Song.* Jenkins, E.

Music for Little People. *Aesop's Fables the Smothers Brothers Way.*

Music for Little People. *Burl Ives Sings Little White Duck.* (*The Little Engine That Could, The Tailor and the Mouse*)

Music for Little People. *Singable Songs for the Very Young* and *More Singable Songs for the Very Young*. Raffi. (*My Dreidel; Baa Baa Black Sheep; Six Little Ducks*).

Music for Little People. *Singing, Moving, and Learning.* Thomas Moore.

Warner Brothers. *Peter, Paul & Mommy.* (*Boa Constrictor; It's Raining; Going to the Zoo*).

BOOKS FOR CURRICULUM INTEGRATION

Sounds and Colors

Carle, E. *The Very Quiet Cricket.* New York: Philomel, 1990.

Martin, B. *Listen to the Rain.* New York: Henry Holt.

Stoiz, M. *Storm in the Night.* New York: Harper Trophy, 1996.

Songs/Nursery Rhymes

Aylesworth, J. *The Completed Hickory Dickory Dock.* New York: Athenum, 1994.

Bullock, K. *She'll Be Comin Round the Mountain.* New York: Simon & Schuster, 1994.

Galdone, P. *Cat Goes Fiddle i Fee.* New York: Clarion, 1985.

Trapani, I. *The Itsy Bitsy Spider.* Boston: Whispering Coyote Press, 1993.

Books about Music

Carle, E. *I See a Song.* New York: Thomas Crowell, 1996.

Melmed, L. *The First Song Ever Sung.* New York: Lothrup Lee & Sheperd, 1993.

Winch, J. *The Old Man Who Loved to Sing.* New York: Scholastic, 1994.

Musicians and Music

Rasahka, C. *Charlie Parker Played Bebop.* New York: Orchard Books, 1992.

Rosenberg, J. *Dance Me a Story.* New York: Thames and Hudson, 1993.

Swore, G. *Cynthia Gregory Dances Swan Lake.* New York: Simon & Schuster, 1990.

Verdy, V. *Of Swans, Sugar Plums and Satin Slippers.* New York: Scholastic, 1994.

Animals in General

Rosen, M. *We're Going on Bear Hunt.* New York: Macmillan, 1989.

Slavin, B. *The Cat Came Back.* Morton Grove, IL: Whitman, 1992.

Musical Instruments

Drew, H. *My First Music Book.* Darling Kindersley, 1993.

Hausherr, R. *What Instrument Is This?* New York: Scholastic, 1992.

Lilligard, D. *Percussion.* Danbury, CT: Children's Press, 1993.

Correlations for The Carnival of the Animals, *Camille Saint-Saëns*

Elephant

Le Tord, B. *Elephant Moon.* New York: Doubleday, 1994.

Mahy, M. *17 Kings and 42 Elephants.* New York: Puffin, 1994.

West, C. *One Little Elephant.* New York: Barron's, 1994.

Swan

Fonteyn, M. *Swan Lake.* San Diego, CA: Harcourt Brace Jovanovich, 1993.

Aviary

Ehlert, L. *Feathers for Lunch.* San Diego, CA: Harcourt Brace Jovanovich, 1993.

Williams, G. *The Chicken Book.* Dell, 1992.

Aquarium

Pfister, M. *Rainbow Fish.* New York: North South Books, 1992.

Wildsmith, B. *Fishes.* London: Oxford University Press, 1985.

Early Childhood Methods Books

Bayless, K., and M. Ramsey, *Music a Way of Life for the Young Child.* New York: Macmillan.

McDonald, D., and G. Simons. *Musical Growth and Development, Birth through Six.* New York: Schirmer Books.

Shared by Mary Pautz, Wisconsin.

INSTRUMENT SOURCES

Magna Music, Inc.
10370 Page Industrial Blvd.
St. Louis, MO 63132

Peripole-Bergerault, Inc.
2041 State St.
Salem, OR 97301

Rhythm Band Instruments
PO Box 126
Fort Worth, TX 76101

Suzuki Musical Instruments
PO Box 261030
San Diego, CA 92196-9877

CATALOGS

Children's Book and Music Center
2500 Santa Monica Blvd.
Santa Monica, CA 90404

Folkways Records and Service Corp.
632 Broadway, Ninth Floor
New York, NY 10012

Kimbo Educational
PO Box 477
86 S. 5th Ave.
Long Branch, NJ 17740

Music for Little People
Box 1460
Redway, CA 95560
(Recordings, books, instruments)

World Around Songs
(Formerly Cooperative Recreation Service, Inc.)
Rt. 5, Box 390
Burnsville, NC 28714
(Pocket-size song collections)

Song Index

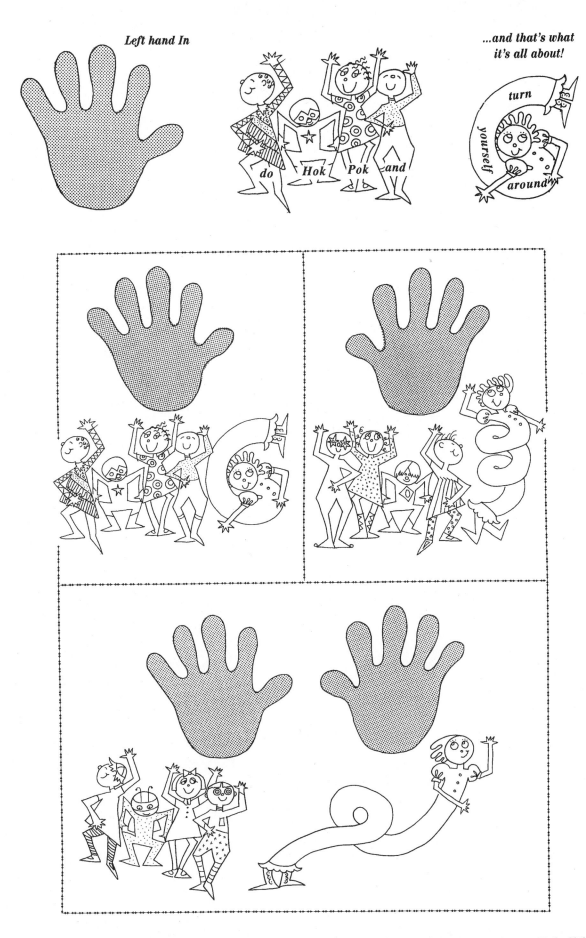

Left hand In

...*and that's what it's all about!*

do Hok Pok and

turn yourself around

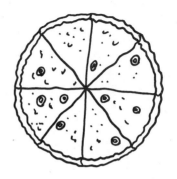

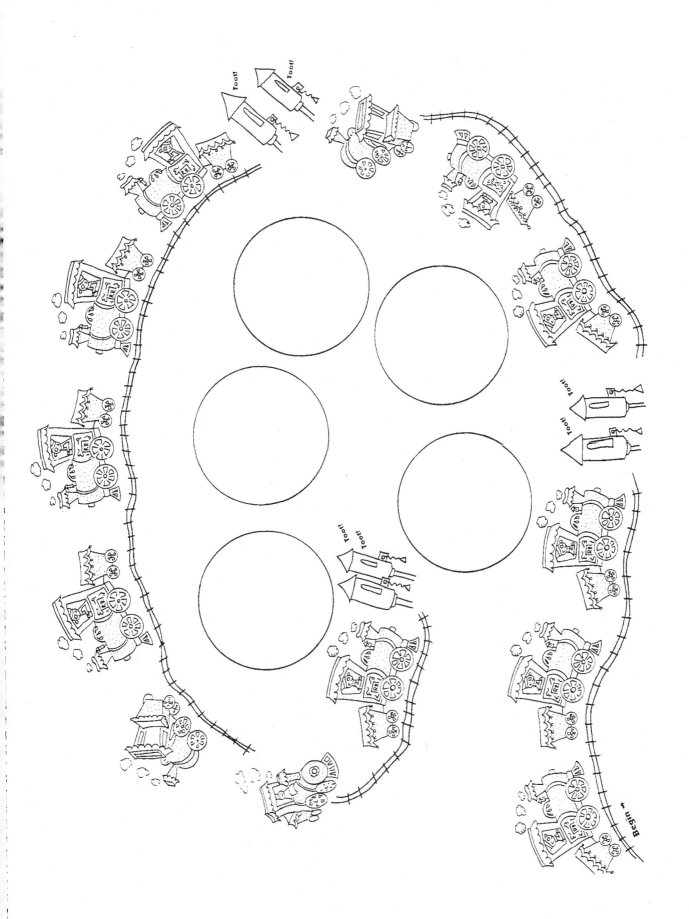

"Comin' 'Round the Mountain," reprint from *You, Your Children and Music*, Vol. IV, Issue 3. Arizona Early Childhood Music Collaborative Project. Used by permission. Permission to reproduce this page for personal use only is granted to users of this textbook.

Pop! Goes the Weasel

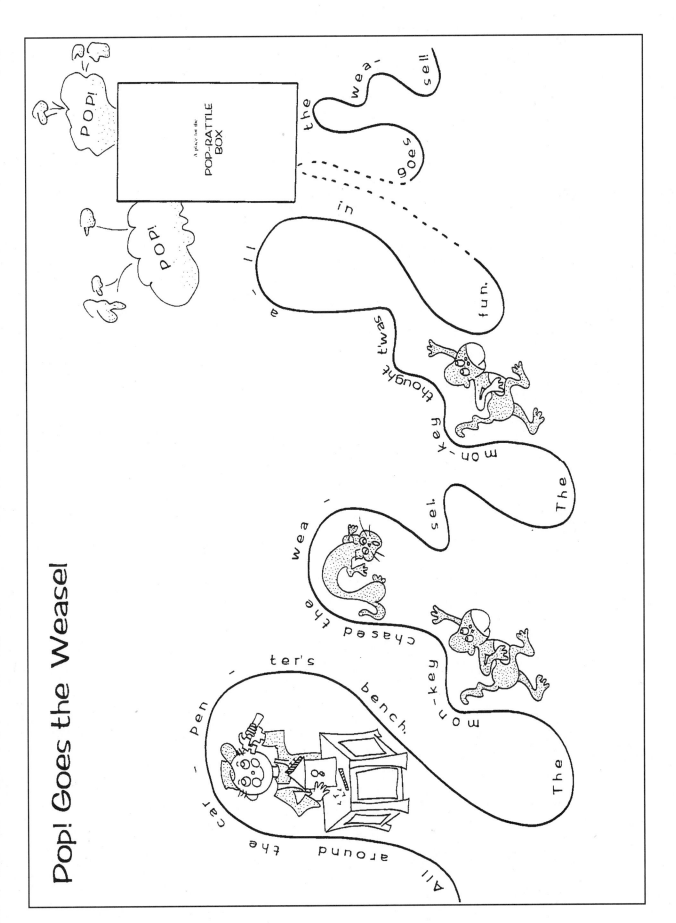

M. Pautz, "Pop! Goes the Weasel," *You, Your Children and Music*, Vol. II, Issue 5. Arizona Early Childhood Music Collaborative Project. Used by permission. Permission to reproduce this play mat for personal use only is granted to users of this textbook.

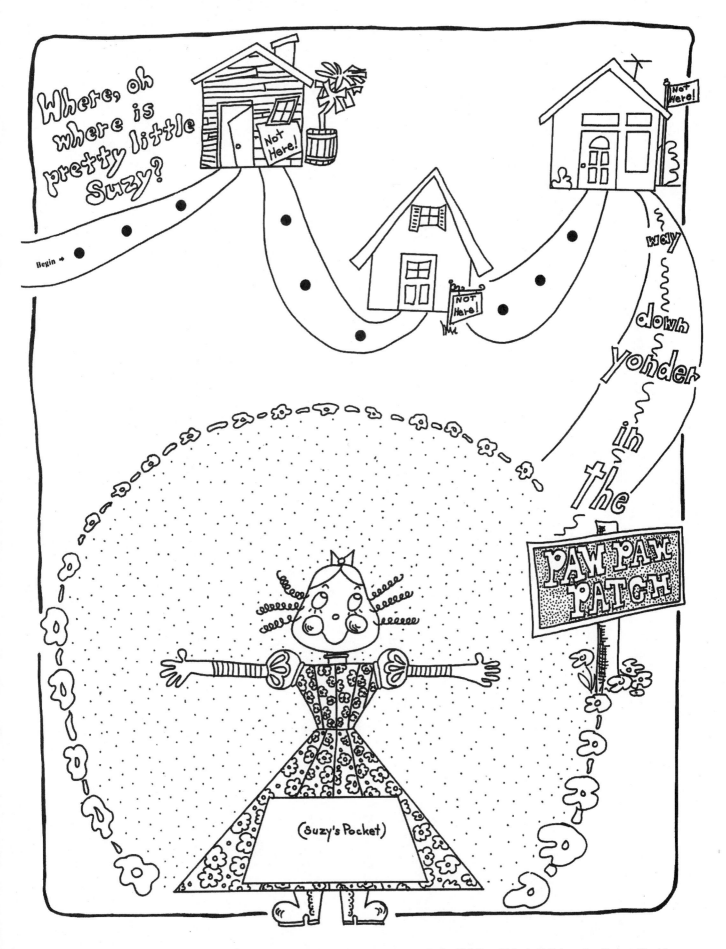

E. Achilles, "Paw Paw Patch," *You, Your Children and Music*, Vol. I, Issue 7. Arizona Early Childhood Music Collaborative Project. Used by permission. Permission to reproduce this play mat for personal use is granted to users of this textbook.

B. Andress, "Little Boy Blue," *You, Your Children and Music*, Vol. II, Issue 3. Arizona Early Childhood Music Collaborative Project. Used by permission. Permission to reproduce for personal use is granted to users of this textbook.